Dick Bangs
&
Lily Bourne

Their story

Paul Bangs
Peter Bangs
2021

Contents

Introduction		5
Chapter One	Dick's earlier years	7
Chapter Two	Along came Lily	15
Chapter Three	Mum's early years	23
Chapter Four	Mum as a young woman	39
Chapter Five	The early married years	42
Chapter Six	The new arrival	47
Chapter Seven	Life during the war	59
Chapter Eight	Dad and his wartime travels	68
Chapter Nine	Post-war events	86
Chapter Ten	Hatherley Gardens	96
Chapter Eleven	Family life continues	112
Chapter Twelve	Travels	122
Chapter Thirteen	The last years together	128
Chapter Fourteen	Life without Dad	141
Appendix A	Mum's 21st Birthday Cards	162
Appendix B	House receipts	165
Appendix C	Dad's Army Pay Book	170
Appendix D	Dad's Army Release Documents	174
Appendix E	Rent documents	188
Appendix F	Silver Wedding cards	201
Appendix G	Travels	206
Appendix H	Dad's death	255
Appendix I	Mum's cake making	256
Appendix J	Mum's 90th birthday cards	261
Appendix K	Mum's funeral remembrances	275

Introduction

This work is by way of being a supplement to the Bangs family history books already published. For the close family, it takes up the story of our parents, Richard (Dick) Bangs and Lilian (Lily) Bourne. In this way, we hope that the details of their progress through life, individually and collectively, will not be forgotten (as if they could!).

The reason for putting this into print is the awareness that electronic media, though they might seem permanent, are in fact ephemeral, depending on technological platforms which change at an ever bewildering rate, leaving "data tombs" in their wake. So many of us have videotapes, floppy discs and the like, with no means of extracting the information contained on them, and that is set to happen with the newer media such as discs.

However, as we know from our years of family history research, paper and other written forms do last. We have been astounded to have been able to read parchments and paper records which date back up to 700 years and more, some of them almost as fresh as the day the scribe set quill pen to vellum parchment.

So treasure the written word, look after the book, and pass it on to future generations. One thing which is clearly common to all of us who seek to learn about our origins and our forebears, is that we always leave it too late to start. So many times we have said to ourselves: "if only I had asked Mum/Dad about that while they were still with us"!

Apart from a few hints in the past about some research and knowledge of our family history, it was only when stimulated by the work of Andrew Peckett, a cousin, that we started to take interest, but the main catalyst was the discovery, when Mum had to move into care, of so much material carefully kept that we knew nothing about. Dad's wonderful letters from India have already been committed to print, and now we are able to share much more through this current work.

The Bangs family history books took the story of our line of the family down to our grandparents. Now we are adding more detail about our parents which would have been inappropriate for a publicly available work. As for Mum's forebears, they have been researched, much has been recorded digitally, and maybe a printed version awaits, though for many reasons there is less material available about them.

Paul and Peter Bangs

1. Dick's earlier years

Richard Charles (Dick) Bangs was born on the 25th November 1909 at Barnby Street, West Ham, the second son of Joseph Bangs and Bertha Jackson.

This section is about him, and, of course, our Mum. We will return to their life together in due course, but first a few glimpses of Dad's life. In fact there is very little photographic evidence of his years before marriage, and we don't know too much about those times, which is rather surprising. Here you can see his birth certificate, which gives us an insight into his parents.

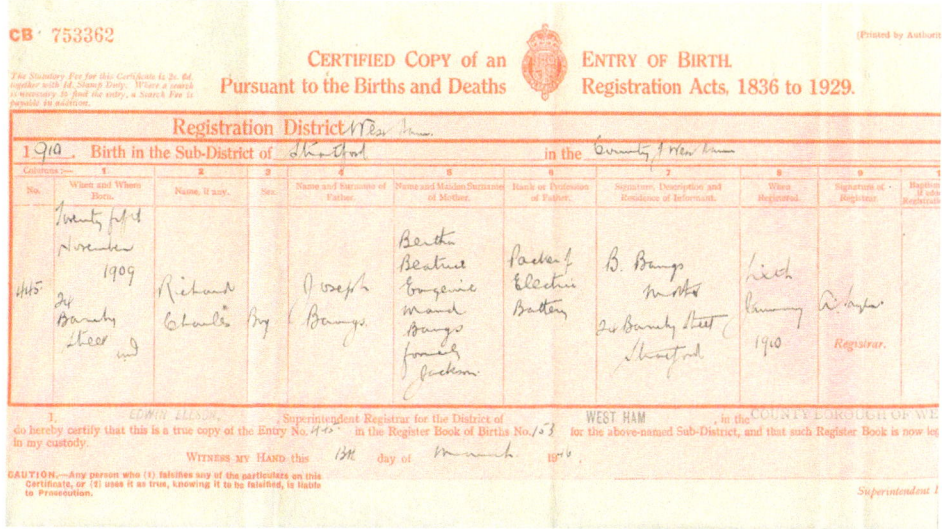

For example, his mother's full name is given: Bertha Beatrice Eugenie Maud Bangs, formerly Jackson. His father's occupation is stated to be "packer of electric battery" which is the only indication of such a job we have seen.

The next photo, Mum assured us, is of the table in Barnby Street in early days. He went to Bridge Road School in Stratford as we can see from his prize certificate, inside a book which we still have. But he did not pursue any education (or was not allowed to) beyond the compulsory age of 14.

What little we know of Dad's family life in his early years was obtained from glimpses, small mentions, and recollections from both him and Mum and some uncles and aunts. We know that the family was a poor one in many ways. The boys, we are told, only owned one pair of shoes each and if they were being mended they were unable to attend school. Speaking of school, it is known that every boy in the school they attended was obliged to learn a musical instrument. We have learnt that his brother Sid played a trumpet, that Wally played violin and mandolin, Ern also played violin and mandolin, and Eugene (Bill) the same. In fact three of them accompanied their cousin Ernie Tyrell in the Hackney Mandolin and Banjo Group. But we have no idea what Dad's instrument was. That he liked music was evident – he had a particular penchant for Gilbert & Sullivan – but the only instruments we ever saw him attempt to play were the "spoons", a "Jew's harp", (the name probably had nothing to do with Jews!), and (honestly) a panel saw (using a violin bow!), all of which were unlikely to have been taught at his school.

For certain, there was always a Jew's harp tucked away in a cupboard at home, and it looked like this – we have no idea what happened to it.

His life was probably a fairly free one. He mentioned on occasions that he would travel around the East End, recounting the districts he visited, such as Limehouse, with its Chinese ethnic population and the Lascar communities nearer the docks.

There are very few photos of Dad before his marriage, but four are shown here - already with his trademark wavy hair, but before the need to wear glasses. The first is dated on the back as 2/2/1933. He worked as a clerk and salesman at Byfords, a builder's merchants, and there are two pictures here taken in the yard with some employees indulging in horseplay. By 1939 he had become a "Cost Manager" at the firm.

Dad was known to belong to what we now think is the Cooperative Comrades' Camps movement. Even Mum was a bit vague about this, but some information from the Cooperative archives centre has clarified this for us. It may be through this connection that Dad first met Aunt Win (in fact, although about the same age, she was Mum's aunt) - he was going out with her until he saw Mum one day, and, as they say, the rest is history! We do know that Aunt Win as well as Dad was very friendly with Laurie Pavitt (she was due to marry his brother Freddy until he tragically died two weeks before their wedding) and Laurie went on to become a Labour MP and a major figure in the Cooperative movement. Amongst the things Mum had saved, we found this lapel badge which we think belongs to the movement, with CCC standing for Cooperative Comrades' Camps, but we are not completely sure.

His "mate" from those days was certainly Harry Thurling (we always knew him as "Uncle" Harry). We can see two photos of him on Brighton beach, and one at one of the Ongar camps, dated Easter 1933 - just before Dad's marriage in 1934. An additional photograph shows an unknown female friend of theirs. There is another photo of Dad and Harry on a Thames boat trip - we think taken at Boulter's Lock in Maidenhead. Dad can be seen leaning over the lifebelt, and Harry to his right. And of course we can see Dad at the camp, resplendent in his shorts!

We have three photos of the wedding of Harry Thurling to Lil Jupp (to us she was always Auntie Lil), but somewhat surprisingly neither Mum nor Dad are to be seen.

We also have two more Christmas cards, from an unknown friend John, and from a Mr and Mrs Poole (neighbours, we think, whom Dad helped out) to "Dear old Dickie".

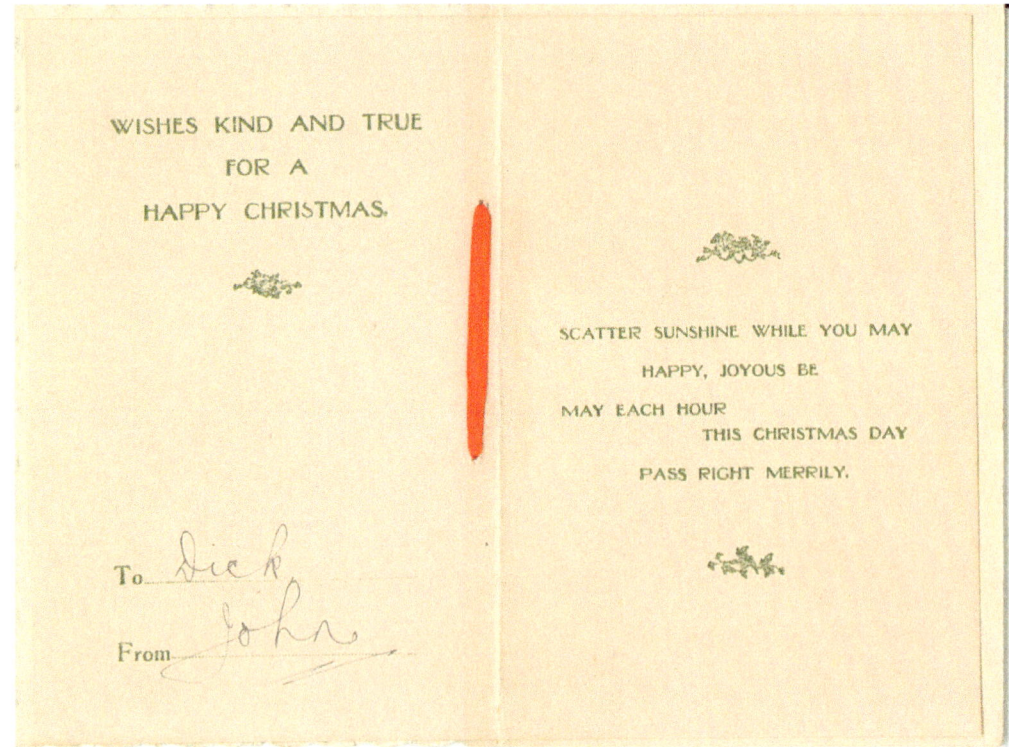

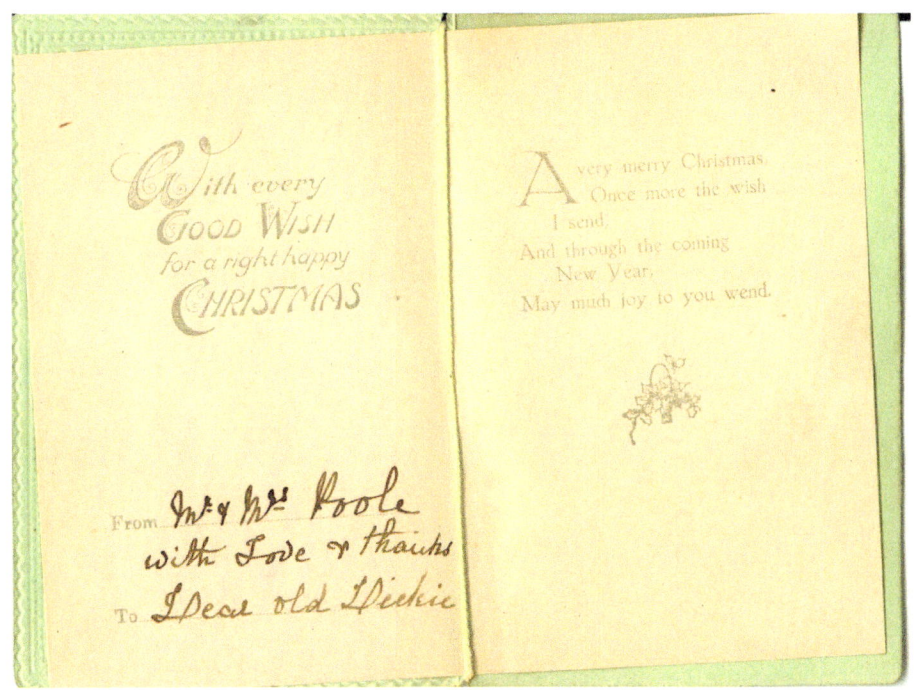

We know that he had another close friend in Bill Flower, who can be seen in the wartime photo taken in India, shown below (he is on the right). There are two Christmas cards from him which Dad had kept and they are shown as well.

The Season's Greetings

To wish for You a day so bright,
Just brimming o'er with gay delight,
Good Friends to cheer You on the way,
Happy Fortune near You stay,
Christmas bring You sweetness rare
And blessings rich beyond compare.

and All Good Wishes.

With every Good Wish, Dick, for
Xmas and the Coming Year.
from Bill.

Christmas Greetings

May happiness and Peace be
with you this Christmastide and
throughout the Coming Year

with Greetings from

Bill

Church Lane, Ledbury, Herefordshire
A lovely example of domestic
architecture in the heart of a countryside famed for its half-timber

2. Along came Lily

The next, and the most important event in Dad's life, came in 1934, when he married Lilian (Lily) Rose Bourne on the 30th December at West Ham Parish Church – a stone's throw from where Dad used to live in Barnby Street (the family had moved to Ferndale Road, Leytonstone by that date), and just down the main road towards Plaistow, where Mum lived at her parents' greengrocer's shop at 78 Stephens Road. We will deal with the wedding in greater detail when we come to talk about Mum. But as for the courtship, we can show a photo here which may have been taken to commemorate their engagement. Dad by now is wearing glasses.

We don't know too much about their courtship, Mum (and to a lesser extent Dad) did tell us a few things. We have already mentioned the transfer of affection from Aunt Win to Mum – though Win was always a great friend to them both over the years. As seen in the photos above, Dad worked in a builder's merchants, Byfords, as a sales clerk. Mum worked for a few years as a dressmaker (we'll come back to that) in Great Portland Street, where Dad would come to meet her after work and take her out. Mum recalled that her workmates would look out of the window and say "He's there, waiting for you!" and comment on Dad's good looks, saying he was "dishy" and a "good catch"! We are told that they would sometimes go to a music hall or to see a show in the West End, including the Palladium. Here you can see a more recent photo of the theatre though it has changed little.

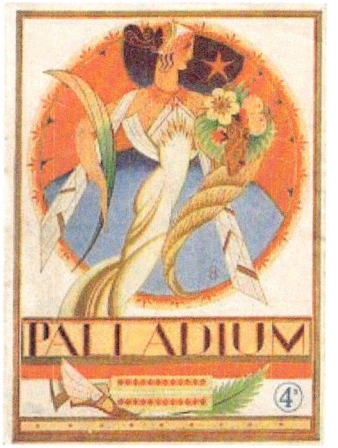

The stunningly designed Art Deco cover for a programme dates from 1928. Theatre seats in the upper circle were relatively cheap in those days, and they probably saw shows such as The Crazy Gang with Flanagan and Allen.

Dad would not have had that much money to spend. Nevertheless, according to Mum he often brought her a box of chocolates and they would go for tea before the show. That may have been in somewhere like the famous Lyons' Corner House. (See the pictures here).

There is an irony in the above information. Whilst they were making eyes at each other over the muffins, little did they know that the whole empire around them (Joe Lyons and Company) actually belonged to Dad's extended family! Another curious thing is that one of the group of musicians that played at the Corner Houses included, in the years around 1930, Dad's cousin Ernie Tyrell, an accomplished mandolinist, playing as part of *Troise and his Mandoliers*. We know that Dad was aware of Ern's part in the group, so it would hardly seem likely that he would not have known that he was playing there – perhaps their paths never crossed! Much more on the rather remarkable Ernie Tyrrell has been discovered and is dealt with elsewhere.

One more thing we discovered that surprised us was that Dad was also a part-time projectionist in a cinema, and got cheap tickets - one of Mum's first dates with him was being taken to see King Kong (the first version!) and she remembered that she was so scared she gripped Dad's arm till it was bruised. It was years before she ventured into the cinema again!

Well, of course the big day dawned for their marriage ceremony. This large photo of the day always stood on display at our home at Hatherley Gardens. Besides Mum and Dad the other people on the photo are Mum's cousin Florrie and Dad's sister Rose, the two senior bridesmaids, and of course Dad's brother Ern, the best man. The small bridesmaids are Mum's cousin Gwen (née Gale, later to be Harper), and sisters Mia and Hailwen Evans, daughters of Mum's neighbours (a photo is seen here).

Gwen told us that the reason for her scowl is because she was taken by car to the photographer's studio, without her mother and amongst a group of people whom she did not know. This is something that in 2011 she still remembered well!

The happy couple feature in another of their treasured photos, shown here.

Mum was still under age (21 was the age of consent at that time) and needed written permission from her parents. That is confirmed by the letter from the vicar which includes a receipt for the Banns and which has interesting information - for instance that the wedding, including certificate, cost just 15/1 - which means fifteen shillings and one penny. Transferred to decimal coinage this would be about 75 pence. But of course, you could get a lot more for under a pound then, than you can now!

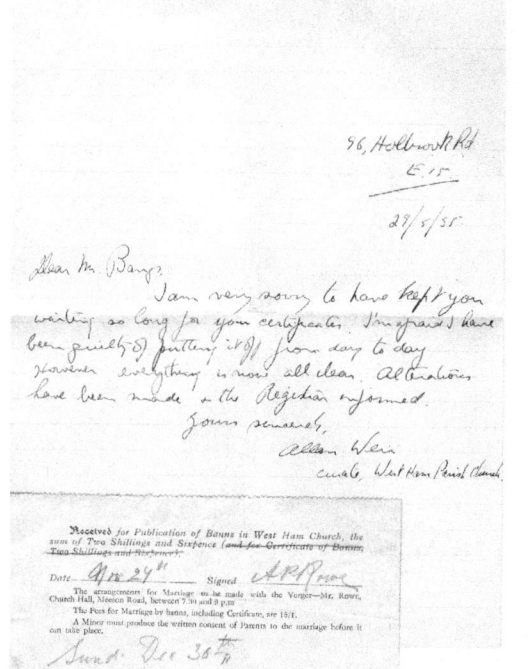

The documents which have survived include, of course, the wedding photos, but also a couple of photos of the wedding breakfast table laid out, (apparently our Nan kept directing everyone to the "top table"!), an invitation card (note the mistake, it's Stephens Road, not St Stephens), some gift cards and letters, a press cutting, the marriage certificate and some receipts for important items such as the ring (£2.15s was a lot of money!), Dad's signet ring which Mum bought just before the wedding, what appears to be the material for Mum's wedding dress, the wedding cars, and, last but certainly not least, the beer! The last one is interesting as the beer was purchased from the Three Mills Distillery in Bow, which is where Dad's father and his brother Ern worked. From the wedding certificate you can see the mistake that was made, putting Mum's age at 19! The letter from Ernie and Vi (Nan's Sister Violet who married Ernest Boon) shows that they were in the licensed victuallers (=pub) trade. Notice the charming card from Grandma Peckett to her "first grandchild".

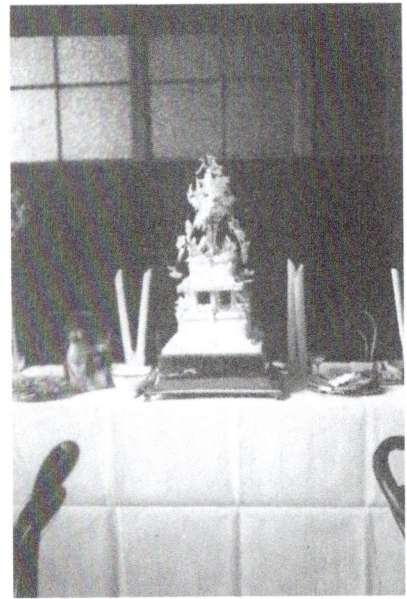

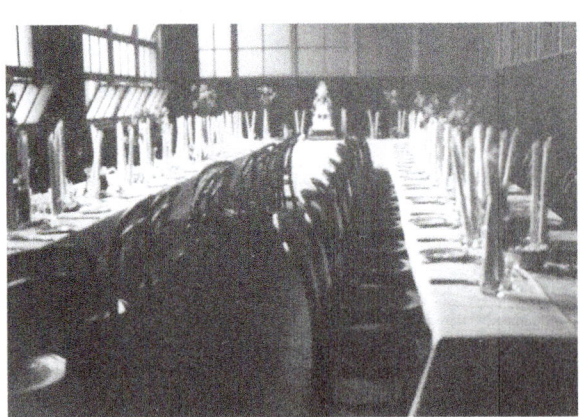

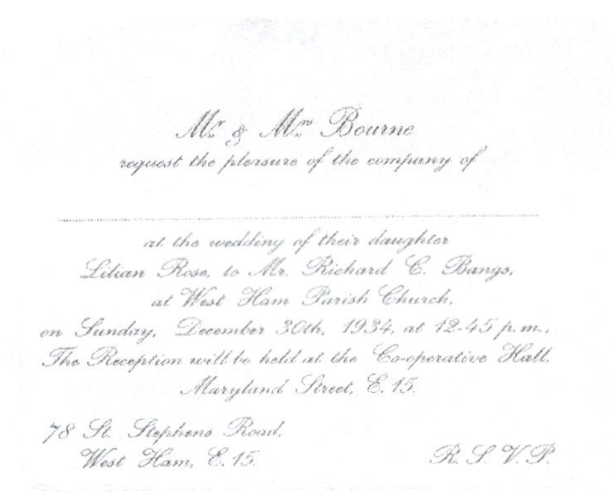

Mr. & Mrs. Bourne
request the pleasure of the company of

....

at the wedding of their daughter
Lilian Rose, to Mr. Richard C. Bangs,
at West Ham Parish Church,
on Sunday, December 30th, 1934, at 12-45 p.m.,
The Reception will be held at the Co-operative Hall,
Maryland Street, E.15.

78 St. Stephens Road,
West Ham, E.15.

R.S.V.P.

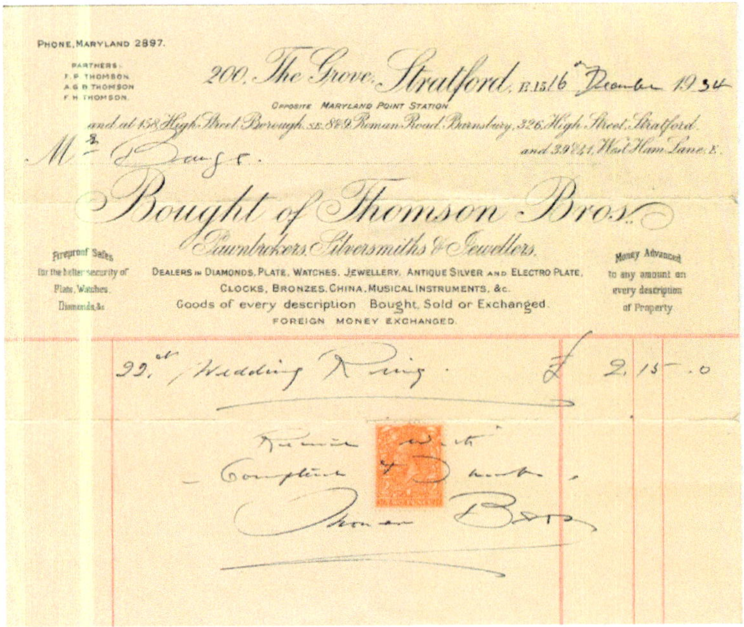

PHONE, MARYLAND 2897.

PARTNERS:
F. P. THOMSON
A. G. B. THOMSON
F. H. THOMSON

200, The Grove, Stratford, E.15. 16th December 1934

OPPOSITE MARYLAND POINT STATION

and at 158, High Street, Borough, S.E. 8 & 9, Roman Road, Barnsbury, 326, High Street, Stratford.
and 39 & 41, West Ham Lane, E.

Mrs Bangs.

Bought of Thomson Bros.

Pawnbrokers, Silversmiths & Jewellers.

Fireproof Safes
for the better security of
Plate, Watches,
Diamonds, &c.

DEALERS IN DIAMONDS, PLATE, WATCHES, JEWELLERY, ANTIQUE SILVER AND ELECTRO PLATE,
CLOCKS, BRONZES, CHINA, MUSICAL INSTRUMENTS, &c.
Goods of every description Bought, Sold or Exchanged.
FOREIGN MONEY EXCHANGED.

Money Advanced
to any amount on
every description
of Property

22ct. Wedding Ring. £ 2.15.0

Received with
Compliments & thanks,
Thomson Bros

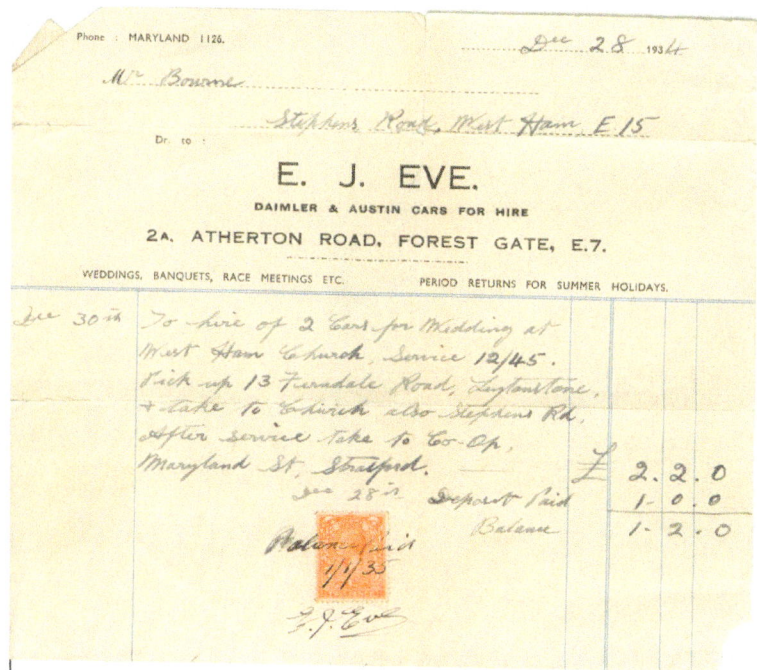

MARRIAGE OF MISS BOURNE

A wedding was solemnised on Sunday at West Ham Parish Church between Miss Lilian Bourne, only daughter of Mr. and Mrs. A. Bourne, of Stephens-road, West Ham, and Mr. Richard C. Bangs, of Ferndale-road, Leytonstone. There was a large attendance at the church, where the Rev. A. Weir officiated.

The bride, who was dressed in ivory satin beaute, was given away by her father. Her hand-embroidered train was carried by little Miss G. Gale, who was dressed in white taffeta. She was followed by two small bridesmaids, the Misses H. and M. Evans, who were in lemon satin beaute; they each carried a posy of carnations. The chief bridesmaid was Miss R. Bangs (sister of the bridegroom), and was accompanied by Miss F. Bourne (cousin of the bride). They were dressed in blue satin beaute, and wore Marina hats to match. The bride carried a bouquet of lilies, and the two principal bridesmaids carried bunches of yellow chrysanthemums. The best man was Mr. E. J. Bangs (brother of the bridegroom). The organist played the Wedding March as the party walked up the aisle.

After the ceremony the happy couple left for the Co-operative Hall, Maryland-street, where the reception and wedding breakfast were held. The bride and bridegroom were the recipients of many presents.

Certified Copy of an Entry of Marriage

D 738410 — Pursuant to the Marriage Acts, 1811 to 1932.

Registration District: West Ham

1934. Marriage Solemnized at Parish Church in the Parish of West Ham in the County of West Ham.

No.	When Married	Name and Surname	Age	Condition	Rank or Profession	Residence at the time of Marriage	Father's Name and Surname	Rank or Profession of Father
335	Dec 30th 1934	Richard Charles Bangs	25	Bachelor	Hardware Salesman	28 Folkestone Rd	Joseph Bangs	Engineer Retired
		Lilian Rose Bourne	19	Spinster	—	78 Stephens Rd	Albert Victor Bourne	Fruiterer

Married in the Parish Church according to the Rites and Ceremonies of the Established Church by — or after Banns by

This Marriage was solemnized between us: Richard Charles Bangs / Lilian Rose Bourne

In the Presence of us: E. J. Bangs / A. V. Bourne

A. Weir, Curate.

I, A. Weir, a true copy of the Entry No. 335, in the Register Book of Marriages of the said Church. Witness my hand this 30th day of December 1934.

HARDWICK'S
Blouse Specialist, Silk and Woollen Merchant

469 Green Street AND 385 Queen's Road
Telephone: Grangewood 1284
Upton Park, E.13
10193
London ... 1934

£5 · 17 · 11

Bought of **Thomson Bros.**
Silversmiths & Jewellers
326, High St, Stratford
22-12-1934

To my first Grandchild.
Wishing you both every happyness in the bigest venture of your life.
Grandma Peckett.

Mullally's Wine House,
Gt. Titchfield Street,
Oxford Circus, W.1.
Also at
267, Walworth Road, S.E.17.
32, Harcourt Street, W.1.

Dec 30th 1934

Dear Lillie & Dick,
Accept our most "Hearty Congratulations" on this your Wedding Day.
Although we are not there, we will be thinking of you both, so "God Bless you Both" on your Future Undertaking.
Your affectionate Aunt & Uncle
Ernie & Vi.

P.S. Leroy has had a turn for the Better.

With every good wish
for your future happiness.
Hilda
&
Bert.

Health and Happiness

Best of Luck! congratulations
Heres to greet the Happy Day
Please accept the warmest wishes
Which my little gift convey.
From Aunt Ciss & Uncle Charlie

From Aunt Ciss & Uncle Charlie
Wishing you Long life & Happiness.
To Dick & Lillie.

With best wishes for
your future happiness
From
Lily Jupp

With all Good Wishes

It's just a simple little gift,
The words are simple too –
But every special wish they bring –
May every wish come true.
From Florrie. to Dick. + Lillie

Wishing you Both
Long Life & Happiness

So Mum and Dad were married. But here we must pause. We have seen what we know of Dad's youth, so it is time to roll back the clock and discover Mum's past until this point.

3. Mum's early years

Lilian Rose Bourne was our mother, born on the 19th December 1914. We think this is the earliest photo of her - a typical studio portrait from those days, wearing the christening robe, which is still in the family, as you can see from the photo. When this was taken she was 2 months older than her birth certificate, seen below. When she was born she weighed just 3 lbs (1.36k) and was washed in olive oil, wrapped in muslin and placed in a large jug. This was then put into a drawer and surrounded with cotton wool. A forerunner of a premature baby incubator, no doubt. It certainly did its job, as she lived to 94 years old!

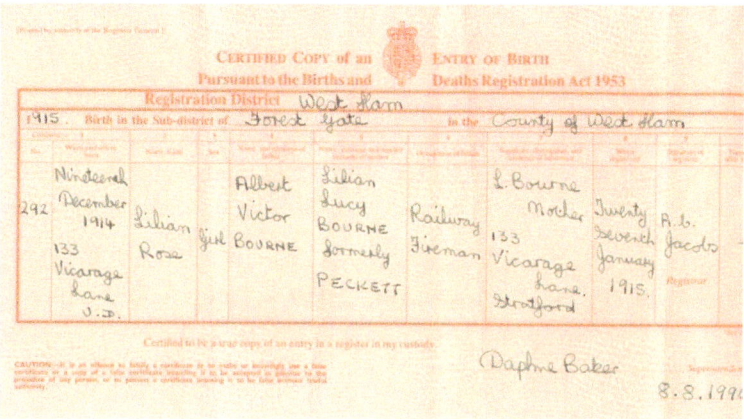

One item we treasure is a letter from Mum's Great Aunt Lucy (Peckett – Nan's maiden name), sent to Mum soon after she was born. The two pages can be seen here. The letter, or "epistle", dated March 1915, accompanied a knitted jacket, and shows how eloquently people wrote in those days. This photo is of Lucy Peckett. The history of the Bournes and Pecketts is written elsewhere, but we can mention here that Lucy was in service, and the wooden trunk in which she kept all of her possessions (literally!) is still put to use today – it contains Paul's camera equipment!

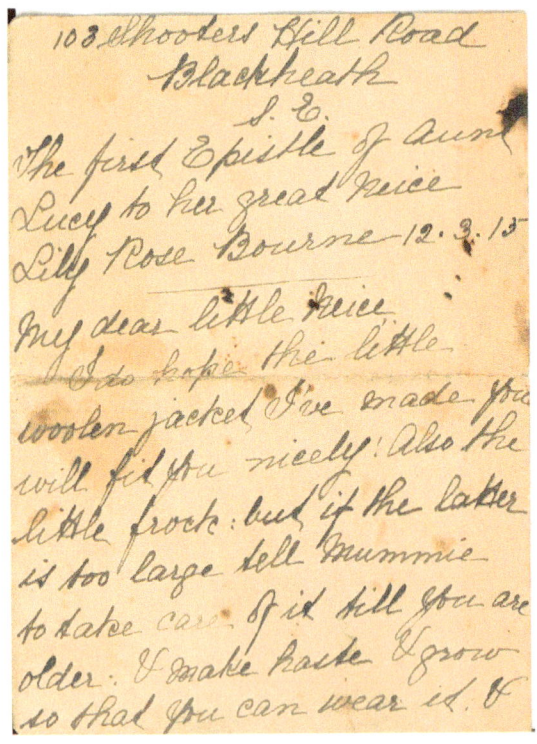

Cards were often sent, as now, to celebrate births, and here we have one from an Auntie Grace about whom we know nothing. Alongside it is the reverse showing the inscription and indicating that of course Mum was born very near Christmas. Auntie Grace remembered Mum's first birthday and we can see another card after that.

Mum's parents, our Nan and Grandad, kept a greengrocer's shop in Stephens Road, West Ham, and as you will see from the photos and the business card, Grandad also had a light haulage business. He had previously worked as an assistant in the same shop, and below you can find a testimonial from his employer, dated 1910.

Removals any Distance

Estimates Free

Personal Supervision

Telephone: MARyland

A. V. BOURNE

Haulage Contractor

78 STEPHENS ROAD
WEST HAM, E.15

In the photo of the shop, we think that the lady is our Aunt Rose, one of Nan's sisters, and the man is Bob Davies a neighbour, close family friend and Aunt Rose's erstwhile suitor; and amongst the group in the other photo, it looks like Mum on the right as a child. Bob Davies is there again, still unwilling to force a smile!

R.L.1.

Licence No. 193

FOOD CONTROL

LICENCE TO TRADE IN FOODSTUFFS BY RETAIL.

The Food Control Committee for the district of

WEST HAM.

hereby license

A.V. BOURNE.

as a Retail Dealer in

Vegetables (Fresh, canned or dried)

Fruit (Fresh, dried, preserved, canned or bottled)

Potatoes

in respect of the business carried on at

78, Stephens Road,

E.15.

Signed on behalf of the Food Control Committee

Signature

Date 9th. October.1939

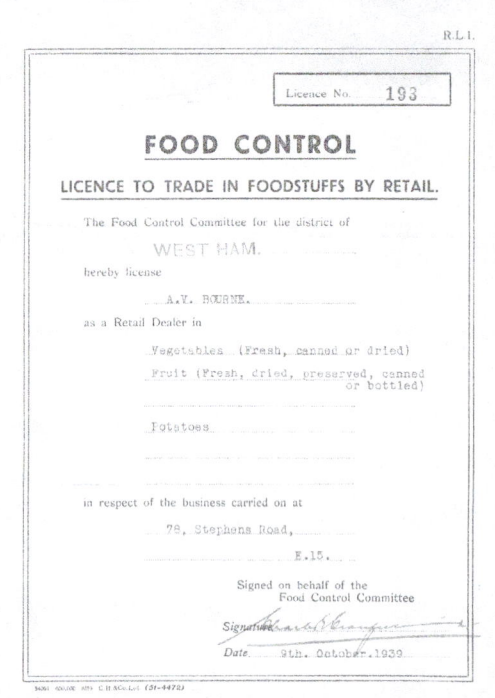

What we are unclear about is how Grandad moved on from being an employee to actually running the business. It seems impossible that they bought the premises, so presumably rented the accommodation and somehow bought up the business, which they were to run until after the Second World War, even in spite of being bombed. Here is a licence to trade from later, in 1939. Living in the shop, our mother as she got older helped out by serving - probably illegal in these days to use her at that age! The rear of the shop had a stable area where they originally had a horse (yes, just like Steptoe and Son!) and later was where Grandad parked the lorry. After the bombing, the business continued under a sort of tarpaulin tent.

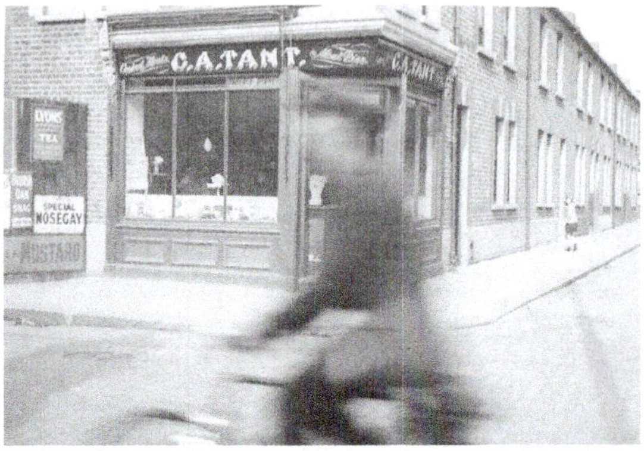

The shop was obviously well linked with all the local community, with Page's, a butcher's, next door and many other shops - here is a picture of another one. In this case it is Tant's cooked meat and pie shop, quite typical of the East End of those days, though sadly mostly replaced by fast food outlets selling burgers and kebabs etc. There are a few examples left however. We can remember also the "eel and pie" shops which had trays of live eels in the window displays. As Mum grew up, she saw difficult times, in spite of the fact that her parents were "in trade". Life was not always easy in that part of the world, and Mum often spoke of families who fell on hard times. The pawnbroker was a regularly visited spot - though not, as far as we know, by our family.

Here is Mum with Nan and Grandad Bourne. You can see from the photograph that, typically, the family was dressed in best clothes. The photos were often taken to be printed on postcards, which were sent as keepsakes and even Christmas cards to friends and relatives. Sadly, although the names of the studios are usually printed or embossed, as here, dates are rarely added.

The next photo is of Mum on the beach - we haven't a clue where it is - it could even be a fake studio shot, but you can see boats in the background. Travel to the seaside was not uncommon - trains from the East End to Southend were easy to take (and much cheaper than today!), and Margate and Brighton were also within reach.

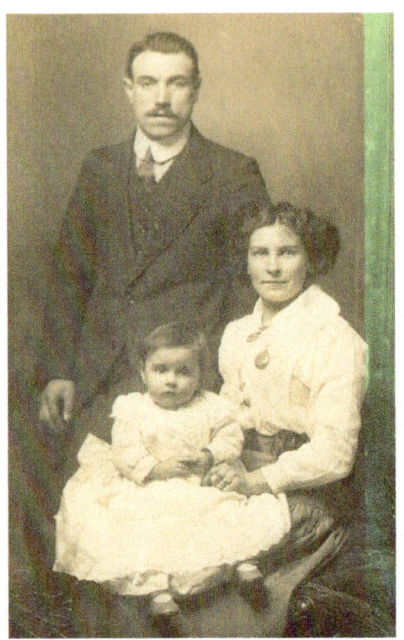

The photo of the boat loaded for a sail "round the bay" includes Mum, Nan and Grandma Peckett - they have been marked with crosses on the original, and there's a note on the reverse which says *"You will see I have my little Lily and Big Lily, x Mum"*.

The other photo shows a typically crowded beach of the time, probably Margate. We don't know who took it but it was probably our Dad, and the guess is it was during the 1920s.

In this first studio photo, Mum has a favourite toy. Visits to the photographer were seemingly fairly common, probably to mark birthdays, although, as here, there is often no indication to help us. The other photo is another early studio portrait of Mum - we don't know the name of the dog! But we believe that Mum was 4 years old.

In the next photograph, the aim appears to have been rather to "show off" the quite elegant clothes. We doubt Mum ever had to go short of such things. The First World War seems to have passed fairly uneventfully for our close family. We know our Uncle Sam served in the army (details on his somewhat fascinating if turbulent history are found elsewhere!). In the photos below Mum was five years old, and in the other, six. The latter photo, in a very large, framed, hand-coloured version, was to hang for many years in the house and still holds pride of place on Paul's staircase.

Mum began Elementary School and we have these pictures of her class from those days. She's not too difficult to spot - especially if you remember the "trade mark" ribbon she often wore in her hair. If there was ever a stereotypical schoolteacher, in the first photo it has to be the lady on the left! And in the second photo, note the nice touch of bringing some plants (including an aspidistra) out into the playground for the photo session.

In 1919 Uncle Albert, Mum's brother, was born, and the two of them can be seen in the above photo. Uncle Albert is wearing the same christening robe which we saw Mum used. They had no other siblings, and were always close for the rest of their lives. The other picture, although very faded, is of Mum with Uncle Albert at the seaside. And we can see Uncle Albert and his rocking horse. Don't be surprised at little boys being dressed rather like girls - it was the fashion at the time.

Mum was always very close to her brother, and kept photos of him – here are a few of them. In the first two he is with the family dog, Prince.

The next photo was taken at Letchworth, where there were Bourne family connections and the other one at the seaside with an unknown friend or relation.

In those days, horse and cart were still used for transport, in this case outside what we believe to be the former entrance to West Ham train and underground station, which was quite close to their home; and in the final picture we see Uncle Albert with a typical cheeky grin!

The set of images which follow are some more photos from Mum's world around the shop. There is Mum in a garden, presumably at their home, and in the same garden the same two people we saw in the photo of the shop - her Aunt Rose and Bob Davies.

Then there is her cousin Leslie with the two Evans girls from the dairy, who were friends and are seen also in other photos (and with their brother who was to die young), and Cissy Davies, a neighbour who later was to bring the good news to the house that Albert had survived Dunkirk. Note Mum's boots – it would be many years before they came back to be the height of fashion!

It is interesting to note, as we move through Mum's childhood, that there are very many more photographs of her than of Dad. This probably reflects the relative difference in financial circumstances between the two families.

Mum enjoyed a pretty normal childhood - here paddling with some unknown friends in an unknown place!

She learnt to do many things - swimming was only one of them, and here we have three swimming certificates of which she was always proud!

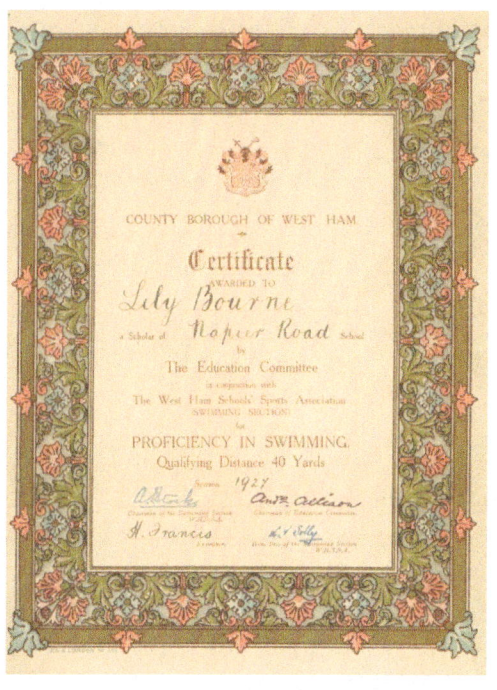
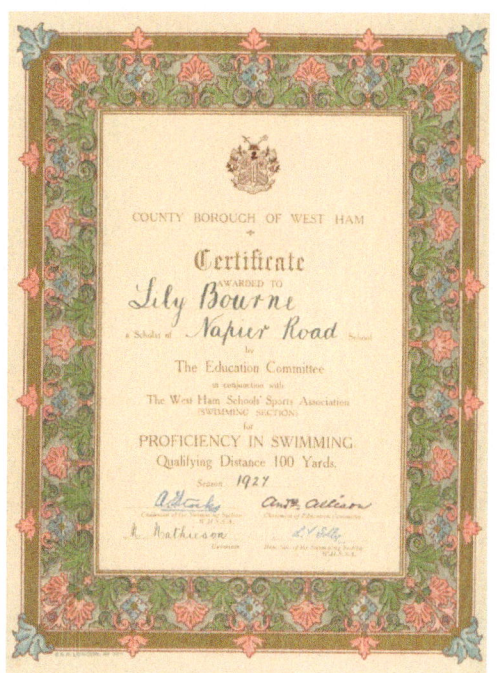

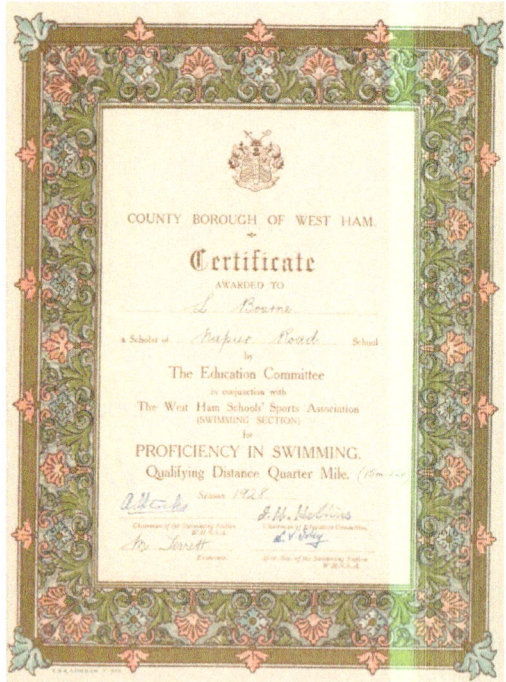
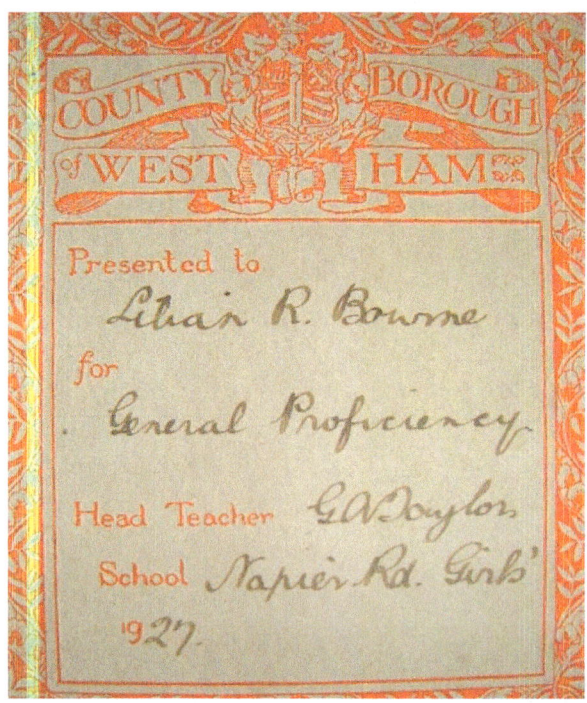

She also received a prize book and we can see the certificate on the frontispiece. She was also given a netball medal that she lost on her way home. Nan went to the park at 5 am the next morning to look for it, but to no avail!

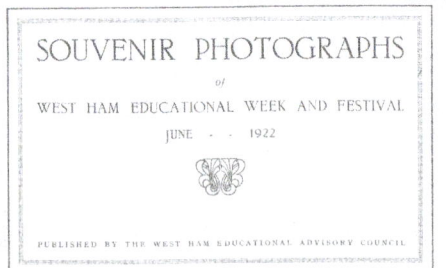

She even featured in a publication to mark West Ham education week, and in the photo she is country dancing - spot her if you can!

Folk-Dancing as it used to be.

Mum was always fond of music. What we don't know is how she learnt to play the piano. We always had a fine Monington & Weston piano at home, bought, surprisingly, during the war. We rarely heard Mum play, but play she could, and read music – there was lot of sheet music in the house, but most has not survived. We can only presume that there was a piano at Stephens Road, and that maybe she learnt at school or her parents paid for lessons?

Another picture of Mum, aged about 10.

As was common with most families, Mum attended many weddings, mostly as bridesmaid. In the photo here she is a bridesmaid at her Uncle Sam's wedding in 1919. Can you spot her?

And here she is at two family weddings - Uncle Perce and Aunt Rose, then later (try spotting Mum!), Aunt Kate and Uncle Jack, both from Letchworth.

And here she is again at the wedding of her Aunt Violet, who married Ernie Boon.

And in these next two photos she is bridesmaid at the wedding of yet another aunt, Alice. The photos were taken in Chapel Street, Stratford. Note that they brought the carpet out into the garden for the photographs!

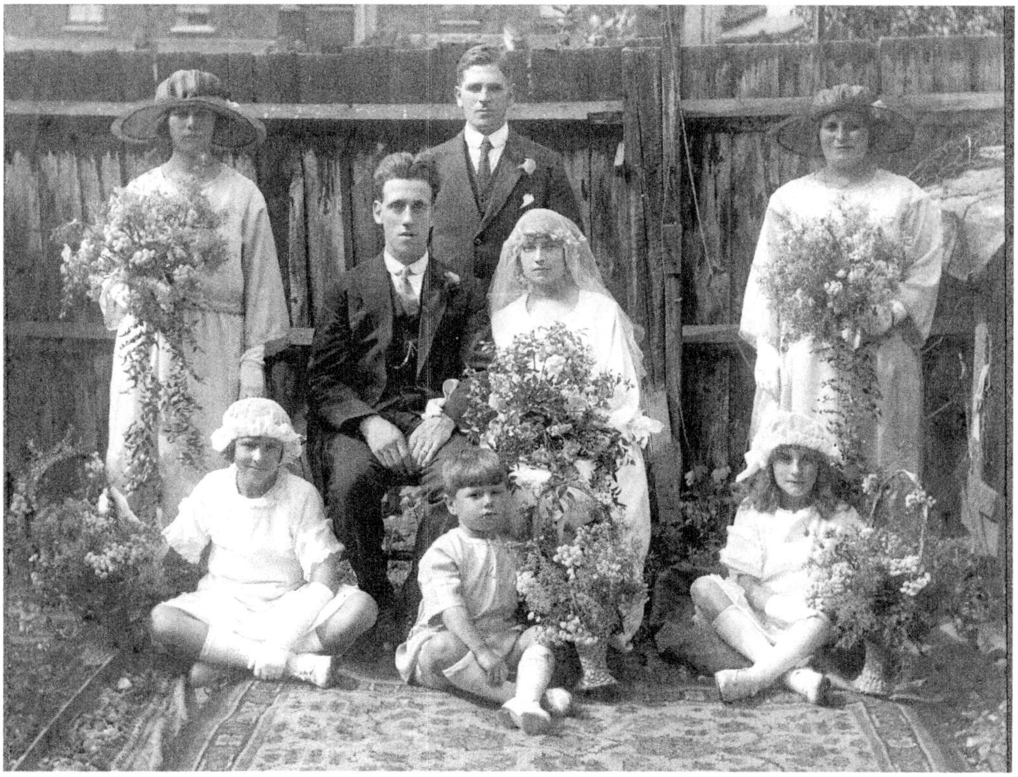

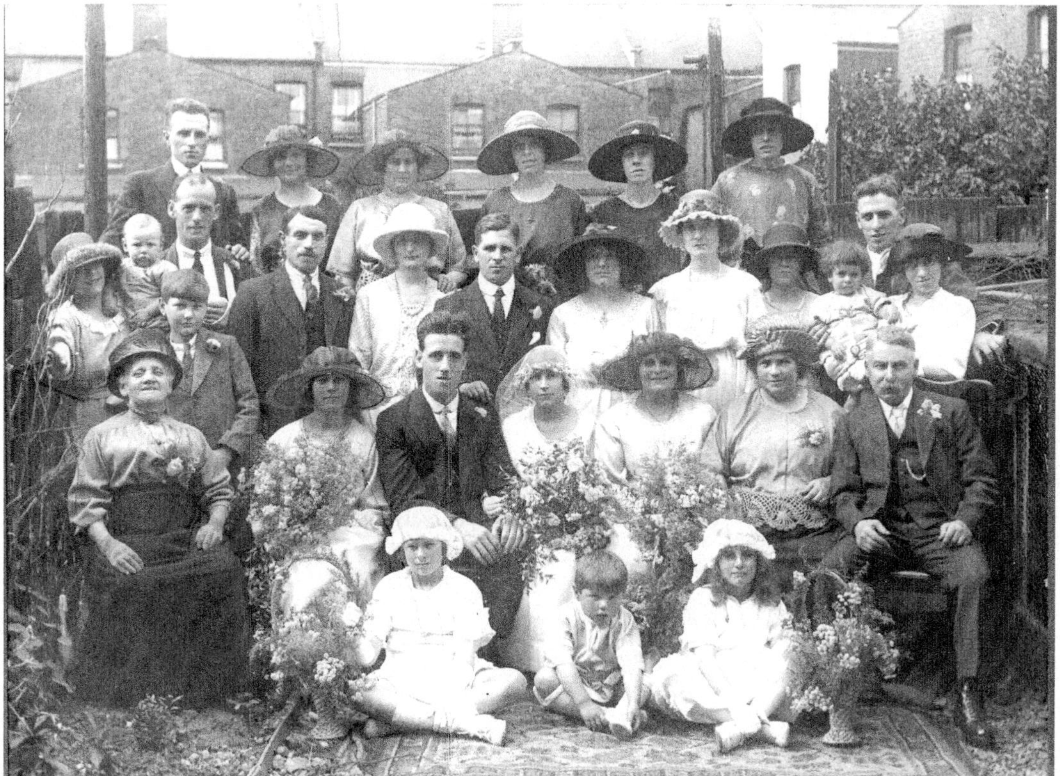

All childhoods come to an end. In those days that was sometimes sooner than one would have liked. Mum was an exceptional pupil at school - her teacher, Miss Burbidge, even came round to talk to her parents to persuade them to let her take up a scholarship to stay on for further schooling. Alas, the attitude towards girls was not what it mostly is today, and Mum's lot was deemed to be to help out in the shop, so she had to leave school at 14. Although Mum in her usual self-effacing way, never mentioned it often, it undoubtedly was something she regretted all her life, and was perhaps the motivating factor behind her sacrifices to ensure that her three children did progress in their education as far as was possible.

So we leave Mum's childhood, at the age of 13, as she starts to wear silk stockings, as in this photo taken with Uncle Albert. Notice that this is a hand-coloured photo. In the photo Mum is wearing a locket and we think it is the very one which we still have and which you can see in these close-ups. However, so far, frustratingly, we have not been able to work out exactly who the little photos inside are of.

4. Mum as a young woman

So Mum is growing up. Here we see her on the beach with her Grandma Peckett (Nanny Bourne's mother) and who we think is her cousin Leslie.

And here again, this time in a garden.

This next photo was taken at Letchworth where relations lived, and below Mum is at the later wedding of Dad's sister Rose. We can see Uncle Sid, Cousin Flo and Great-Aunt Sarah. Mum could never recall why she had her thumb in her mouth!

We know so little about her teenage years and her life as a young woman before she met Dad.

Although in this faded photo she is on a motorbike with our Grandad, and she did recall refusing to go on a date with the milkman when he turned up on a similar machine!

We also recall very occasional mentions of meeting boyfriends at, for instance, the *Cherry Tree* pub in Barking. Looking the way she did then, she surely had no lack of admirers!

Mum was already married, and came of age (21 was the age in those days) and she carefully treasured and kept the cards she received, many of them delightfully Art Deco in style and which we display in their entirety in Appendix A.

We're not sure when this next photo was taken - it was probably after her wedding. And she's wearing the same dress as in the other photo, taken with friends or relatives in Erith. Although Mum became slightly forgetful in her final years (though thankfully never succumbing to severe dementia) she always remembered the colour of her dresses – this one was blue with yellow! The Erith connection, however, is one which Mum could not recall and which we have been unable to unravel so far.

This is another rare photo because it shows Mum with Grandma Bourne. We think that next to Mum is Aunt Rose with her daughter Denise, on a trip over from Canada, to where she had emigrated. The man looks like Uncle Charlie.

We are not sure when exactly Mum met our Dad. What we do know is that she was working as a dressmaker or seamstress in a company in Great Portland Street. This move happened because our Nan insisted that she was not going to spend the rest of her life in the shop. It was a shop customer who arranged for Mum to begin at the dressmaker's, through her connections. The other photo here is of Mum's friend Blanche, who was also her mentor at work.

5. The early married years

So Mum and Dad are married. Many of the photos we can show from now on were taken by Dad himself. He was always fond of photography. People had cameras in those days, however no such thing as digitals! And you have to bear in mind that film and processing was not cheap. So if you want to see what sort of cameras were used - here is a photo of Dad's bellows Kodak, which has survived in remarkably good condition.

If you look closely you can see that there is a sort of "stylus" to the left of the lens. This enabled you to open a small panel at the rear of the camera and write a title for the picture, which would appear when processed, rather like the digital metadata we have today (all that hidden technical detail about date, format, size and so on that gets saved with every digital camera shot). Having said that, we haven't found a single photo where this seems to have been used! The countryside did seem to figure greatly in Mum and Dad's courtship, as did trips to the seaside. But this may be more a reflection on the fact that that is where you took your camera!

The definition of when you should be informal was a different matter in those days compared with the informality we enjoy today. Mum is seen here, almost certainly on Brighton Pier. Probably not particularly dressed up to impress Dad – it's just what you wore to the seaside, perhaps! We can see that the dress she is wearing under the coat is one of her favourites which we have already seen in other photos.

Here is Dad looking, for him, quite informal - it was not uncommon for him to wear a tie on the beach! We think this picture is also on Brighton Pier but the weather seems warmer so it can't have been taken at the same time as the one of Mum. The strap round Dad's chest in fact belongs to the camera seen in the picture above.

This photo is of a crowded Brighton Beach from the pier - long before the days of package tours to Benidorm, this is where people spent their holidays!

The photos below are from Margate. The one on the left is clearly labelled on the back "Margate beach" and Dad is not wearing glasses. But notice the same "pullover", as in the one on the pier, and, oh! those socks ..... The picture on the right is almost certainly taken at the same time. On the back, Dad has written "I am shy, Margate beach". Mum is still rather formally attired - note the stockings!

This rather faded photo shows Dad on what looks like Brighton beach, in quite informal attire, newspaper in hand, camera again slung around him. It could be his friend Harry who took the photo.

There is a tragic story behind this photo taken in Letchworth. Uncle Albert is pretending to drive the lorry, and the other two boys are Aunt Alice's Laurie with the cap, and Albie, from Letchworth. Apart from Nan and Mum, we can see Aunt Alice, and at the front, Aunt Doll. The nonchalant young man is Freddie Pavitt, who was due to marry Aunt Win in the same year as Mum and Dad wed, but who was tragically killed in a road accident just before the wedding.

Let's leave the seaside for the country. When Mum and Dad were courting, and after their marriage (but before they were tied down with the arrival of Joyce!) they often went out for a walk in the country on a Sunday. We can remember them telling us about going up to London Bridge station, getting the first convenient train out into Kent, then walking across country to another station and catching a train back up to London. Seems amazingly laid back, but reflects the frequency and density of trains and railway lines in those days.

Here we see Mum relaxing with our Grandad in the country - probably Devil's Dyke near Brighton. That might be Grandad's lorry in the background.

But, country or seaside, lo and behold, Dad is still sporting his favourite "tanktop"!

On these walks Dad enjoyed taking photos of Mum, and here we've a selection of typical shots. The one on the left is entitled "At the bottom" but we have no idea where it was taken.

The other is titled "Maid of the Woodlands, Pennebury Heath" on the reverse. Unfortunately Dad seems to have made a mistake as we cannot find such a place!

And here is Mum, all coy again, swinging on a country gate. This was taken at Barkway in Hertfordshire, where relatives lived. And what's this? Not only Dad on the same gate, but the only photo we have of him smoking a pipe!

And here is Mum in another Barkway cornfield.

Mum is again in Letchworth, with a relative, Jean, on a swing.

This one was taken at Keston Lakes and is labelled "The lady of Ye Post".

This one Dad has entitled "Close your eyes, or Where is he?"

After the wedding, Mum and Dad set up their home in a flat (actually half a house) in Albert Square, Stratford. Here is a photo of them in the garden with their landlady and another from their window of their landlord mowing the grass.

Obviously, they needed to set up their new home. Many receipts for items were kept and can still be viewed, so we have included a number of them in Appendix B.

6. The new arrival

On March 19th 1936 Joyce was born.... This quite lovely and moving letter from Dad to Mum was written on the back of one of Grandad's blank invoices. It must have been written just after Mum had given birth to Joyce and was still in hospital, and seems to have been written in the evening after he had visited her for the first time – the equivalent of sending a text message today!

Here also is the traditional "four generations" photograph, showing Joyce, Mum, Nanny Bourne and Grandma Peckett.

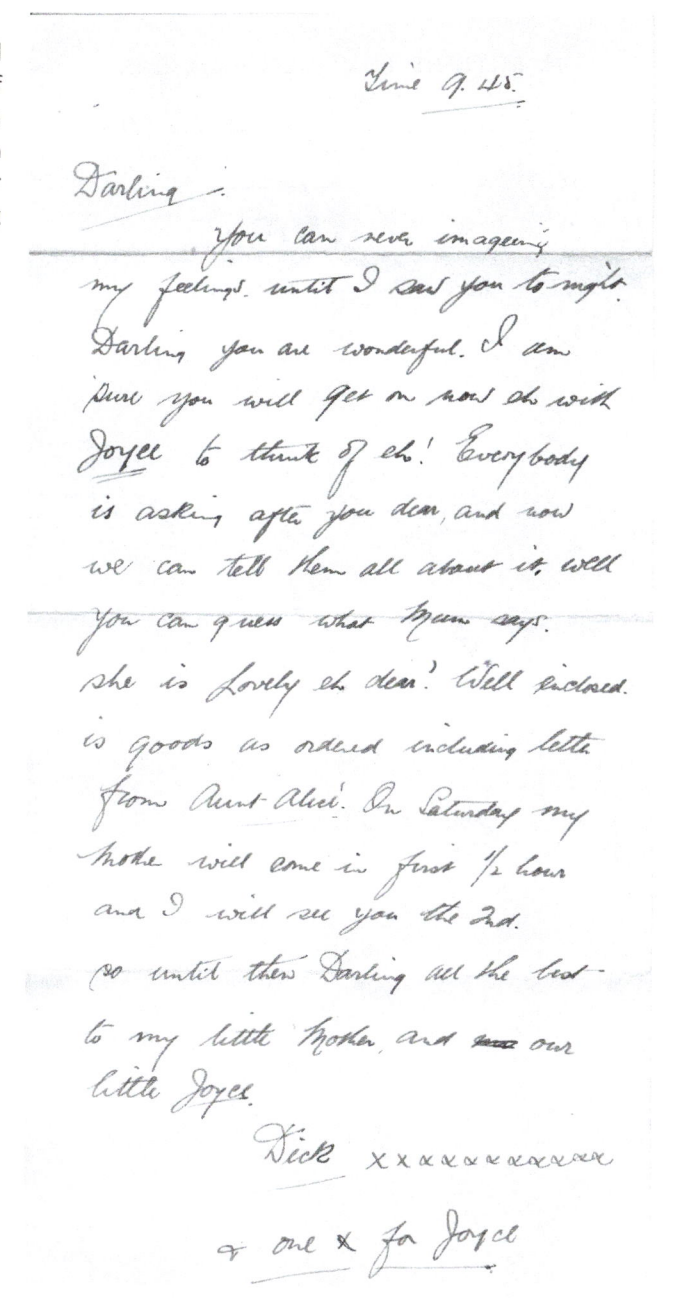

Two photos survive from Joyce's Christening. In the first you can see Mum and Aunt Rose, with Grandad on the left and Nan on the right. Looking over Mum's shoulder is Nanny Bangs – Dad's mother, and this is one of the few photos we have of her. In the second one you can see Auntie Clara, and Grandma Peckett with our Nan on the right.

In this photo Joyce is about 4 months old, and here also is the proud father with his little girl.

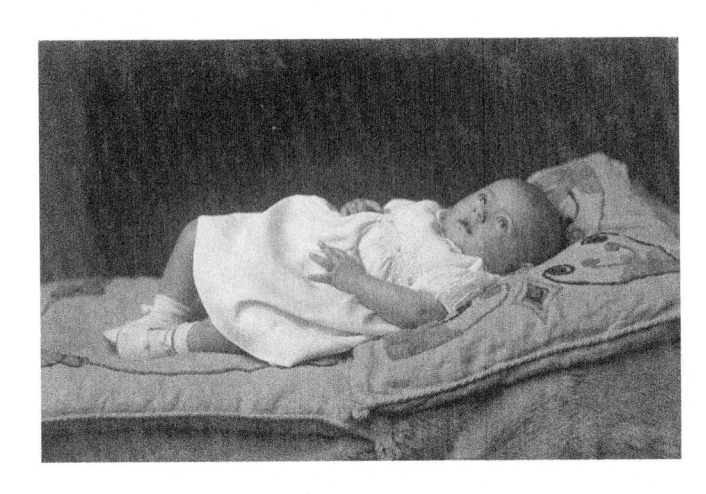

Two photos follow, taken in the garden at Albert Square, presumably taken at the same time, on the right including Dad's sister, Rose (nonchalant cigarette in hand!).

Even at an early age, Joyce was taken to the seaside. This was taken on Brighton or Southend pier and Joyce is in Grandad Bourne's arms. Note the care taken with the bonnet and the rather fetching parasol!

These two shots were definitely taken near Brighton - a favourite spot on the South Downs, The Devil's Dyke. Mum and Joyce are with Nanny and Grandad Bourne. The beauty of the spot can be appreciated in the photo on the right.

This is at Westcliff, where Joyce is getting used to the comfy life in a deck chair! But what would we say now about safety and welfare!

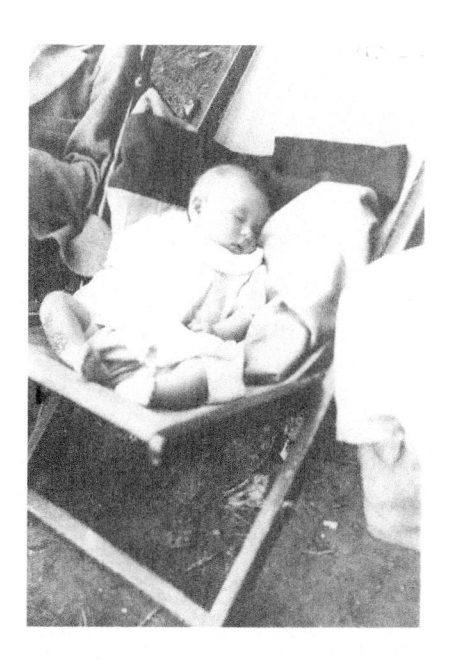

This further example of risking child injury was taken, Mum assured us, in Brighton.

Here we have two photos of Joyce, continuing the studio tradition, taken to celebrate her first birthday.

And life with Joyce continued, at home and on holidays. Whoops! Must have forgotten the sun-hat. Never mind, a hanky is traditional anyway... This was probably taken on the Isle of Wight, where there were a few holidays.

Still on the island, the giveaway that this is the Isle of Wight in the photo below is the wording on the Pickfords removal van in the background. Mum and Dad are holidaying with some friends, and Joyce is bidding for future dental treatment!

In this snap Joyce is clearly older, but it looks like the Isle of Wight once more.

And here are Mum and Joyce with the same friend posing at what might be Carisbrooke Castle on the island.

"Please Daddy, don't make me wait here until the tide comes in!"

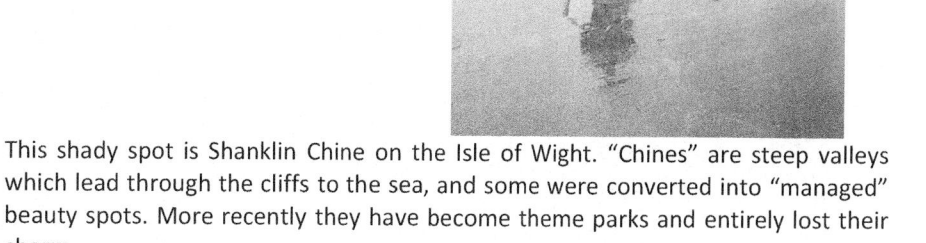

This shady spot is Shanklin Chine on the Isle of Wight. "Chines" are steep valleys which lead through the cliffs to the sea, and some were converted into "managed" beauty spots. More recently they have become theme parks and entirely lost their charm.

The next photo was taken at a similar spot - Blackgang Chine. We know that Dad won a prize for this snap, but we don't know what the prize was.

This snap shows a very happy Joyce with her Nanny and Grandad at an unidentified wedding.

Probably the last of the studio shots, this was taken on Joyce's second birthday. What a happy girl!

And this rather blurred photograph of a cheeky face has written on the back: "Sez me at lunch". It was taken at Dad's family home in Ferndale Road, Leytonstone.

The two photos here show Mum and Joyce with the landlords and those same friends (from Dad's work at Byfords) they went on holiday with to the Isle of Wight.

Mum and Dad really loved their holidays on the Isle of Wight, and Dad used his camera to good advantage on those occasions. Below is a selection of the photos he took with his Kodak on the island and elsewhere.

900 year old cottages in Shanklin.

Alum Bay, where the famous coloured sands were there for the taking - banned now, probably on grounds of health & safety! Or could be something to do with sales of pre-packed sands....

Nearby are the famous chalk stacks of The Needles.

And a shot of Sandown.

Here are four more views of Blackgang Chine and its small inhabitants...

These two snaps are of Shanklin Chine and its "Lovers' Cottage".

On the left, a view of Black Rock, to the east of Brighton's beaches

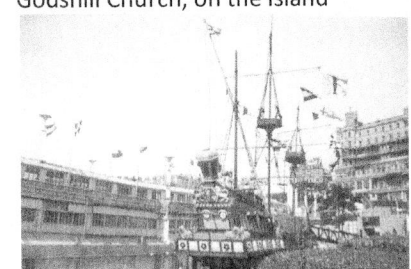

Godshill Church, on the island

The three photos above were taken in Southend-on-sea, famous for its annual illuminations, its pleasure pier (the longest in the world) and its mud.

Back in London, Dad's photographic efforts continued. And of course, Joyce was the most important focus of his attention, as will be seen in these images below.

Joyce in the garden, presumably again at Albert Square.

Joyce again trying hard to see the dentist... This must be an early photo from Hatherley Gardens - before the air raid shelter was installed. Note Dad's bike behind her.

There was a family dog, a cocker spaniel who was Nan and Grandad's dog. Joyce entered him into a dog show at Saturday morning pictures in 1948/9. She was most abashed when the judge asked her to open Roy's mouth! Roy didn't win!!!

At the age of 2½ years, Joyce was a bridesmaid for the first time, at the wedding of Dad's sister Rose to our Uncle Reg. Here are two photos of her.

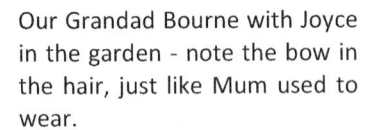

Our Grandad Bourne with Joyce in the garden - note the bow in the hair, just like Mum used to wear.

A rare photo taken by our Uncle Ern of Joyce in the garden at 140 - must have been soon after moving in.

This is also an early photo taken in the new house in Hatherley Gardens, which Mum and Dad (and Joyce) moved into in 1939. You can see to the right and behind Mum, an object which in fact is the half-built air raid shelter which most people had in their gardens.

In this photo, taken with Dad's sister Rose, Mum is wearing the same dress, but the air raid shelter seems complete, so it has to be a later date. And it would also appear that Mum is expecting another happy event...

In this one, we see Joyce with Mum, Nan and Grandad, at Hatherley Gardens. On the reverse it says that the baby is our cousin Margaret, Uncle Albert's first child. So this was taken during rather than before the war.

Joyce is on the left here at a birthday party next door, whilst her little brother Paul is the mucky one on the chair on the right.

Joyce was also a bridesmaid at the wedding of Mum's cousin Florrie.

Joyce is going so fast to win the egg and spoon race at Brampton School sports that her image is blurred!

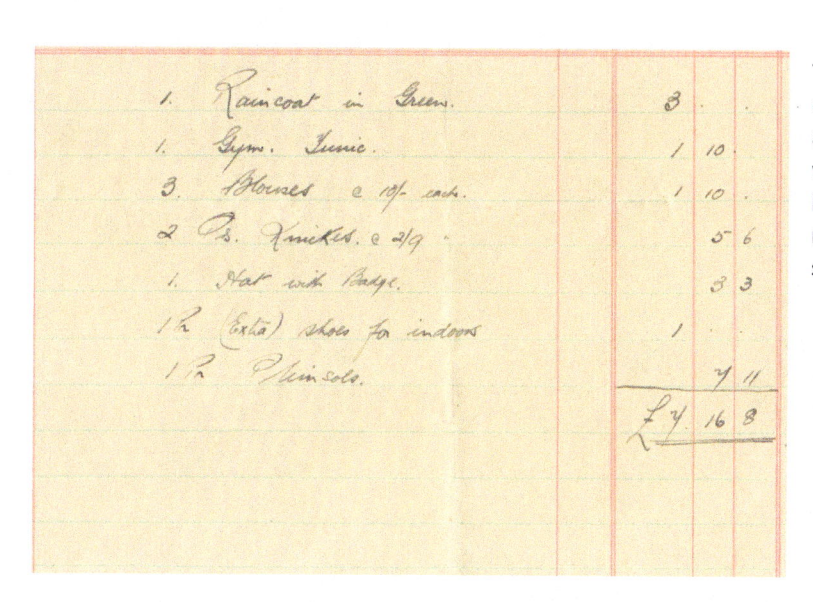

This is a note, written by Dad, of the school uniform list for Joyce's secondary school – but we are jumping the gun here. We first have to deal with what was obviously a major event in all their lives – the advent of war. Afterwards we will return to the progress of Joyce (and her new siblings) and to details about the house.

This seems like a good moment to show some recently discovered images of the family. In 1935, Dad's cousin Ernie Tyrrell, by then a successful business man, had purchased a cine camera, which he used frequently over the coming decades. Many of his films have survived and have been restored. From these it has been possible to extract some stills of interest to us here.

The first is a shot of Dad in Ernie's garden from about 1938. To judge by the pencils in his jacket pocket he must have come straight from work!

The remaining pictures were taken at the 1940 wedding of Dad's brother Wally.

7. Life during the War

To understand what life must have been like for our parents during the Second World War, you first have to realise what the situation was, and this means understanding where they lived. East Ham was close to the Docks. Nowadays the name Docklands is used (it never was then) but most people understand this as smart loft conversions of quayside properties or ultra modern office blocks. In those days the reality was very different. London was a working port, surrounded by industry of all sorts. There was also the largest gas works in the world, and a major sewage treatment plant (well, part-treatment, if our recollection of the smell of the Thames is to be trusted!) - all this was a prime target for the Hitler bombers during the Blitz in 1940-41 and later when the planes were replaced with the V1 and V2 rockets.

We include two maps of the area. If you look at the first map below you can see how close Hatherley Gardens (arrowed) was to the targets at the Royal Docks and others. The map was drawn up in 1936. In the second map, which is a close-up view, we have highlighted two areas, which is where our Grandad had successive allotments. The first one was just across the "Sewer Bank". This is the raised bank inside which is the "Northern Outfall Sewer", a masterpiece of Victorian civil engineering, which was created after Parliament could no longer stand the stench of the Thames outside their Westminster offices (though less concern had been shown over the many years when other Londoners just had to put up with it!) and set about the major engineering project of sewage works which exist to this day. It has to be said that they have improved. Our childhood trips on the Woolwich ferry were accompanied by smells which we still remember and which is why we never cease to be amazed that the river now attracts cormorants, herons, terns and many others, and that even salmon pass upstream. Somewhat euphemistically, the sewer bank, now a major cycle route, is known as the "Greenway"!

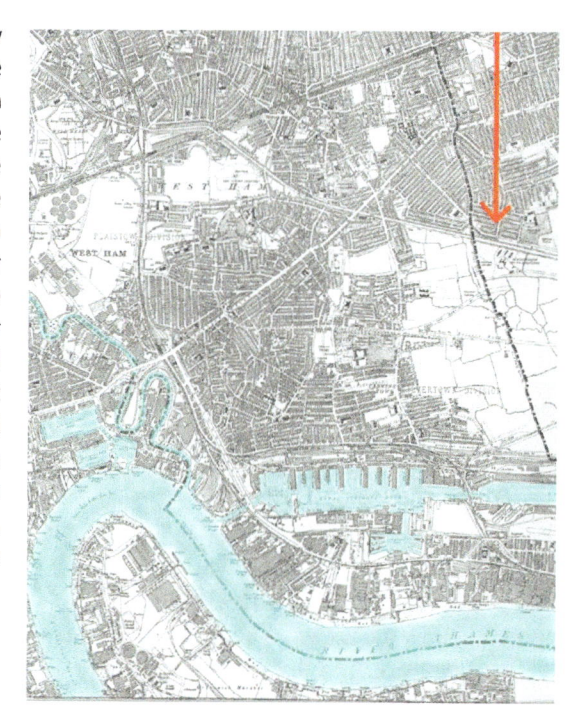

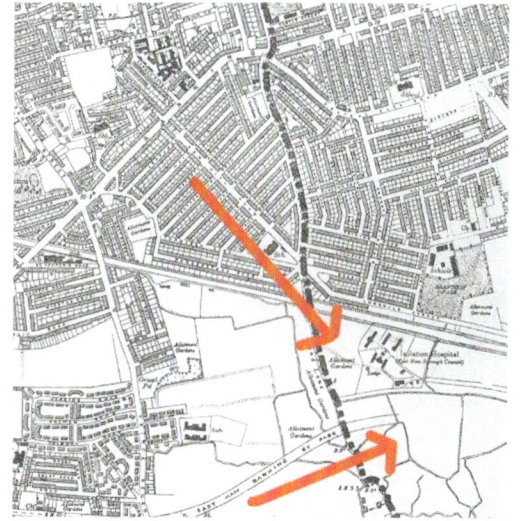

On a more fragrant note, Joyce recalls that after school she was often sent over to the allotment to take Grandad his flask of tea, and she often went with her friend Iris. On one occasion, for a special presentation of flowers which she needed for an event for the Girls' Friendly Society, Dad painted a basket, and she and Iris went to the allotment where Grandad allowed them to fill the basket with wallflowers (no money for florists in those days).
To this day the smell of wallflowers brings that moment back for Joyce. Later, Grandad had to give up the first allotment due to "impending redevelopment" – which didn't actually happen for years.

The second allotment was on the other side of what became the extremely busy A13 trunk road, a major route out of London to the east. In 1936 you can see that it was unfinished. When Pete and Paul were young, they used to go down to the main road with a wheelbarrow and wait until someone helped them across or got our Grandad to come and do the same. You wouldn't last long if you tried that today!

In those days, and until well into the 1960s, the area was marshland, small fields given over mostly to allotments, with tidal creeks - we remember seeing moorhens, yellowhammers and even skylarks, but today it is all the Beckton Housing and commercial estate, and all built on marshland!

In this final map of the area, you can see the close relationship between our house (in blue) the allotment, and our early schools (Brampton Infants and Juniors - in yellow). The isolation or fever hospital has long since gone, though as children we remember the odd ruin on the site. The allotment is now the site of Brampton Manor secondary school. The house we lived in was in what was known as the Central Park Estate, a large area of well-built Edwardian houses of various sizes, and which had some legal restrictions on commercial activities. Above all, there is to this day NO PUB! Referring again to the allotment, years later, after the site had lain derelict and overgrown for over a decade, Pete had one of his first summer holiday jobs, helping to lay out the playing fields for the new secondary school that was being built on the site.

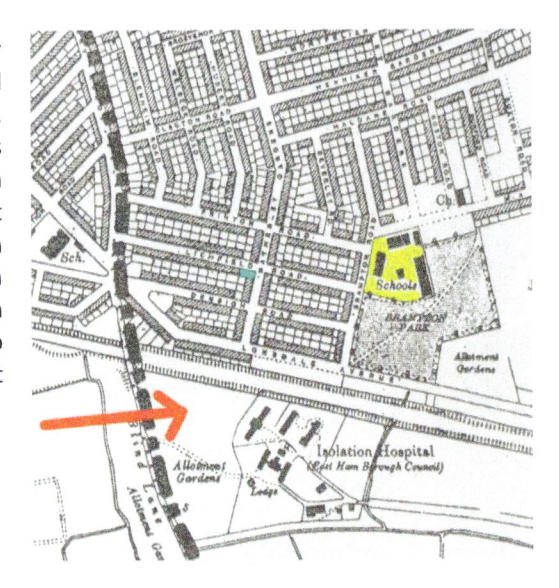

But to return to the war years, we have already seen how most residents had air raid shelters ("Andersons") in the back garden, (if they had one). The bombing was at times intense, especially during 1940 and 1941, and we are all familiar with this dark part of European history. There is of course the inevitable saga of solidarity in the face of adversity, the "cheeky Cockney" spirit of the Blitz, enhanced by the admirable fact that the Royal Family stayed in London throughout, even though urged to go to Canada for safety. But alas, as often happens, the myth was either created or enhanced for propaganda, and the reality was often quite different. This is not to gainsay the enormous heroism of many who worked in the emergency services, but there were also many "on the make" through black market and other corrupt or downright criminal behaviour. To bring the general down to the specific level, our house suffered some blast damage, and not long after builders had been in to effect repairs, it was noticed that a quite valuable clock had "gone missing". Mum always maintained that the builders had stolen it. It took some time, but eventually we believe that compensation was received.

Again relating the general to the individual, among the many properties that were bombed, our Nan and Grandad's shop in Stephens Road was hit. Nan and Grandad for some time came to live at Hatherley Gardens. But unrelated to this event (at least we suppose so!), is the question of evacuation. The situation must have been so hard to bear - and very hard for us to fully understand as we look back. Both Dad and Uncle Albert were called up, Dad to the Royal Army Pay Corps - as befits a treasury clerk as he was by then - and our Uncle in the Engineers as a mechanic. Here you can see them in their uniforms.

Of course, a familiar wartime situation, wives and mothers were left behind to look after the family. The levels of stress on both sides can only be imagined. But the way the British government came to the assistance (we won't say "rescue"!) was to begin the scheme of voluntary evacuation of non-essential residents from vulnerable areas, including, of course, the East End of London. Sometimes children were taken (not by force, we hasten to add) and went on organised train trips to rural areas, often without either parent, to be looked after by local families who took them in. This well documented phenomenon, for all its good and bad points, was spared for Joyce.

The first place Mum and Joyce went was for a time to Barnet, north of London. Joyce has some memories of this as she and Mum both spent a while in hospital, but in separate wards, rather traumatic for both of them. Dad's medical card shows their address.

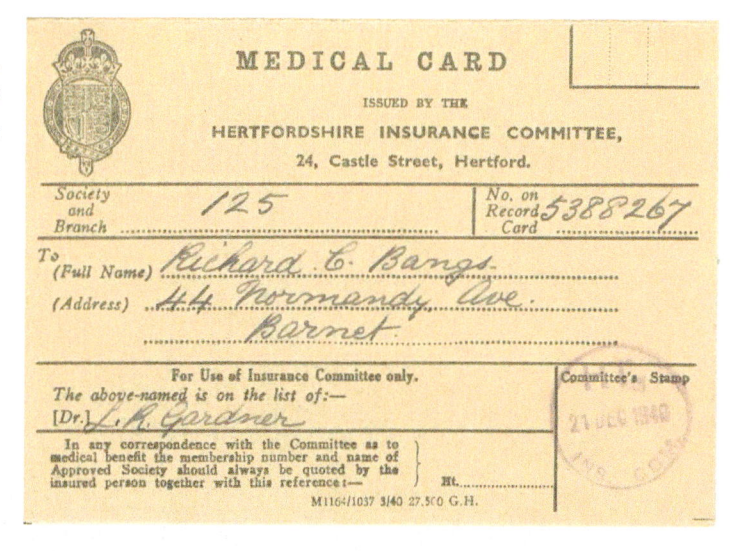

Then a better solution was found, because we, like others, had family already living in the country. Our Great-Aunt Doll, our Nanny Bourne's sister, at that time was living in Norfolk, married to our Uncle Mac Chamberlain. Aunt Doll had been married before and had two sons, Leslie and Michael. They lived in a tiny hamlet not far from the town of Diss, and that is where we go next. So off to East Anglia it was to be. Sadly, we have no real general view of the thatched cottage, which has long since been pulled down. But it was located in the hamlet of Short Green, near Winfarthing, which is the place name we always used.

In the maps which follow you can see the environs of Winfarthing. To say it was very rural is an understatement! Note the railway line passing close to Gissing. This is quite near where Aunt Doll, much later in the 60s, had another cottage. Pete and Paul remember putting pennies on the line for passing trains to flatten ..... ah, those townies.....

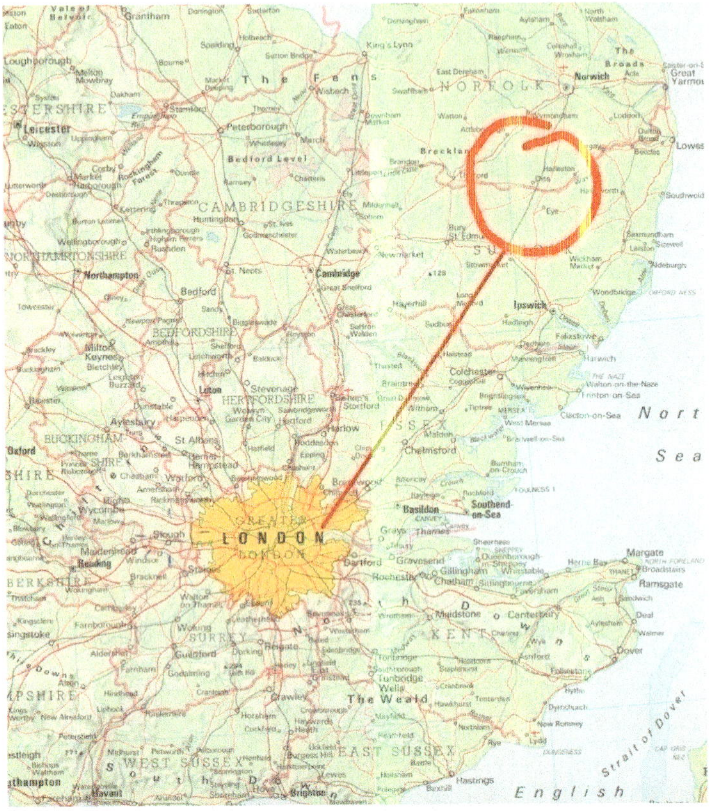
NORFOLK
Norwich
CAMBRIDGESHIRE
Cambridge
Ipswich
Colchester
Chelmsford
Southend-on-Sea
GREATER LONDON
LONDON
HERTFORDSHIRE
KENT
North Sea
English

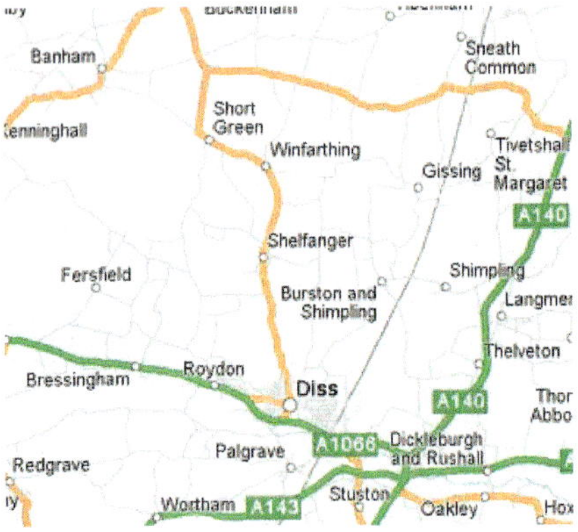
Banham
Sneath Common
Short Green
Winfarthing
Tivetshall St. Margaret
Gissing
A140
Shelfanger
Fersfield
Burston and Shimpling
Shimpling
Thelveton
Roydon
Bressingham
Diss
A1066
Dickleburgh and Rushall
Redgrave
Palgrave
Wortham
A143
Stuston
Oakley

Short Green
Winfarthing
Boyland New Fm
PH
45
High London Fm

WINFARTHING

WINFARTHING

All Saints V.A. C.E.
Primary School
Winfarthing
THE STREET

The photos were taken fairly recently, but still show the church, the school and the pub. Joyce will have attended some of these, though her lips are sealed as regards the pub! Dad's favourite local however was not the *Fighting Cocks* but *The Oak*. Banham can be seen on one of the above maps - this is where, in 1942, our great grandmother, known to us as Grandma Peckett, died.

The war meant many changes, not the least of them separation. Our Uncle Albert was due to be posted abroad (more on this later) and as happened with many in those times, rapidly married his girlfriend, our Aunt Bet, on Christmas Day in 1940. He did well to do so, as he was away from home for an incredible four long years! These are some photos of his wedding which took place in Bethnal Green but was celebrated afterwards in Barnet, North London. It's Joyce joining in the snowball fights.

The war also meant the introduction of identity cards. Here are Mum's, Paul's and Joyce's.

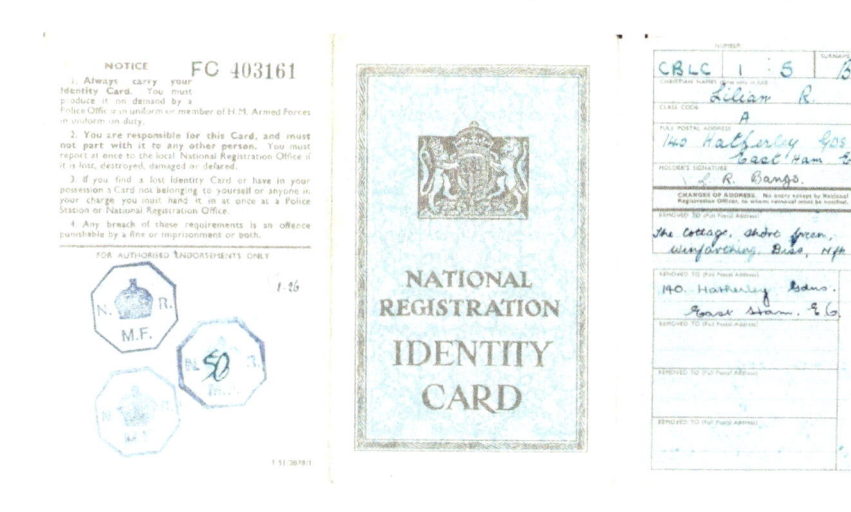

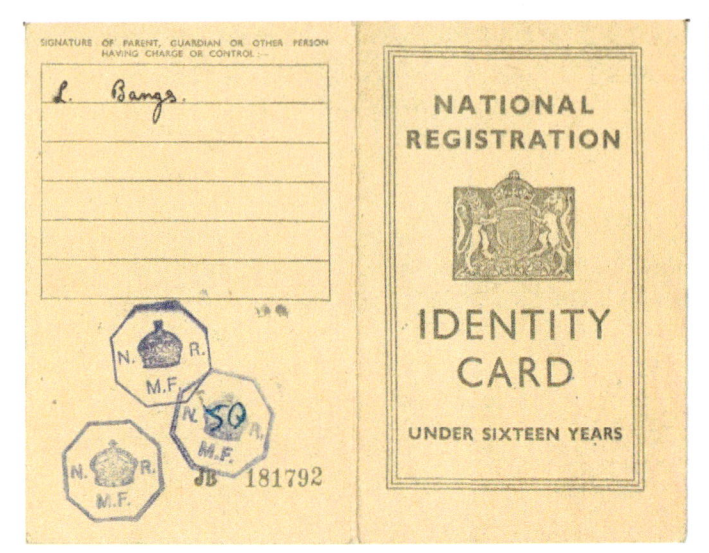

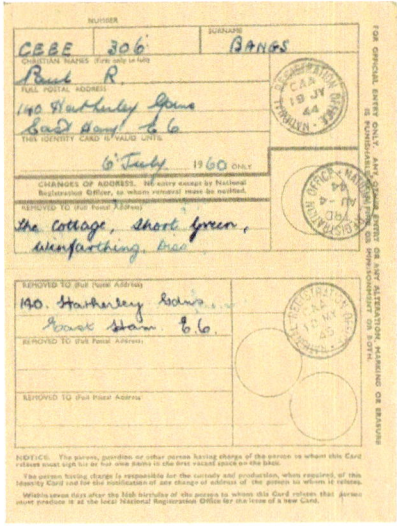

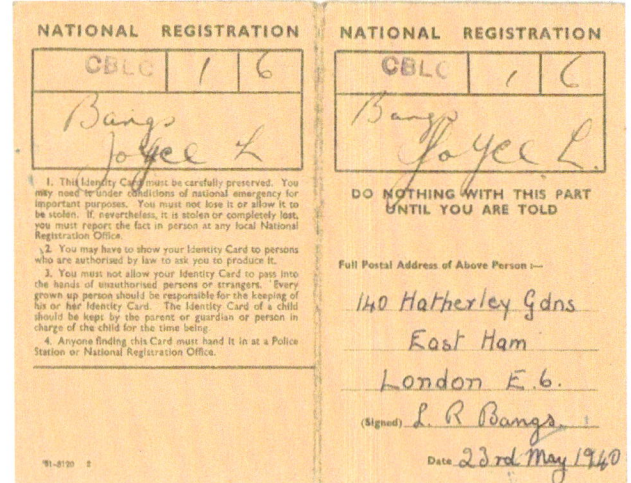

And here is Dad's. He, of course, had been conscripted – "called up" – into the army, and we will catch up with him in a special section in a short while.

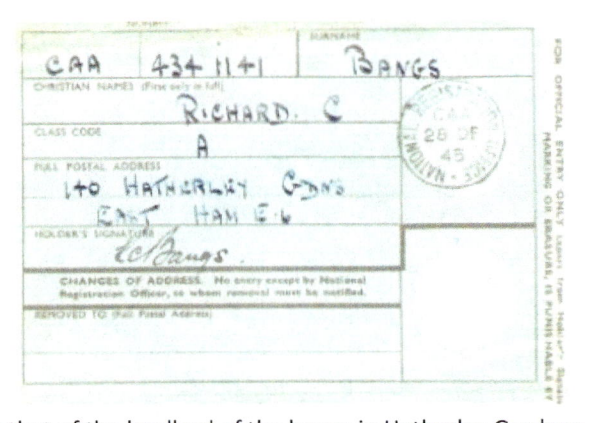

Of course it wasn't just our family affected. We have another example: that of the landlord of the house in Hatherley Gardens. We'll come back to the story of the house later. In the letter here you can read that he has been called up and therefore changes the arrangements for paying the rent.

Dick Bangs & Lily Bourne – Their story

> 16, South View Drive,
> E.18.
> 10/7/41
>
> Dear Mr. Bangs,
>
> I am very sorry indeed that I did not reply to your letter dated 10/2/41. I am afraid that it was just one of those things one ought to have done but has left undone. However, I did get the necessary roof repairs done promptly.
>
> I hope you and your family are keeping fit & well, and that you are finding Army life not too bad.
>
> We are all well here, but my turn for call-up has come. I shall probably go sometime in August.
>
> I shall then unfortunately be unable to attend to my mother's affairs, and my sister Mrs. R. J. MOXOM of "Highlands", 97, Queens Rd, Hertford, Herts will be doing this.
>
> When I hear from you that you have received this letter, I will forward to you a new bank paying-in book for A/c R. J. MOXOM, Barclays Bank Hertford. The rents should then be paid in at any Barclays branch, commencing at a date which we can arrange later. I hope this will be convenient & that you will be good enough to reply as soon as possible.
>
> I am going into the R.A.F. as a ground-gunner & so the Jerries had better beware.
>
> Kind regards to yourself & wife
> Yours sincerely, [signature]

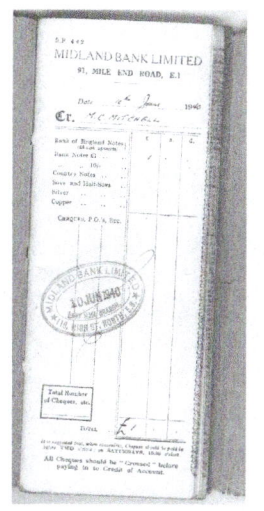

So the rent was moved from one paying-in book to another - as we can see ... and in the letter, note the threat to the enemy! And here is the actual paying in book referred to. Note that it is Mum who has had to do the honours – presumably Dad was already away from home.

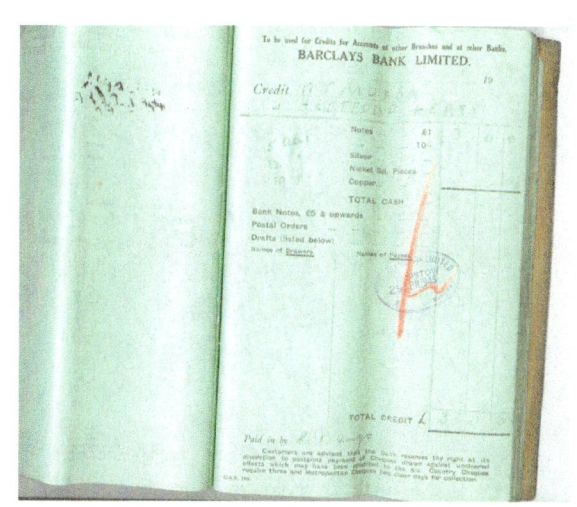

The rent book has survived – strangely, the amount here seems to be more than the amount paid in.

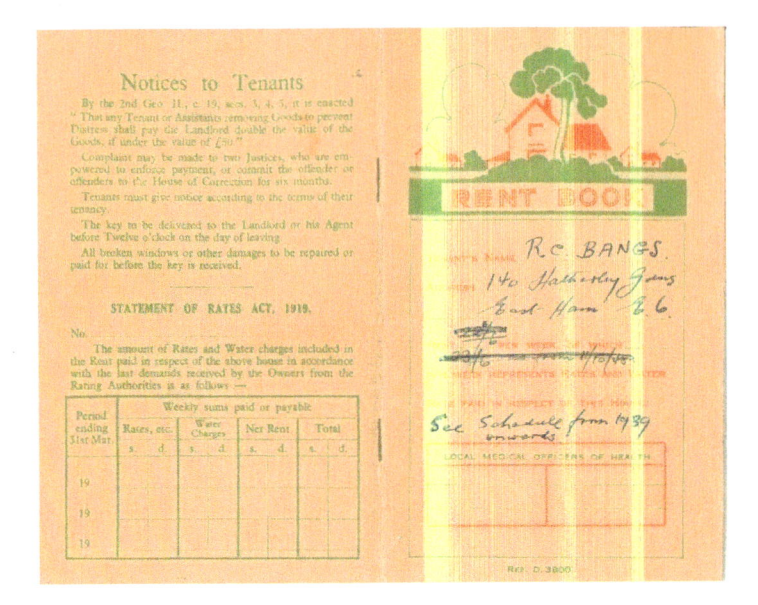

The figures on the sheets below only partly explain the discrepancies. But in any case, the rent was not much more than £1 per week!

Things, presumably, ticked over as best they could for a few years. Dad was for some time based in Foots Cray in Kent, not too far from London. Mum and Joyce continued to be at Winfarthing. Other family members were also called up or had what were known as "reserved occupations". For instance our Uncle Sid was a chef, and our Uncle Bill suffered from "petit mal" a mild form of epilepsy. In this photo you can see Uncle Bill in Home Guard uniform.

This photo is of Mum's uncle, Ernie Peckett, in uniform with his family. He had married Clara, a German national. We don't know if she suffered in any way during the war years. Uncle Ern was in the intelligence service, presumably for his linguistic skills.

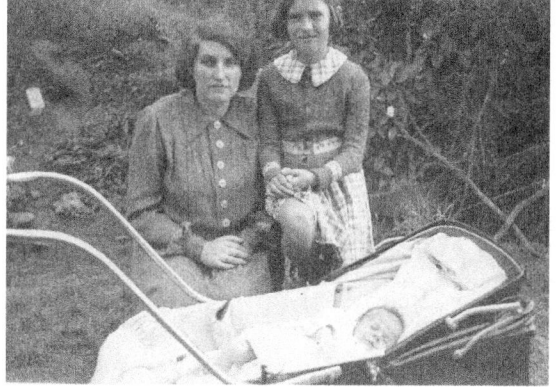

Then, as if the separation they had was not enough to bear, the news came to Dad that he would be going abroad. He was not allowed to divulge where he was going to be taken (if indeed he knew) and we don't know when this became apparent. Why this matters is that on July 6th 1944, their second child, Paul, came into the world, and he was just a few weeks old when Dad was taken off and did not see his son for about one year.

Whether the knowledge of impending parting accelerated the family expansion or not is impossible to judge - however it was not uncommon for soldiers to leave this type of "present" with their wives before departure, presumably responding to an innate desire to procreate the family in case of no return. We don't know what the real story is. In the photos here, we can see photos of Mum and Joyce with the new infant, taken in East Ham, another, taken in Winfarthing, probably whilst Dad was on embarkation leave, (so must have been taken between July 27th and August 8th 1944), and one more of Paul with Nan and Grandad Bourne at Hatherley Gardens. You can just glimpse Dad's prize tomato plants in the greenhouse.

We'll return to Paul (of course) in another section, but first we need to find out what happened to our father on his travels, so read on.....

8. Dad and his wartime travels

We mentioned just a while back that Dad had been called up to join the Royal Army Pay Corps. We don't have all the details of his service, but can piece together an awful lot. One thing which survived has been his Army Pay Book, seen here:

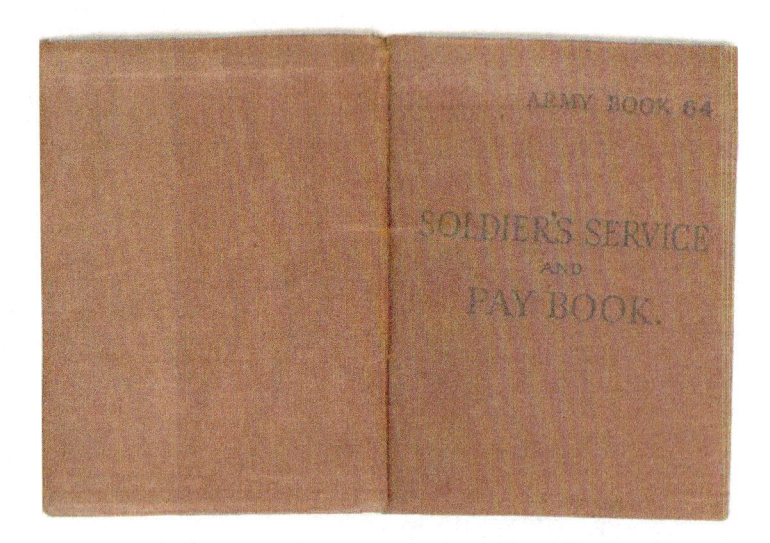

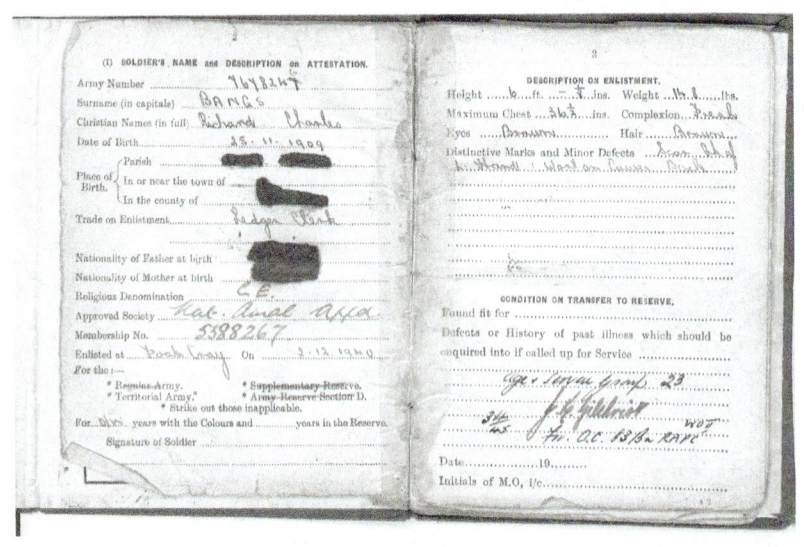

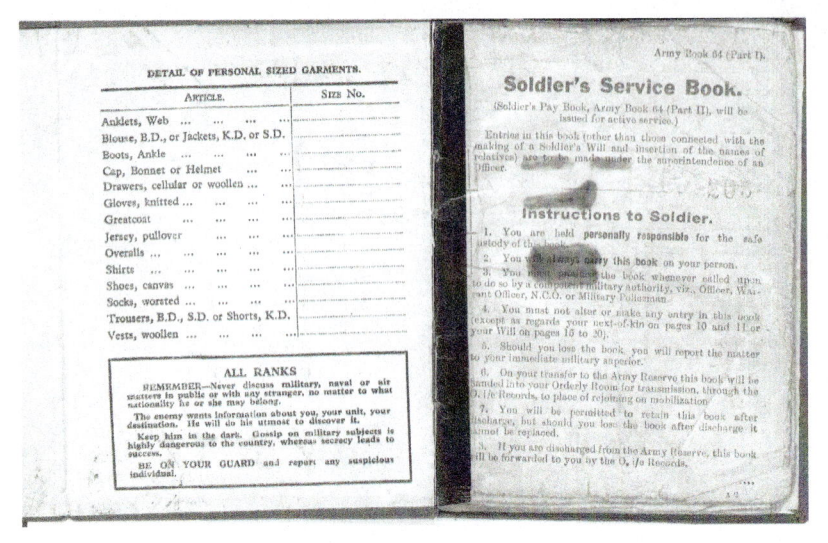

These are just a couple of pages from his service book. Full coverage of its contents can be seen in Appendix C. There are some interesting things to be gleaned from a closer reading. Apart from finding the identifying marks on Dad's body (!), we note that Dad initially seems to have been registered for the Territorial Army. Perhaps this was just a technicality for those called up - after all he wasn't a "regular". We can also see that Mum in 1940 had been evacuated to Barnet, which happened prior to the Winfarthing decision. And Dad's leave has been entered. In 1944 there was "Special" leave from the 27th July to the 8th August – presumably this was pre-embarkation leave before travelling to India. Later there was Privilege leave in May 1945 - this is useful information, as we can see that it almost certainly means that Dad was back in the UK (we believe in Edinburgh), by May 8th, although we think he didn't get to see Mum as he was ill at the time. And finally, Pete thinks the Privilege leave in August 1945 important for some reason. Work that one out for yourselves! Dad did not fill out the Will form – probably because he was not on what was designated as "Active service" – i.e. combat.

Although there are some things we don't know about Dad's travels, we are fortunate in remembering his tales, and in particular because some documents survive, and we will return to those. For instance Dad always told us that he travelled out to India (details in a while) on the famous liner, the *Queen Mary*. He was proud of that fact and remembers that it went first across the Atlantic to New York. The ship travelled alone rather than in convoy because it was so fast that it could outrun any waiting U-boats (German submarines).

However, our research tells us that it is most unlikely that he travelled back across the Atlantic and through the Mediterranean Sea and Suez Canal to Bombay still aboard the *Queen Mary* (which concentrated at that time on rapid trips just across the Atlantic ferrying soldiers in from the US for post D-Day operations). So we think he must presumably have been transferred to another, unknown ship, probably in New York. The best people, even Nelson, can suffer from sea-sickness and Dad was no exception, or so he wrote in a letter written on board ship.

In this picture, the Queen Mary is in wartime colours, and if you look carefully you can see that a strange "pipe" goes all round the ship. This is what was known as a "degaussing" strip, designed to reduce the magnetic "signature" of the vessel to avoid the attraction of magnetic sea mines. Here you can see a huge number of troops mustered on the ship's decks. The *Queen Mary* raced across the Atlantic carrying troops in both directions, and broke record passenger numbers as it brought US troops to D-Day and subsequent operations in Europe.

So where did our father end up? Read on .....

Dad was posted to Meerut, to the northeast of Delhi, in Northern India. You can see it on the map. He was at a headquarters camp which dealt with the pay and conditions of many soldiers who were in the Eastern theatre, mostly on the way to fighting the Japanese troops in Burma.

Meerut had been a well-known army town for many years of British Imperial control - the "Raj". It was even famous for a mutiny in the nineteenth century. The military area was known as the "cantonment", a term we often heard Dad use. Surprisingly, there are still vestiges of it left - the headquarters building is now a bank but can be seen in the modern photo.

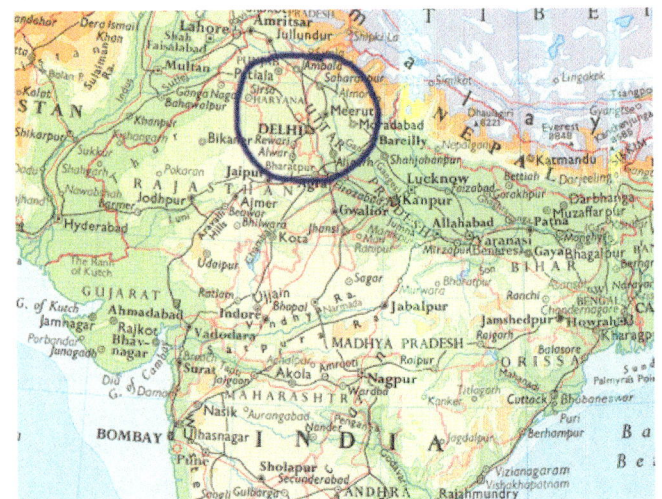

We sadly have just that one photograph of Dad in India, and here you can see him relaxing with friends, including Bill Flower, probably post-"tiffin". We know quite a bit about where he was, mainly because his letters home to Mum have survived. They are very personal, which is why we decided to publish them separately. We have, however, included a few selections here to give a flavour of some of the things he wrote.

Dad brought very few things back with him which have survived, but we have this menu of a Chinese restaurant which he presumably patronized. The prices are in Rupees and Annas.

CHINA CAFE

MENU OF CHINESE

AND

EUROPEAN DISHES

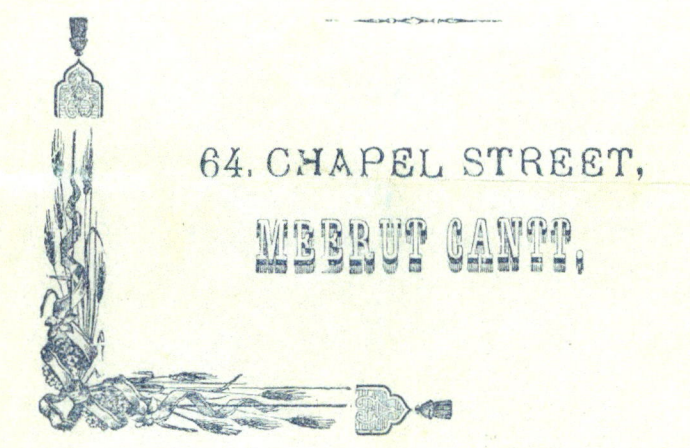

64, CHAPEL STREET,
MEERUT CANTT.

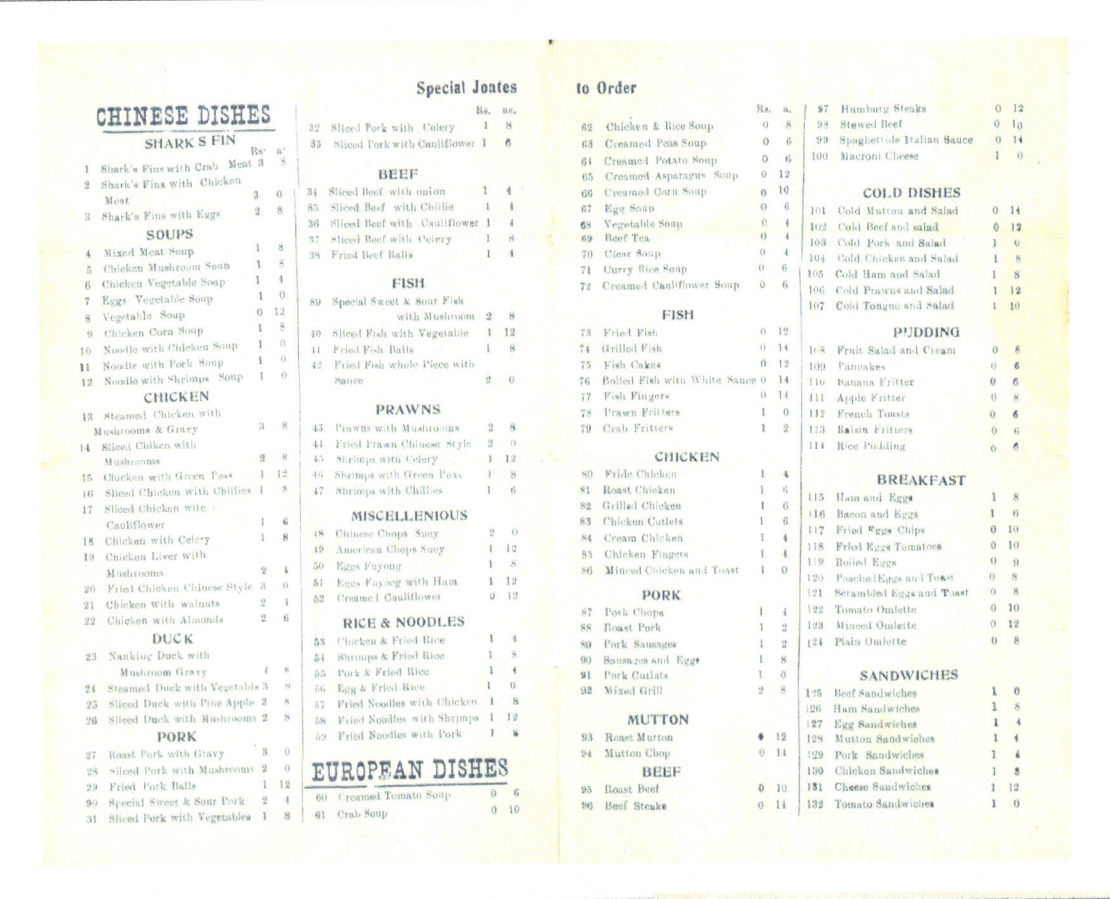

Amazingly, Dad was able to write every few days to Mum, and also to his own parents. The letters were sometimes on very thin paper, but more often written inside special covers, often referred to as "Airgraphs", like the one shown here. Note the military censor's stamp on the envelope.

We can with certainty know that letters to and from India and rural Norfolk were amazingly swift, taking as little as seven days! Of course they often crossed, but Mum and Dad soon adopted a system of numbering them so that they did not arrive at any misunderstandings.

In this letter, the first we know of after Dad left, he is writing on board ship. It is very hot, he has been seasick for three days, and is rather abusive about both cruises and, for some reason, Littlehampton!

> 7678246 Pte Bangs.
> RAPC
> RYHKK
> APO. 4015
>
> 30.8.44
> at sea
>
> My Darling,
>   I dont know when these few lines will reach you, but I am hoping you will receive them before we reach our destination as we are trusting our letters will be posted at first port of call. Well dear I have just about got my sea legs now, I must admit (as I knew I would) I have been under the weather for about 3 days. If anybody was to pay me to go on a cruise I should refuse. I would sooner go to Littlehampton. The weather at time of writing is lovely very hot. Well dear so
> (wearing shorts now)

And in this fragment of a letter we see much that was typical of what Dad wrote on many occasions. He shows concern about his family's well-being, about "dear old Topsy" (Joyce) and as here, little Paul. Above all he is continually worried about any possible return or visit to London, because of the bomb and rocket attacks. Life was not too bad for Mum in the countryside if she could eat partridges and mushrooms!

We in fact learn so much more about life in London and Norfolk than we do about India, which, given that he was in what was for him a really exotic place, is quite surprising.

One concern centred in a good number of letters on the possibility of Mum and the children attending Uncle Bill's wedding. We only have one half of the correspondence, but it seems as though at one stage Mum just put her foot down and said she was going! But the letters display how much tension and worry there must have been for separated loved ones at that time, as we can glimpse Dad's frustrations at not knowing whether they had returned safely until the next letter was received least a week after the event. Did Mum go to the wedding? Well you can judge for yourself from the photo. And yes, that's Joyce as a bridesmaid again.

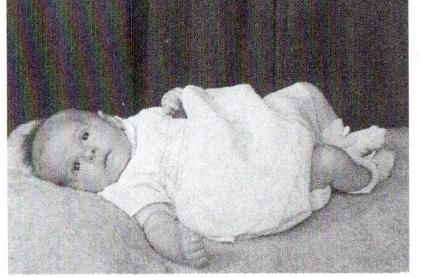

Dad did receive the occasional photos of his family, such as this one of Paul, aged seven weeks, but it was to be over a year before he saw him again - on which occasion Paul screamed when he saw this unknown man!

Dad was not the only one of our family to be in India. Mum's brother, our Uncle Albert, also served there, but on active service as a mechanic in the Royal Engineers. As we said earlier, he was away from home for an incredible four years, first serving in Europe, where he was involved in the retreat and evacuation at Dunkirk, then in India. Although he was in contact with Dad in Meerut, they never managed to meet up as hoped for. His letters to Mum and his parents show once again a remarkable degree of concern for what is happening in London, especially with regards to the suffering of the children. Here we have a few pictures taken on those long travels.

Not all members of our family were lucky enough to survive the war. Our Aunt Doll was informed in January 1945 that her son Leslie, serving in the Royal Air Force, was missing in action. His death was later confirmed. The even sadder thing is that his death was due to so-called "friendly fire" as his plane was shot down by US forces. Here we show his photograph, a letter from his commanding officer, a message of condolence from the King and a photo of his last resting place in Belgium. This is one small way we can honour all those who gave their lives in such circumstances, in the same way as we can see that there is a memorial plaque to him in the church in Winfarthing.

Here is a brief extract from the Commonwealth War Graves web site about the cemetery: *"The British Expeditionary Force was involved in the later stages of the defence of Belgium following the German invasion in May 1940, and suffered many casualties in covering the withdrawal to Dunkirk. Commonwealth forces did not return until September 1944, but in the intervening years, many airmen were shot down or crashed in raids on strategic objectives in Belgium, or while returning from missions over Germany. There are about 35 original burials in Leopoldsburg War Cemetery associated with isolated engagements in or near the town in May 1940. Of the remainder, some are burials from a military hospital which was established at Leopoldsburg during the latter part of 1944 and others were brought into the cemetery from the surrounding district. There are now 767 Commonwealth burials of the Second World War in the cemetery, 16 of them unidentified, and a number of Polish and Dutch war graves".*

No 218 (Gold Coast) Squadron,
Royal Air Force,
Chedburgh,
Bury-St-Edmunds,
Suffolk.

2nd January, 1945.

Dear Mrs Chamberlain,

      I am writing to offer you the sincere sympathy both of myself and the whole Squadron in the anxiety you have experienced since learning that your son Sergeant Leslie Peckett is missing from air operations.

      Your son was Flight Engineer in an aircraft detailed for operations against the enemy on the 1st January, 1945, and which subsequently failed to report back to base.

      In view of the fact that each member of the crew was thoroughly conversant with the procedure to be followed in the event of emergency it is quite likely that they may have been forced down in enemy territory in which case they will become Prisoners of War. In that event any further news as to their whereabouts would be received by the International Red Cross, and transmitted by them to the Air Ministry, who would then get into touch with you at once. The request in the telegram regarding casualty of your son was inserted in order that his chances of escape might not be prejudiced by undue publicity, but does not mean that at the time of writing any further information is available. It is merely inserted as a precaution in the case of all missing aircrew.

      On behalf of the whole Squadron I wish to convey to you our very deepest sympathy for you during this trying time of waiting news.

Yours very sincerely,

Squadron Leader Commanding,
No. 218 Gold Coast Squadron.

Mrs. Chamberlain,
The Cottage,
Short Green,
Winfarthing, Nr Diss Norfolk.

BUCKINGHAM PALACE

The Queen and I offer you our heartfelt sympathy in your great sorrow.

We pray that your country's gratitude for a life so nobly given in its service may bring you some measure of consolation.

George R.I.

Mrs. D. Chamberlain.

PI

IMPERIAL WAR GRAVES COMMISSION,
Wooburn House,
Wooburn Green,
High Wycombe,
Bucks.

18th. September 1953.

Dear Madam,

The permanent headstones have been erected on war graves in many parts of the world, and the headstone engraved with the personal inscription chosen by you is now in place. Although you may already know this, the Commission feel you will like to have this formal notification.

In an earlier letter, the Commission referred to the desire known to be felt by many relatives to contribute towards the cost of engraving the personal inscription and added that an opportunity to do so would be given to them later.

If you had thought of making a contribution would you kindly complete and detach the slip below and return in the enclosed envelope. You may send any sum up to £1, which is the average cost of engraving these inscriptions.

I would like, however, to make it clear that relatives are under no obligation to send a contribution unless they wish, and if the Commission do not hear further from you, the cost of engraving your inscription will be met from their funds.

Yours faithfully,

SECRETARY.

Detach by tearing along the dotted line

Personal inscription for the headstone for: Sergeant (F/Eng) L. Peckett, R.A.F.(VR) in Leopoldsburg War Cemetery, Belgium.

In reply to your letter, I should like to contribute to the cost of engraving the personal inscription chosen by me for this headstone and I enclose..

Signed.. Date................

From:—
Mrs. D. Chamberlain,
The Cottage,
Short Green,
Winfarthing,
Diss, Norfolk.

To:—
IMPERIAL WAR GRAVES COMMISSION,
P.I. DEPARTMENT,
Wooburn House,
Wooburn Green,
High Wycombe,
Bucks.

(48768) WT.P.0389/2827 20,000 6/53 A.& E.W.LTD. GP.685

The months went by, marked by this correspondence. Rocket attacks became more frequent in London and our Grandad became ill with heart trouble, which stayed with him until he died in 1953. Apart from the obvious concern, Uncle Albert shows another worry which soldiers must have had when serving - what employment fate awaited them when the war was over? If Grandad no longer had the lorry and business, what was he to do? All these worries are shown at long distance in the many letters.

Dad didn't only write to Mum. Some letters have recently surfaced in which he writes to his brother Bill and to his own parents. In October 1944 he sends this to his parents (the original is not too easy to read).
R Bangs
Date 1.10.44
RAPC ....
British Army Pay Office
Meerut, India

Dear Mum Dad and Family
Here I am again with a few more lines to let you know I am still OK and settling down. I received a letter yesterday from Lily dated 14. 9. 44, the first since leaving, and she informed me that Albert was now out here. I made enquiries and found that he landed about 9 weeks before me I have his address and have sent him a letter today so should know in a few days where he is actually stationed. All that I am hoping is that he is not too far away, and that it won't be long before we can meet, but still that remains to be seen but will let you know later. Lily said that Peggy was coming home so I expect things are not too bad these days. I hope so. How is Bill getting along OK I hope. I expect he is looking forward to the great day eh. Was it the 12th of Nov. Please let me know. I hope and trust that Dad is still keeping well, and how are you Mum still the same eh. I expect Sid is still at it, I hope he is in the same game. Any news of Wally and Ivy these days. I hope they have wrote you. Has Rose returned yet? If in touch with her please give her my love and hope Jean is keeping OK. According to Lily the baby is progressing OK and Joyce is going to school so things are not too bad up there.
Well folks space is short so here's hoping to hear from you soon. So for time being will say Cheerio Folks
Best of Love. Your son
xxxxxxxxx "Dick"

As we said earlier. Dad and Uncle Albert never did get to meet up. A fascinating thing to note is that Dad had received a letter from Mum which she dated 14th September, and which he received within 2 weeks. The reference to Peggy was that she would be coming home after giving birth to her daughter Mary. And Bill's "great day" would be his wedding to Jean Clapp. And of course, the "baby" is Paul. The post may have been good, but the army wasn't expecting it to be that good, as the cover of the "Aerogram" was a Christmas issue, shown here.

There are also two letters from Dad to his brother Bill, the first of them dated 26th November 1944:

7648346 Pte Bangs R.
R.A.P.C. (ABW)
British Army Post Office
Meerut, India Command
06.11.44

My Dear Bill,

Many thanks for yours of the 14th, as you can guess I was very pleased to hear that things went off OK, and that Lily managed to get along. With the exception of Sid standing in the wrong place, things went according to plan eh? It appears that everybody had a good time, and as you speak of the well filled table, not to mention the Beer etc, I don't think anyone had cause to complain. So you think my son is grand eh? I hope you and Jean took the pattern eh! and Joyce had not forgot her previous do's eh? Well how do you like married life Bill, I hope and trust that it will be as happy as mine. I understand that you are stopping at 13, and am very pleased to know that Mum & Dad were to on their own, as I expect Sid is still away. How are things going at the Vic & Vis. I do hope that things are not too bad Bill, as you hear very little of home news out here. Many thanks for ordering the Papers No 3, & also for the newspapers, will let you know when I receive them. Have not received any yet, but they should be along shortly now. I hope and trust that by the time you receive this Peggy will have got over her event, and that things are OK (daughter?) Please give them my love Bill. How is Mum & Dad going, I expect these new doings have not done Dad any good, but at any rate hope & trust that they are both keeping well. I had a letter from Alfie today, and am awaiting until he manages to get some leave, and I hope to arrange for him to come up here, so it looks as though we shall meet in due course. I also had a letter from Rose last week she told me that Reg has gone, and she has sent him my address in case he should get near here, one never knows eh.

My thoughts were with you on the 12th October by now I am afraid I could only manage to drink your health in Tea, but as you know the wish was there. Was so glad that Wally managed it, and as Lily said he is looking fit & well. I hope he manages to stay put. Well Bill I hope you are feeling better these days, and that you are managing to find plenty of work. I can assure you there is plenty out here, but as the time goes very fast, and the weather is really good these days, things are not too bad. Please give my love to Jean and many thanks for her good wishes, and I sincerely hope that it will not be long before I shall be able to Kiss the Bride. Well folks space is short once again so please give my love to Mum & Dad, and remember me to Aunties, and to You & Jean all the best, happiness etc & trusting that things remain quiet.

So for now all the Best
Yours as Ever
Dick. xxxx
xxxx
x
(the Bride).

Once more we can praise the army postal service – on the 26th Dad is replying to a letter he has received dated the 14th – just over a week for a letter from London to India! The letter was written after Bill married, and confirms that Mum had attended (something Dad had advised against), and that Bill has seen his son (of course that was Paul), although we know that he travelled with Mum but was not at the ceremony. There is a continuing worry about the V1s and V2s, the rockets that dropped on London around that time. Peggy's "event" was the birth of our cousin Mary – curious how direct mention of words associated with such "events" was avoided! Also of interest is the fact that Dad has had a letter from Albert – the army postal service really was an efficient one. And finally, the reference to Bill being unwell is because he suffered from "petit mal", a mild form of epilepsy, which rendered him unfit for active service.

A second letter to Bill is dated 19th December.

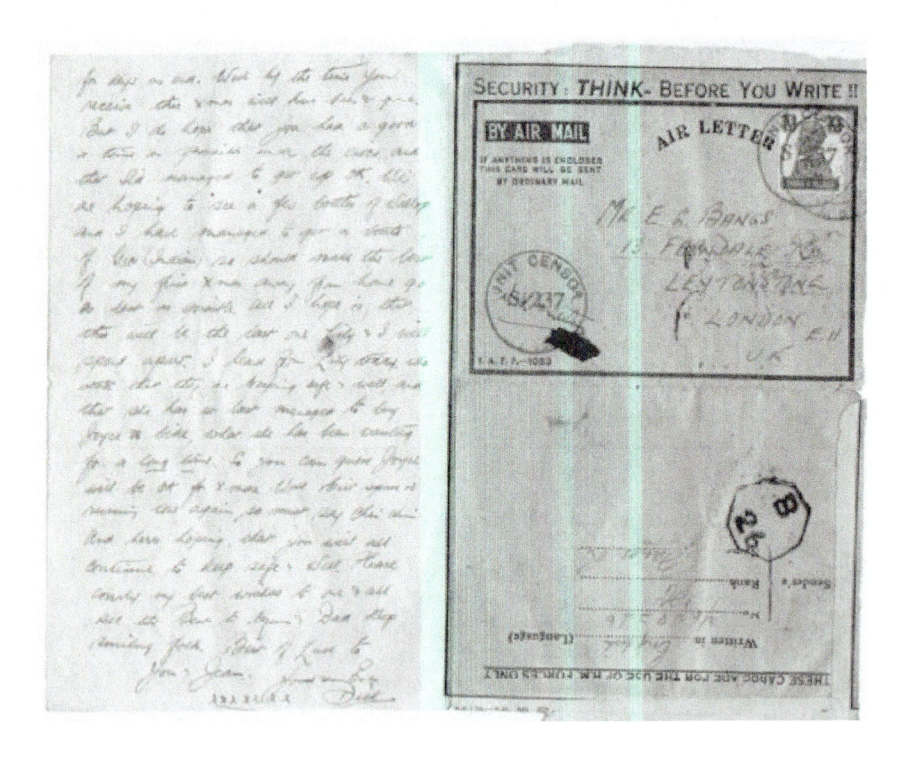

This is now after the wedding of course, and we can note Dad's lovely reference to not wanting to be single again himself. "Auntie" is their Aunt Sarah (Tyrrell) from Walthamstow, whose house received an indirect bomb attack and was being repaired at the time. The "B – things" are of course the Nazi rockets. Dad's usual concern for other family members is apparent, and then he makes one of the very few references to his situation in India, where is is at that time surprisingly cold! He then mentions that Joyce (lucky girl!) will have a bike for her Xmas present.

Meanwhile, back in Winfarthing, Mum, Joyce and Paul survived the cold Norfolk winter and waited for the end of the war. Joyce amused herself by looking after Paul (when she didn't drop him in a ditch!), pole vaulting a stream when sent to fetch water from the well, and riding her bike to the local school, where she did well, in spite of problems with "her sums". Oh, and Mum got into trouble with the authorities for what we would now call "unauthorised absences" - presumably when they went to London for the wedding!

Another occupant of the cottage was a monkey, known as Flakky, and as you can see Joyce adored him. He was left behind by a US airman from the nearby base, who, sadly, did not make it back from a mission. Alas, Flakky was not so popular with others, and when he eventually sat on Paul's head and bit him, he had to go, despite Joyce's anguish, to Banham zoo. Paul has never looked back!

In Dad's letters, rumours abounded about the impending end of the war and "demobilization" of the forces. Mum continued to live in Winfarthing, still under war-time conditions - here you can see the clothing ration books we all had to have - even the Royal Family, apparently!

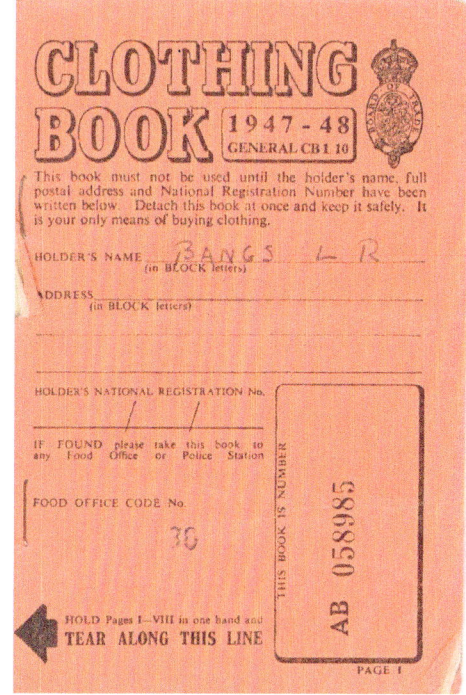

Eventually, Dad travelled home. He travelled on the *Strathmore* - perhaps not along the lines suggested in the tourist brochure, though! The pictures are of the *Strathmore*, including the one showing troops being unloaded at Southampton. There is also a picture taken from an unknown troopship as it passed through the Suez Canal. We have still a mystery about exactly where Dad disembarked – at Southampton or Liverpool.

We always knew that he was in Edinburgh for a while as he was ill in hospital. However, when we received all Dad's army records (below you can see the three pages which detail his "career") we were surprised at a few things. Firstly that he had spent two overnight stays in hospital in 1941 and 1942 (the latter in an isolation hospital) for reasons we are unaware of. He was moved around in the RAPC (Royal Army Pay Corps) as you can see by the abbreviations SOS (*struck off strength*) and TOS (*taken on strength*) and we can see the exact dates of his arrival in India (22/09/1944) and at Meerut three days later. Later he embarked for the return in Bombay on the 12th April 1945, and disembarked in the UK on the 5th May 1945. The name of the ship is only referred to by code.

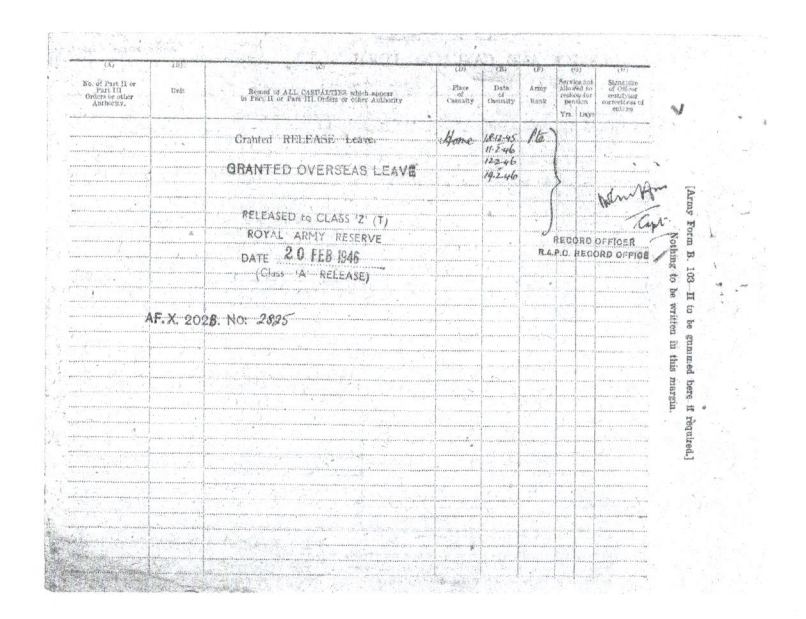

We have some more proof of his whereabouts in the Edinburgh library card you see here, along with a cut-out address from a letter he must have sent, presumably to Mum, but which has not survived. From his Army Passbook we know that he was on leave, and in the UK, from May 8th.

After his leave finished (on May 21st) he wrote to Mum the next day as we see from the address torn off the letter. However, the library card carries the date of 7th July, the day after Paul's first birthday. In the meantime we know that he was admitted to the Astley Ainslie Institution in Edinburgh, but the records do not show the reason. He was admitted on the 9th July, just after the letter was written, and discharged on the 17th August. He must have been home not long after that, as Peter was born in the following May - work that one out for yourselves!

There is a photo of the hospital as it is today, and it seems to have changed very little. Apart from this information about dates, there is little else in the records, apart from Dad's eligibility to gain the Defence Medal, which we know he declined - in case it is of interest, there is an image of what he might have had!

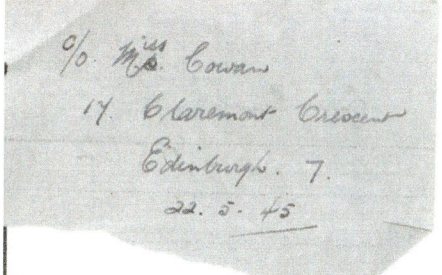

9. Post-war events

Dad came back from India and before long was "demobilised" on the 19th February 1946. But he had to remain on the army reserve register for a time. We know that there was a burning of his army boots - during the incredibly harsh winter of 1947. Below you can see part of his Release papers, one page of which gives a testimonial –

"*Excellent clerk of quick intelligence and steady application. Punctual, loyal reliable.*" The entire set of documents is included in Appendix D, where there is also part of his reserve transfer document.

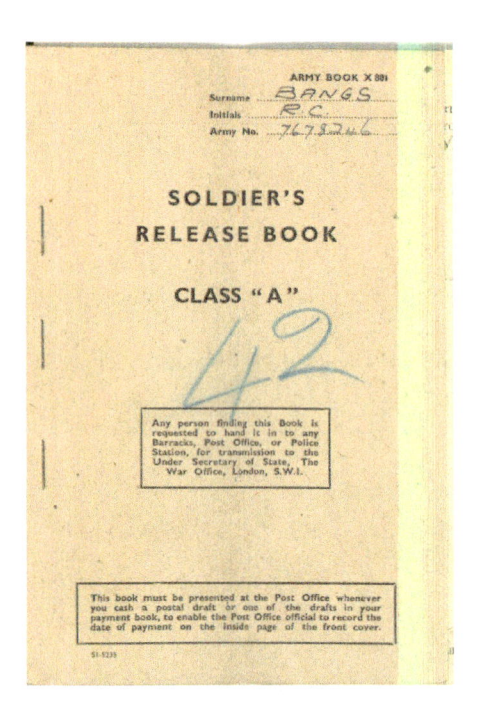

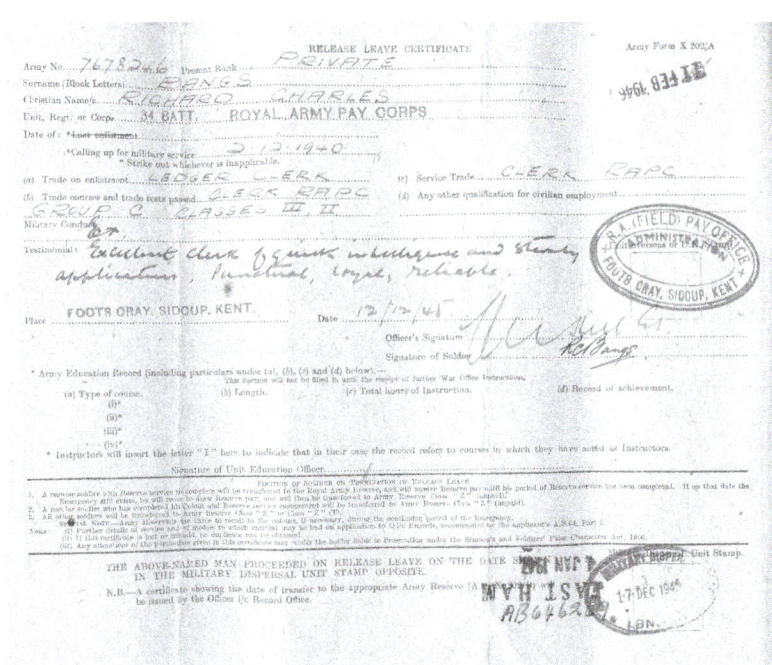

Whilst not exactly poor, money was in short supply in those days. Dad was fortunate in getting his old job back - in fact to a certain extent there was some protection for returning soldiers. As you can see, Dad kept a copy of his letter of application to the Council for his job and we also have the letter sent back immediately inviting him for interview. He worked in the same job until he retired in 1974.

COUNTY BOROUGH OF EAST HAM

W. H. WILLIAMS
F.S.M.T.A., A.S.A.A.
BOROUGH TREASURER

TREASURER'S DEPARTMENT.
TOWN HALL,
EAST HAM, E.6.

TEL. GRANGEWOOD 1430

BTJ/EM.   14th January, 1946.

Dear Sir,

I have received your letter of the 10th instant notifying me of your release from H.M. Forces.

I enclose an application for temporary clerical employment form, which I shall be obliged if you will complete and bring with you to my office on Wednesday morning, the 16th instant, at 11 a.m. When you call, please ask to see the Deputy Borough Treasurer.

Yours faithfully,

Borough Treasurer.

Mr. R.C. Bangs,
140, Hatherley Gardens,
East Ham,
E.6.

Army Form B 2072
(Revised 1945)

UNEMPLOYMENT INSURANCE ACTS.

MEMORANDUM FOR—

(No.) 7678246
(Rank and Name) PTE. BANGS R.C
(Regiment) ROYAL ARMY PAY CORPS

The Ministry of National Insurance has this day been requested to credit you with the number of contributions to which you are entitled under the Unemployment Insurance Acts, in respect of your Army service. No stamped Unemployment Books are issued by the War Office, but an Unemployment Book will be forwarded to you by the Ministry of National Insurance at an early date, for presentation to your employer if you are proceeding to insurable employment. If you require assistance in obtaining employment, or are unable to obtain employment and wish to claim unemployment benefit you should apply at once (taking your Unemployment Book with you, if you have received it) to the nearest local office of the Ministry of Labour and National Service, which Department acts as agent for the Ministry of National Insurance in this matter.

The credit of Unemployment Insurance contributions is made on the basis of one contribution for each week of approved service. The effect of this is to place you on your return to civil life in the same position in relation to unemployment benefit as if you had been employed as a civilian in insurable employment for the same period. A soldier discharged in consequence of a conviction on any proceedings under the Army Act or by any civil court will not be eligible to receive unemployment benefit during the period of six weeks next after his discharge. No deductions are made from a soldier's pay in respect of Unemployment Insurance while he is serving. The contributions are for benefit purposes only and in no circumstances can any cash payment or allowance be made in lieu of the credit. Further, the credit of these contributions does not in any way relieve the employer or employee from payment of contributions under the Unemployment Insurance Acts for employment in an insurable occupation in civil life, even if such employment occurs during a period of furlough.

It should be understood that the contributions credited in respect of Army service will not be available for benefit in Eire or the Isle of Man or the Channel Islands. They will only be so available in Great Britain or, in certain circumstances, Northern Ireland, as and when you are unemployed there.

His war record was also used as a credit for National Insurance contributions as the document here shows.

Now back, of course, in East Ham, we all settled down to family life after the war. Rationing of certain items continued for a while - hard to explain to kids today in these times of plenty that, even if you had the money, you were only allowed to buy a certain (small) quantity of sweets! Nan and Grandad still had the shop, though under a tarpaulin roof on a bomb site. The first big event was, of course, the arrival of Pete. We have been pondering why this bundle of joy does not rejoice in as many photos as his siblings, and our conclusion is that, rather than being an example of "third child syndrome", it reflects the added burden of photographic costs in the post-war period. Pete thinks that quality, not quantity is what counts. Never mind, there are some cute pictures of his early years as you will see here. This is the earliest picture we can find of Pete, in his pram in the front garden at Hatherley Gardens.

Here is Pete as a toddler, and then two more of him aged about seven and ten.

It's not difficult to spot Pete in this school picture, with the oh so archetypical schoolteacher, Miss Jones!

The other photos are of a May Day pageant at school.

So the family is complete, and Dad has his job back. Paul's days as the only son are over, but here is one early photo taken in the road at Letchworth, where Mum had relatives.

Now of course Paul has to get in on the act as a big brother, and there are photos of the two together - saving on film? They were often dressed alike - bear in mind that Mum's skills as a dressmaker were employed to the full and many of the clothes were made by her.

Visits from family also became frequent. In this photo Pete and Paul are joined by cousins Jean and Vivienne and Aunt Rose in the garden.

Here we both are with other cousins, Reene and Rita. In these photos notice that the air raid shelter has now been removed and in the background you can see the rudimentary shed which was where the coal was stored.

Whilst on the subject of family, Bill and Jean had an arrival in 1945 of their son Roland (now known as Roy), and when he was just two, he was with Grandma Bertha near their home when a car ploughed into them on a pedestrian crossing and knocked them down. Roland was unhurt, but Bertha needed hospital treatment. Roy says he can even remember the event, as he had to be taken into someone's home nearby until help arrived. This misfortune was marked in a card and a letter which have survived. The birthday card is written by Mum, and mentions her recovery on the back.

The letter was also written by Mum:

> 140 Hatherley Gdns.
> East Ham E6.
> 18.11.47.
>
> Dear Mum,
> I hope these few lines find you comfortable, although I expect you are feeling rather sore now the bruises are coming out. I must say I was surprised to hear of your accident as I know how careful you are of the road. You must have known it was going to turn cold and wanted to stay in the warm.
> Still joking apart mum I do hope you are not feeling too bad. don't forget what you tell us "keep your chin up!". No doubt it helped you to know that Roland was O.K..
> Dick will be coming in to see you this evening. He said what a lovely baby Vivienne is. Joyce sends her love and hopes you will soon be well.
> Mum and Dad send their best wishes for a speedy recovery.
> Cheerio for now. Mum.
> Lots of love. from
> Lily xxxxxxxxxxx

The jokey style does not disguise genuine concern. Vivienne was of course, the second child of Dad's sister Rose and Reg. Another fascinating insight into postal services is seen: in the first instance Mum says that Dad would be going to visit that same day – but then changes it to "tomorrow" – perhaps she just missed the morning post? A service that has long since disappeared.

Back to our own family. Excursions were also made, but we have no idea where this rural picture was taken.

Paul still had some photos of his own - as here in the garden and others, aged about six and seven.

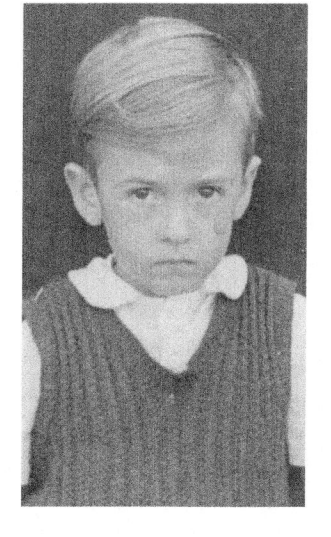

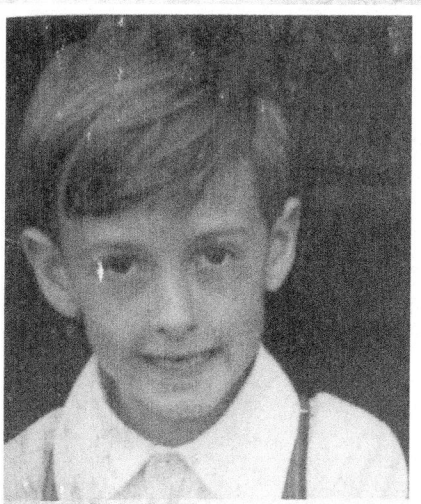

By now Dad had replaced the garden lawn with concrete to make it more pleasant for Mum to hang out the washing in the winter! The concrete was always cracked! Dad delighted in planting the border flowers, which were always the same – alyssum and lobelia, referred to as "blue and white".

You may think we were deprived in having to play at sandcastles in the back garden, as in the next photo, but as you will see from the one following that, there were trips to the beach. In the background of the first you can see the home-made barrow we had for years and which we used to take to Grandad's allotment to bring home produce. It was also used to go with Dad to collect off-cuts of wood from a local furniture factory which we used as kindling for the coal fire.

Still photographed together, you can see that Paul has begun to wear glasses. And in the rather blurred photo, Dad is with us in the garden.

In this photo, taken by our Uncle Ern, we are with that wheelbarrow again! The long-gone greenhouse can be seen, where Dad grew his tomatoes, along with the ladder stored gift-wise for burglars, and on the left the "pig-bin" where we put food waste for collection.

And in the next one you can see Paul and Peter with cousin Mary and Uncle Ern - we think Aunty Peggy took the photo.

Paul also had school photos and May Day pageants (definitely no starring roles though) and also photos with his school chums (John Day and David Gibbard) taken outside their classroom.

In the photos below we can see that there were more seaside trips - we think this was Southend, a short (steam) train ride away. Do note the vests tucked well inside the trunks! We'll return shortly to travels.

Here we have photos taken either in a park (possible Greenwich?) or at the seaside. The alternating personnel suggests that it was Pete and Paul who were taking the snaps....

The next pair of photos were taken at our Great-Aunt Rose and Uncle Henry's house in Whitstable, Kent.

But no sign of Joyce. However, at this time she was starting at her Teacher Training College, Rolle College in Exmouth. We do have a picture of her from about 1950 in school uniform, as you can see. After Brampton Junior School, Joyce attended East Ham Grammar School for Girls and eventually Paul and Pete were at East Ham Grammar School for Boys - neither school survived the transition to comprehensive secondary schooling.

There are three other pictures. Firstly one of Joyce in her choir girl's surplice at St George's Church. Then a later one of her visiting a wishing well, something she does not remember - but it probably wasn't wishing for "Mr Right" to come along as by then she had already met Wally!

And finally, here he is, with Joyce in our garden.

10. Hatherley Gardens

We have regularly referred to the house we lived in at Hatherley Gardens, so it is a good moment to say a little more about the home which was always ours, but which we never owned.

Mum and Dad, with Joyce of course, moved into 140 Hatherley in May 1939, from their 'half a house' in Albert Square, Stratford. With Joyce now aged three they would have needed more room. Perhaps, too, they felt it was time to 'upsize', as it was at about this time that Dad changed his job – from a clerk/salesman at Byfords' builders' merchants to a clerk in the employ of the County Borough of East Ham (later to merge with West Ham to form the London Borough of Newham in 1964). It would appear from the 1939 register that at first they stayed with Mum's family at 78 Stephens Road, West Ham, but perhaps this was temporary whilst waiting to move in.

The house in Hatherley Gardens was to remain Mum's home until the last few months of her life, when she moved to Ebury Court residential care home in Romford. Apart from periods spent at Barnet, Letchworth and Winfarthing to escape the danger of German air raids during WW2, Mum spent little time away from the house. There were the times while giving birth to Paul and Pete (best part of a fortnight was the norm in those days - but Mum was sent home a few days after Pete was born, as there was gastroenteritis in the ward; Dad looked after Mum and Pete for several weeks, and Joyce can still remember the smell of Dettol); and then on family holidays (few and far between until we children were 'off hand'); and visiting each of us once we had set up our own family homes. Once we had all moved out Mum and Dad did get away on quite a few holidays on their own (more on this later).

140 Hatherley was the only childhood home for Paul and Pete, but Joyce has memories of life both at Barnet and at Winfarthing. But what was the house and the area around it like?

Firstly, a little history of this interesting area of London. East Ham hardly existed until the early years of the twentieth century.

If you look at the two maps wich follow, you can see that in the first, in 1800, West Ham was there, and so were the West India Docks, and you can even see Maryland Point, near the house in Albert Square. But look for East Ham and all you will find is a cluster of houses, plus, beyond "South End" (which is about where the 'Hammers' pub is now), the old, partly Saxon church, St Mary's, which is situated clearly in the marshes.

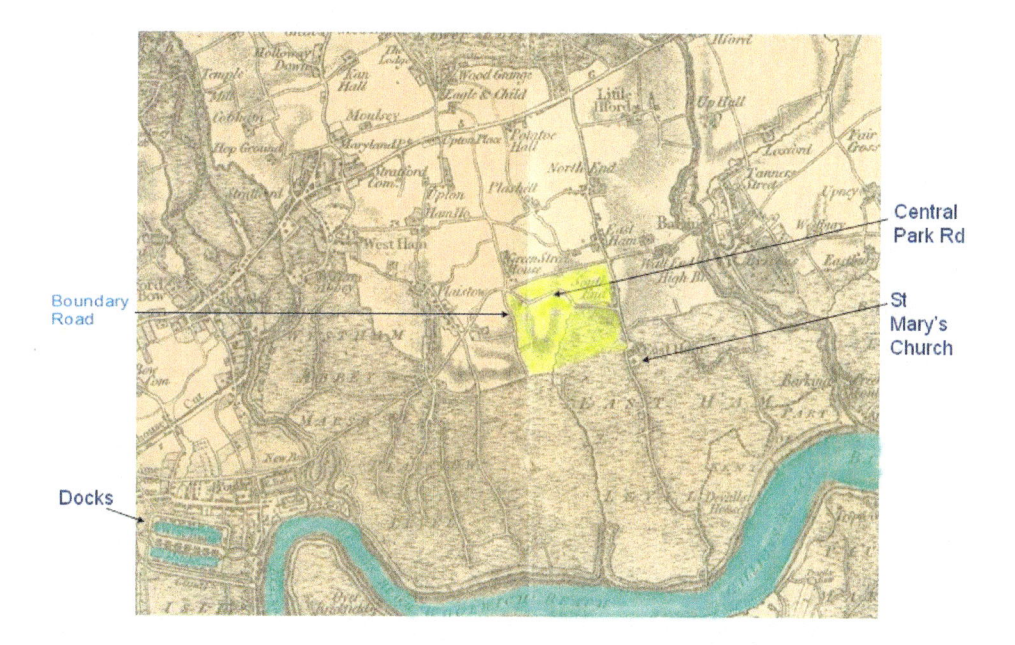

The map includes some contour shading which explains much. Although it is difficult to trace today, we can see that this was the boundary between some slightly higher ground and the East Ham levels (or marshes), and you can clearly see that what is now part of Central Park Road, then Henniker Gardens, finishing at what used to be the "White Horse", is a lane which goes down to the only road to cross the marshes, past the church and to presumably what will have been a ferry across the Thames at Gallions Reach. The other locally identifiable road goes south from Green Street House (the site of the former West Ham Football ground!) and is now Boundary Road, stopping at where it stops now, but which was in those days the edge of the marshes. We have shaded in yellow the area which is now the Central Park Estate.

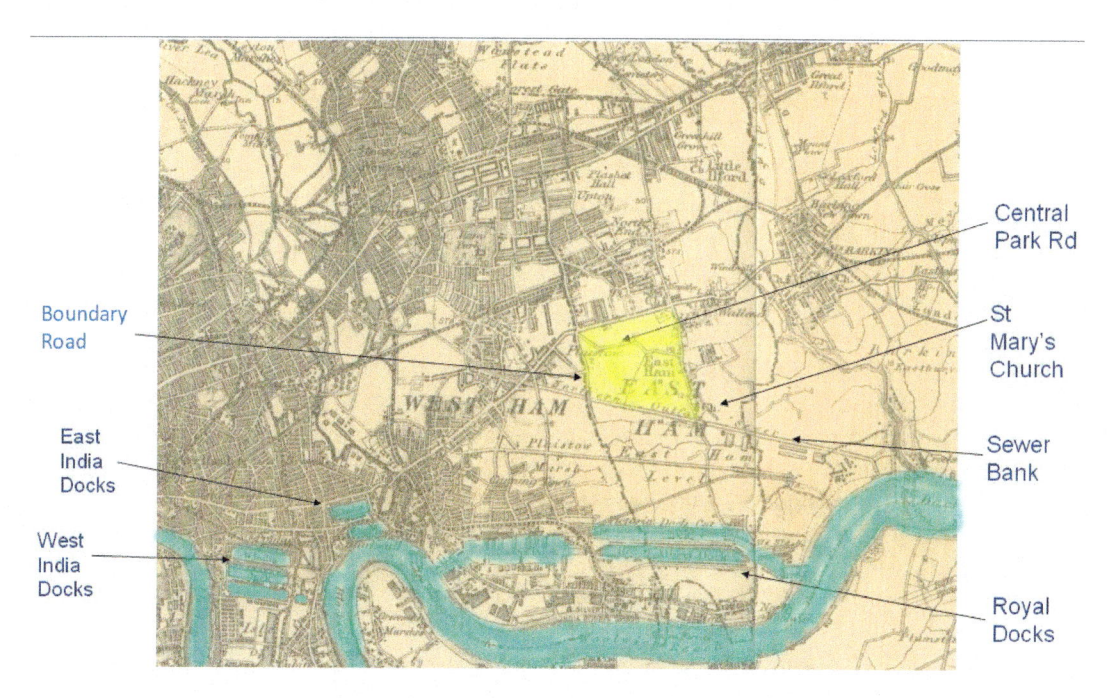

Now look at the second map, made in 1900, a century later. The huge boom in international trade gave rise to the construction of the Royal Docks complex. Of course, to build these, the land had to be at least partially drained. There are no significant housing developments in East Ham but West Ham and Canning Town are encroaching.

What we can also see is the construction of the "Sewer Bank" – the Northern Outfall Sewer – built to take drains from around London to be (more, or less, according to stages of development) purified before discharge into the Thames. Thus a "safe area" was created, and it is precisely this area, bounded by the Sewer Bank, Boundary Road, Central Park Road and East Ham High Street South, which was used for building on.

Not long after the 1900 map, the estate was built. So by the time this next map was completed, in 1936, we were not far away from moving in. You can see Hatherley Gardens, almost "nestling" against the sewer bank, on the other side of which are the allotments, one of which was Grandad's. 140 is on the corner of Lichfield Road, a short walk from Brampton Park and our primary schools. So Hatherley Gardens was part of this large Central Park estate. Whilst it had schools and parks and corner shops, what it didn't have (and still doesn't to this day) was pubs (there was some sort of covenant tied to the land from the time it belonged to the church). Now Dad liked a pint of beer on Sunday mornings before lunch. Many were the times when Paul and Pete, and Joyce before them, were sent to the nearest off-licence to fetch his pint of Guinness or Whitbread Pale Ale. (The licensing laws were much different then.) Sometimes it was Worthington Green Label we had to fetch. This was a bottle-conditioned beer, which had sediment at the bottom. On those occasions there were always strict instructions from Dad not to shake the bottle. Woe betide us if it came back cloudy!

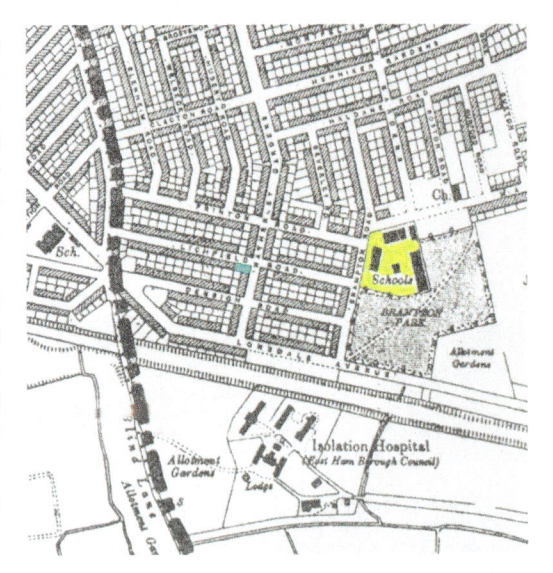

Built about 1912 '140' was an end of terrace house with three bedrooms upstairs and two 'reception' rooms and a kitchen downstairs. The 'bathroom' was an area of the kitchen that could be closed off by some folding doors. When not in use the bath was covered by a hinged lid that acted as a kitchen work surface. The toilet was outside – no heating, plenty of ventilation, and spiders too, as Joyce remembers well! Also outside was a lean-to greenhouse – mostly used as a DIY store, workshop and bike shed, but early on it was used to grow tomatoes as we have already mentioned. At a certain stage, Dad kept hutches with rabbits in – Paul just about remembers the line-up of baby rabbits on the living room floor being fed milk with a dropper. We don't suppose he ever linked their cuteness with the reason they were being kept..... and strange how we never associated them with the rabbit stew Mum served up!

Most of the early photos we have of the house feature the garden – where there was enough light for photography in those days, and we have already seen many of those early photos. They also bear witness to the changes in the property. When Mum and Dad first moved in the garden was lawned, but that soon changed with the construction of an 'Anderson' air raid shelter. After the war the shelter was dismantled and Dad laid a serious amount of concrete – all mixed by hand! – to leave the garden with the layout we all remember.

Dad enjoyed caring for the garden and was quite strict about how we played in it. Paul still feels the sting from the slap he got for picking green tomatoes and proudly telling Mum they were plums! But in fact, we never really worried too much about playing space. We were two minutes walk from Brampton Park to play football and cricket, and in any case, unlike today, the streets were deserted so we could play tennis in the road or cricket up against the side wall. When we were a bit bigger, the boys (at an age no-one would dream of doing now) would be given a sixpence (2½p in new money) for the bus fare, and off we would go to Wanstead Park with a jam sandwich, two fishing nets and a jar to bring back sticklebacks, which we would sometimes keep for a good while in a tank in the greenhouse. We even once brought back a lizard from the forest which lived free in the garden for a good while!

Apart from the photos already seen, here are a number of extra ones which show the changes to the house and garden.

This is Aunt Bet with our cousin Margaret. Note the typical way in which the London Plane trees in the street outside were pruned by the council.

In this next shot, Pete and Nan are showing off the rubbish bin and the greenhouse, now no longer used for tomatoes, but useful for drying clothes in bad weather.

We mentioned our famous home-made barrow earlier, and it was used as a prop in many photos, as can be seen here.

In these shots the boys are in secondary school uniform. And Peter offers us a glimpse of the neighbours' gardens.

The garden changed over the years, and next to Paul you can see asparagus fern, and on Mum's right her beloved camellia.

Not much had changed by the time Peter had met Jen. The asparagus and camellia are seen again in this lovely snap of a happy Mum and Dad. Grandchildren came to know the garden as well: first we see Keith.

Then Laura and Helen got to know the same garden.

But by the time the grandchildren were growing, the house underwent a radical change. The landlord made improvements, demolishing the greenhouse to make way for an extension which included a proper bathroom and (at last!) an inside toilet. This was less a philanthropic move, more a way of increasing the rent, which was very low as the house was subject to a "controlled" tenancy. (We'll return to that). And so, in the photo below, Laura now shows us, behind her, the new construction.

In this shot, Keith and Ann, along with Andrew and Kate, show that Dad had a new shed at the end of the garden.

At its best, the garden could be really quite colourful, and Mum and Dad both enjoyed it.

Let's leave the garden and go indoors.

On entering the house there was a narrow passage dominated by a wooden hallstand which had a chest at the bottom, coat hooks and a mirror on the wall at eye level (when you were old enough to have reached that height). A narrow staircase finished with a curve at the top, leading to a small landing and a turn to go up a step towards the front bedroom. There was a spindle rail and banister which finished at a cupboard on the landing just outside the bedroom. Inside the house was quite a bit of storage room as two of the bedrooms had built-in wardrobes and downstairs there were two cupboards 'under the stairs'. The small one housed the gas meter, and was also home to boxed board games, jigsaws, the "shove-ha'penny board" (if you don't know what that is, ask Paul who still has it!) and clothes airers. The taller one housed the electricity meter, and had shelves storing things that went on the dining table – jam, salt and pepper, plates, etc. In the kitchen there was a larder. Actually this stuck out of the building next to the lavatory, so it was always cool. This was important, as there was no refrigerator until well into the 1960s, when Mum and Dad acquired a cast-off from 'Uncle' Harry and 'Auntie' Lily. It was a small thing, but with an enormous motor that could be heard all over the house. The lack of a refrigerator had an impact on our way of life. With no way to keep perishable food fresh for more than a few days, shopping had to be done regularly. Mr Wise from a local grocer's shop – the 'Economic Stores' – delivered a box of groceries every Thursday, made up from a list we handed in. (You can see that we were such good customers that in 1959 they sent us a Christmas Card!). But as well as this, Mum usually went shopping in Green Street (for the Queen's Road street market) on a Friday and to East Ham High Street on a Saturday morning.

Vegetables were often purchased from Alec's – the greengrocer on the next corner. Both Mum and Nan, having been "in the trade" were often quite condescending about the quality of the goods on offer there! One thing that has disappeared from those shops is the fact that they also sold shellfish – prawns, sold by volume in pint or half pint pots, though other shellfish were purchased from a cart that came round. Other perambulating visitors were the milkman, with in the early days his horse, Nobby, and the baker who left Hot Cross buns on the window sill on Good Friday - the only time in those days that you could buy them. Joyce remembers (and Paul just about) the Walls ice-cream man on his tricycle.

In summer things like cheese did not keep very well, so were never bought in anything other than small quantities. If Paul or Pete wanted to go out for the day – for a bike ride or fishing – and wanted a packed lunch, then one of us would be sent over to the next corner shop – Edna's – to get 2 ounces of cheddar! Buying meat was also part of the chores for the boys, who would be sent to the Co-op in Boundary Road, to buy "four chump end chops" or some stewing lamb and so on.

Across the road, on the next street corner, there was a sweet shop. You can just see it in these photos from, probably, the early sixties. The rainbow in the second is coincidental, but for us it might have meant the "crock of gold" for when we were very young, sweets were still on ration – and no matter how much money you had (which we didn't) you were only allowed a small "ration". Sweets were sold from those large, old-fashioned glass jars, and carefully weighed out and dispensed in small, white paper bags.

None of those corner shops still exist.

Whilst we are on views of the street, here are a few other photos taken from the house over the years. In the first of these, taken in the early 1960s, you can see the sweetshop on the corner of Frinton Road, long gone now. It's still there in the photo with the rainbow. This and the photos with the snow show just how little traffic there was in those days. We have no idea what the fly-past was commemorating.

Originally the house was built with no electricity. The gas lighting brackets remained upstairs, and were still 'live' until Dad capped them off in the 1950s. When electricity was added – before Mum and Dad moved in – a water heater had been provided next to the kitchen sink. This was a small affair, with a tiny tank that took ages to heat. It was just meant for washing up. There was no means of providing large quantities of hot water until the landlord provided a 'gas copper' in the kitchen, installed for £5. We still have the receipt and letter from the landlord for this. This just boiled the water. To get it into the bath, it had to be drawn off via a tap into a small enamel bowl, then decanted into the bath. A dangerous operation.

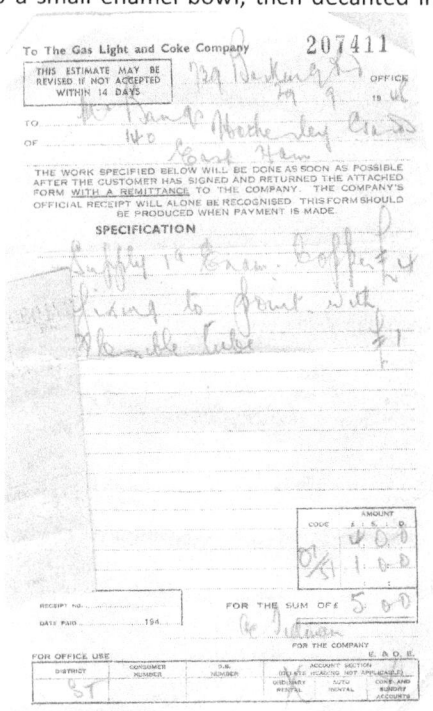

Notice that the company supplying the gas for the copper was the "Gas, Light & Coke Company". The days of competition among a myriad of energy suppliers were still a long way off. "Coke" referred not to a refreshing narcotic (!) but to a smokeless fuel which was a derivative of the process of producing town gas, hence the connection. In fact, quite close to the house was the largest facility in the world for producing town gas, at Beckton Gas Works, and Paul recalls a scientific school trip round the place, from which the odd photo has survived, as you can see.

Of course there was no washing machine. On Monday mornings Mum had to light the gas copper and boil up water for the weekly wash. This was mostly done in an oval galvanised tin bath placed on the bath top. Much use was made of a scrubbing brush and wooden scrubbing board. Cottons with stubborn stains were sometimes boiled in the copper itself. After rinsing them in the sink (using a 'blue bag' to enhance the whiteness of sheets) Mum would wring out the bulk of the water, before putting the clothes through the wringer. For those who don't know, a wringer (or mangle) was a hand-cranked machine with a set of rubber covered rollers under pressure, that squeezed excess water from the wet clothes, prior to them being hung out to dry.

In the late 1950s Mum was treated to a luxury – a Hotpoint washing machine! This was not an automatic, or even a twin tub machine. Just a top loader, but it had a major advantage – an electric wringer above the washer, which saved Mum a lot of hard work. Later still she had a spin drier, which extracted even more water from the clothes, and reduced drying times. By then the copper had gone – replaced with an 'Ascot multipoint' water heater. At last we had unlimited continuous hot water on tap – both at the sink and the bath.

For cooking there were fewer problems, as there was a gas stove in a recess (which replaced the original "range" cooker with chimney) and utensils and basic foodstuffs were kept in the "Maidsaver" – a typical kitchen cabinet with a drop-down work-surface. Although we were far from being well-off, we ate quite well, with meat and fish regularly – they were relatively cheaper in those days. But chicken, for instance, was unthinkably dear! Mum's routine was clear – roast dinner on Sundays, cold meat or shepherd's pie on Monday while she did the washing. We never lacked for fruit and vegetables as long as Nan had the shop. And Christmas was full of surprises, not just the tangerines in exotic wrappers, but the fact that we had a turkey which came from Pages, the butcher's next door to Nan's greengrocers' in Stephens Road. Paul recalls the odd pheasant which came down from Norfolk, and was probably provided thanks to Uncle Mac's shotgun.

It was never a warm house – cool in summer and cold in winter. The reception rooms were heated by open coal fires (with wonderful Minton tile side panels to the fire grates), as were the bedrooms. The bedroom fires were only lit when Dad took to his bed with 'flu'. (This happened most winters, and Joyce always wondered if it was a recurrence of malaria, picked up on war service in India.) The reception rooms were separated by folding doors that could be opened up to create a large 'through lounge', but this was for summer. In winter the 'front room' was closed off, unheated and cold. Paul remembers how cold it was when he played with his electric train set in the only place where there was room for it! The only exception was at Christmas, when the doors were folded back, both fires lit and the house once more had 'breathing space'. To conserve heat there were curtains that hung across the doors to reduce draughts and 'sausages' or 'crocodiles' – tubes of material sewn by Mum and stuffed with old newspaper, placed on the floor against the doors.

Going to bed in winter was never a relaxing occasion. It was up the stairs, into pyjamas and under the eiderdown as quickly as you could – often with a hot water bottle. There was never any 'central heating' in the house, but over the years some improvements were made. First there was the 'all night burning stove'. Dad, using his well-practised DIY skills, fitted these to both downstairs fireplaces. Instead of an open fire basket the front of the fire was sealed in with 'fire cement' at the bottom and sides, allowing much greater control of the airflow to the fire. This enabled two things – the burning of coke as well as coal and the ability to keep the fire 'in' all night. To do this Dad would bank up the fire with 'coal dust' - mainly small chippings from the bottom of the coal bunker and close the air flow to a minimum.

Coal was ordered at the beginning of winter from George Newman, a relative. Delivered in open sacks each weighing 1cwt (50 kilograms) it came on an open lorry and the sacks were tipped into the coal bunker in the garden. (See in the background of the photo).

The coal often came in very large pieces, and had to be broken up by hammer when filling the coalscuttle to take indoors. It was this operation that generated the 'coal dust'. Banking up the fire at night was a common practice in London in the 1950's and while very effective in helping keep houses warm and avoiding the need to light the fire afresh each morning it had some alarming environmental consequences. As the coal dust heated up, many pollutants were driven off and carried up the chimney, especially sulphurous gases and small dust particles. In cold wintry conditions these often got trapped under a 'temperature inversion', creating the infamous (and deadly) London 'smogs'. In the worst of these the air turned greeny-yellow and visibility was reduced to a few yards. Buses had to be guided by the conductor (who used to collect the fares in those days) walking in front holding a flare aloft. On one occasion Dad took over an hour to walk home from his office at the Town Hall – just a mile away. In 1952 so many Londoners (mostly the elderly and those with chest problems) died during a 'smog' that there was an outcry. However it was not until 1956 that the Clean Air Act was passed by the Government. Only 'smokeless' fuel was allowed, and London's air quality improved dramatically. Grants were available to update fireplaces, and Mum and Dad eventually opted for subsidised gas fires to be fitted in both the downstairs fireplaces.

In the late 1950s and early 60's Mum and Dad supplemented the coal fires with 'oil stoves', in the hall and bedrooms. Made by 'Valor' these burnt paraffin – a cheap fuel at the time, which partly made up for their tendency to be a bit smelly. Dad had a regular regime of trimming the wicks of the stoves to help them burn properly and keep this odour down. Mostly the paraffin was delivered by our Uncle Albert, Mum's brother, who had a door to door delivery round, using a large bulk tank on the back of our late grandad's lorry. Looking back, these were highly dangerous apparatuses!

The tenancy.

Before leaving the house, we will spend a while examining the form of tenancy which we had. In these days when tenancies are returning in "popularity" (or maybe necessity), it is often forgotten that tenancy was the norm for most people some decades ago, with house purchase an aspiration which relatively few achieved, though the relaxation under the Thatcher government's "Right to buy" act moved things along – not always in a good direction. Mum and Dad stayed as tenants their whole lives. In part this was due to Dad's obstinacy (he was offered the purchase of the house but refused to consider it) but also because of the protection long-term tenants then enjoyed.

We'll start by seeing how such protection helped the improvements seen a while ago. It was only after all three of us children had moved out that 140 Hatherley saw any substantial 'improvements'. In 1970 the landlord proposed building an extension to provide a 'proper' bathroom, (see the letter), and even the 'luxury' of an indoor toilet.

He did this not from any philanthropic motive, but because it was the only way that he could make a substantial increase in the rent! Amazingly (it seems to us now) Dad actually resisted this move as you can see from his draft reply below – probably because he feared the rent increase would be too much. (The landlord politely ignored his objections as you can also see). Indeed the rent did increase substantially - from £2.57 per week to £6.50, albeit phased in over three years. Rents on private tenancies such as this were regulated by the Government since the 1960s to prevent exploitation of tenants by landlords. Only by making improvements could landlords substantially increase the rent on a property. Later the Fair Rent Act was passed, whereby landlords could apply to a local Fair Rent Officer no more frequently than every two years, with a proposal for an increase in the Registered Rent. This scheme still applied to 140 Hatherley when Mum eventually gave up the tenancy. It still seems incredible to us that Dad could object to this, and prefer to carry on using the outside toilet! As seen above, his objection was simply ignored.

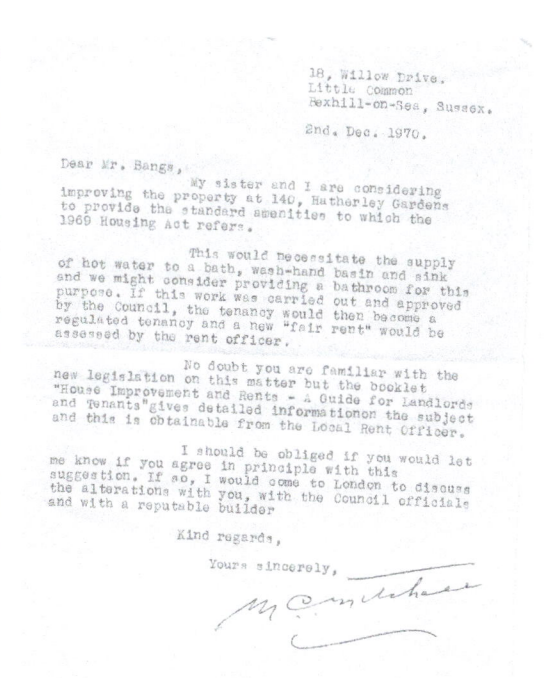

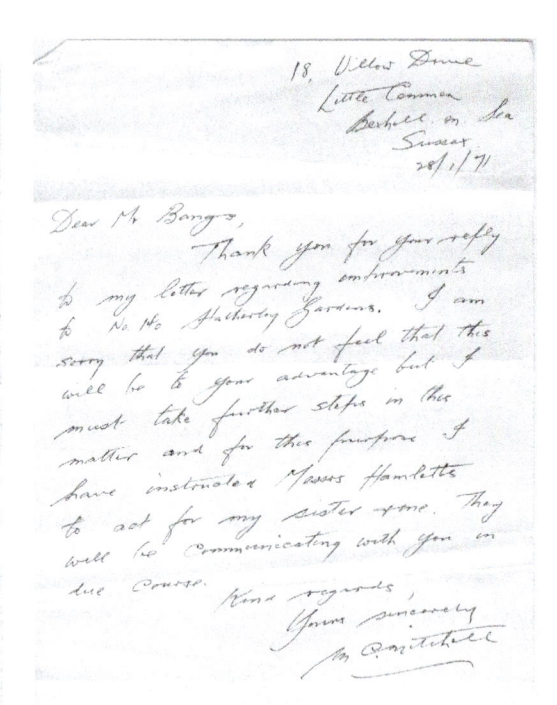

You can see the changes to the back of the house by comparing these two photos. The one of Paul in school uniform still has the greenhouse. It was demolished (it was well past its sell-by date!) and replaced by a solid brick extension which can be seen in the next photo behind Mum and Dad.

Whatever Dad may have feared (he was very resistant to change, it has to be said) it was a major step forward for them.

The only other major 'improvement' to the house was when it was rewired. This was not really an improvement – just a necessity as the original wiring was condemned as dangerous.

The landlord at 140 was originally a Mr Mitchell, shared with his sister, and this was the case up to 1998, when Mr Mitchell and his nephew Mr Moxom (who had inherited his mother's half-share in the property), and the general relationship between Mum and Dad and Mr Mitchell (his sister was never actively involved in managing the house, except for receiving the rent into her bank account during the war when Mr Mitchell was in the Air Force) was quite benign. Mr Mitchell only visited about once a year, and was happy to let Dad maintain the property inside. If work needed to be done by the landlord, there was not usually any difficulty in getting him to arrange it, and sometimes Dad actually paid the workmen himself, being refunded by a grateful Mr Mitchell later.

The rent on '140' was paid to Mr Mitchell, along with an amount to cover the rates and water rates. Each year Mr Mitchell would get the new demands for these two items, then write to Dad to get him to increase (usually) his payments. There is a typical letter here from 1967.

It is all the more remarkable that this situation lasted for so long, when you consider that the actual rent on the house only increased once between 1939 and 1972! The arrangement eventually came to an end when rates were replaced by the Poll Tax. This was a tax on people, not property, so the landlord could no longer pay it. Mr Mitchell quickly took steps to pass over responsibility for the water rates as well. See his letter on the right. There is a continual grumble in the letters each time the rates were increased, and Mr Mitchell even asked Dad, quite ridiculously, if he could not get something done about it!

Looking at the rent levels over the years of the tenancy, it is no wonder Mr Mitchell wanted to provide 'modern amenities'. The rent started off at 16s 1d (approximately 80p) in 1939, and increased to 24s 10p (approximately £1.27) in 1959. Once the bathroom was provided he, and later Danriss, (a property company who bought the house from Mr Moxon with Mum as "sitting tenant") applied for increases in the Fair Rent at every opportunity. As Dad had feared, the rent increased steadily. In later years Mum, who for a long while refused to challenge any of the sometimes excessive amounts applied for, was eventually sheltered from these increases as she qualified for Housing Benefit, which increased in line with the rent each time it went up.

The rent for the house rose steadily (along with all other costs) over the years. We already saw the original rent book and the letter from the landlord explaining arrangements to pertain whilst he entered the armed forces during the war. And we have already seen how the only way in which rents could be increased was by making improvements, and how this culminated in the building of the extension and a new kitchen and bathroom. Of course the rent did increase considerably due to that, as the landlord applied on every possible occasion to increase it as much as he could.

There are many letters from Dad (we are grateful he kept copies of his important correspondence) first objecting then withdrawing his objection to a rent increase. After Dad died, Mum would, in her usual way, not allow us to object on her behalf and the rent increased sharply, until the realisation sank in that if she claimed Housing Benefit (to which she was fully entitled) she would be cushioned. But that was much later.

As mentioned, many items of correspondence and forms to be filled in have survived. Too many to place them all here, but for historical or social interest we have placed copies of a lot more in Appendix E. They include applications for rent increase, drafts which Dad kept of his objections (which he usually later withdrew), and letters dealing with the transfer of the tenancy to Mum after Dad's decease.

Now we come to the sorry saga of the house being sold over Mum's head, with an inspection being carried out under false pretences - again Mum would not let us object (as this was illegal because she should have been offered the sale as first refusal). Most outrageous is the letter from Mr Moxom, Mr Mitchell's nephew, in which he states that *"both he and my mother had been hoping that the opportunity might arise to sell it some years ago and then spend some of the money on a few nice things in their old age. But no suitable opportunity ever arose"* – meaning it was a shame that Mum had not died or moved away so the landlord could realise his asset - so much for social responsibility and a slap in the face for Mum's loyalty over the years. And as for Mum's "few nice things", much of the following years was blighted by the long battles with the new owners over repairs, sorely neglected. In later years Mum was pretty much house-bound and so could not see the external state of the property.

Once Mum moved out, the owners put the house on the market, at a price that acknowledged that much work needed doing to bring it up to modern standards. The maintenance of the outside of the house – the landlord's responsibility – had been woefully neglected by Danriss, as the photo shows.

It is difficult to say what our memories of the house really are – they are so inextricably bound up with our memories of events as we grew up. The house was just a backdrop to that. However Pete distinctly remembers serving as Dad's 'decorator's apprentice' in his early teens, learning how to paste wallpaper, and eventually how to hang it. When it came to painting, at first he was only allowed to work with undercoat, but gradually Dad let him loose on topcoat. He also remembers exploring the extreme ends of the house. When Dad wanted to put a power socket in the reception rooms it needed a cable threading though from the kitchen under the floorboards. Pete became the 'human mole', actually crawling through in the space beneath the boards! Later, he helped Paul install some insulation in the loft, once again crawling through tight spaces, this time into the extremities over the back bedroom.

Curiously, when Paul went back to the house after Mum had left, he felt no sense of belonging. We might add a final note about the neighbourhood. In common with a long (very long) history of the East End of London, waves of immigration made their mark in the various areas, and the immediate surroundings of our house were no exception. The "estate" changed drastically over the years, and very few of the original neighbours we knew had remained by the time Mum left – though notably, she still had some wonderful "good neighbours" in the proper sense of the word. The influx of various ethnic groups over the years has had something to do with this, and communities have been fragmented. But the vibrant diversity of East Ham and other areas continues, as it did when Dad told us of the Chinese in Limehouse and the Lascars nearer the docks, as well as the Jews in Whitechapel (which as we now know, were closer to our family than we thought!) and which have now been replaced by Bangladeshis. At the time Mum moved out, the neighbourhood was changing once more – central and eastern Europeans providing an additional layer, and yet more headaches for the local teaching force!

Let's leave the final word with Joyce. She has a special memory of the house, on her wedding day, 5th April 1958.

"Everybody says love and enjoy every minute of your Wedding Day, because you will not remember it afterwards. This is true because after nearly fifty two years I remember the day but, the service itself is a hazy memory. Dad woke me up with my cup of tea on Easter Saturday morning, and, pulling open the curtains casually remarked that it was snowing. I thought it was one of his huge jokes, but no, it was true and I told him to go round to Wally and tell him the wedding was off (notice no phone!) It was not a serious request as subsequent events will show.

After breakfast I walked up to the hairdressers at the Boleyn. She seemed to take forever and after 3 hours to my surprise, Uncle Sid was waiting outside in his car as it was still pouring with rain.

On returning home the house was full of people. Mum and Dad were cooking lunch for fourteen people (yes fourteen). We had boiled ham and pease pudding, home cooked, and potatoes. After we had eaten, everything was cleared away and washed up, and the kitchen was cleared and the table top lifted up (see the previous description of the kitchen) and I was able to have a bath.

My six bridesmaids were all there by now and when we were all dressed, (Mum had made all the wedding clothes) Nan came up to see us and it was quite an emotional moment. Then Dad and I were left in the quiet house and we made our way to the waiting car. I cannot remember exactly what we spoke about in the car, probably the weather, but I do know that when we reached the altar he related to Wally the current West Ham score (sotto voce!) How important was that?

Mum and Dad worked very hard and I have been forever grateful for such a wonderful Wedding Day."

We'll come back to Joyce shortly. But leaving the house, we can return to family life.

11. Family life continues

The children are growing up, and photos are even in colour, as here. And on the subject of photography, Paul got his first camera, a Kodak Brownie 127, which he still has, and it is shown here, along with a later Hanimex.

Many photos Paul took from his youth have survived. Some have already been seen and a further selection is shown here, some of them taken by Peter. In some of them you can see that they are in grammar school uniform. In the photograph of Peter with Nan, you can see both the greenhouse, long demolished, and that coal bunker on the right, long since made redundant with gas fires being installed. Others are holiday pictures - the Isle of Wight being a favourite once more. The photo of the family on the beach at Frinton-on-Sea (the penultimate image) was taken during a family outing with two of Dad's brothers and their families, and some cine film has survived of the occasion. In the very last picture you can see that it was sometimes all too much for Dad!

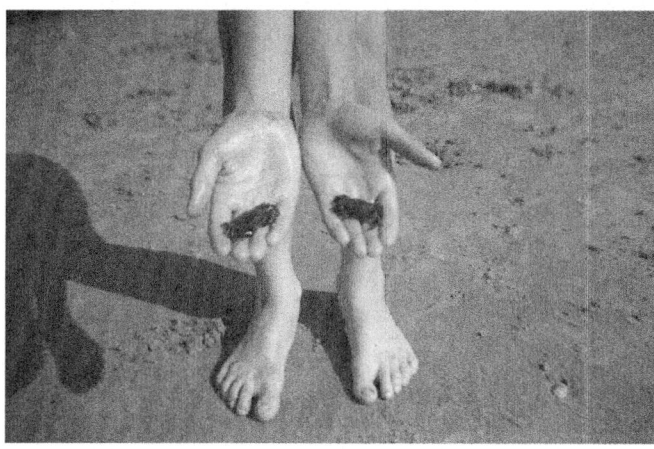

More family events follow. In these first pictures we are at a picnic on Frinton beach with many of Dad's family. From left to right in the first picture: cousins Mary, Sandra & Jean, Aunty Ivy, Uncle Ern, Aunt Rose, cousins Christopher and Vivienne, Uncle Wally, Aunty Peggy, Pete, Uncle Sid, cousin Michael and Uncle Reg. In the second picture there is a shuffle around, and Dad, Mum and Paul have appeared. Notice that Paul is carrying the Brownie 127 camera.

The three photos below were taken on the way to and at a family holiday on the Isle of Wight. Please keep the boys' dress code a secret!

Dad enjoyed fishing with the boys, and as you can see, even Mum joined in at times. The first two photos were taken at the "Ornamental Waters" in Wanstead Park, the others at South Ockendon pits, where we often went (small) carp fishing, on this occasion accompanied by Uncle Ern and Christopher. Even a cine film of that event has survived.

More family events. In the first picture we are at Aunty Molly and Uncle Jack's wedding. In the picture you can also see Wally, Nan, and cousins Margaret and Irene and their mother, Aunt Bet. Speaking of these last two, in the next photo Mum is with their little sister Joanna, and in the next one we are at Margaret's wedding. In the fourth photo, Peter is with our cousin Christopher in their house at Buckhurst Hill.

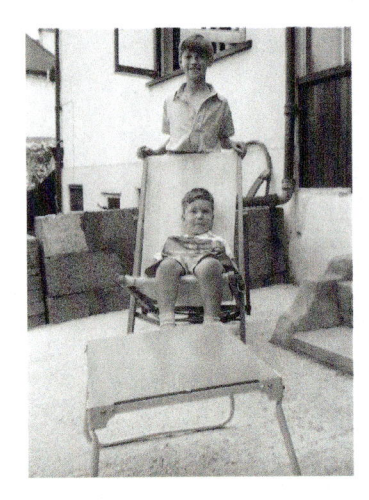

A sad connection with the last of the above photographs is the memory that our Grandad Bourne died in 1953, just a few days before the Coronation. Pete and Paul were deemed too young to attend the funeral so instead we stayed for a few days at Uncle Ern and Aunty Peggie's in Buckhurst Hill. We always enjoyed being there - their garden seemed huge to us, and you could also play great games in the gorse tunnels on the green opposite the house, and it was almost on top of Epping Forest. But the final advantage on this occasion was that they had television! Thus we got to watch the Coronation - the world's first TV outside broadcast, live. It may seem hard to believe today with our hundreds of channels, satellites and so on, but these were the early days of TV. Until (later) we got our own set, we were invited to a neighbour's house, (Mrs Hartshorn) to watch the children's programmes at five o'clock.

But we've been neglecting Joyce's story. She completed her studies at Rolle College, Exmouth and started working as a fully qualified teacher at Hartley Road school (after embarrassing at least one of her brothers by doing her teaching practice at Brampton School!). In 1958 she married Wally, the local boy (!) at St George's church, as we see in the photos. The weather, in April, was foul as it snowed that morning, but that wasn't the only reason for it being a less than auspicious day to choose, as West Ham were playing in an important match that afternoon ..... priorities ..... Dad also had Joyce nearly in tears by threatening to wear his bowler hat, as seen in the picture....

In the photos of the event (we also have some cine film), note Peter and Paul in very "grown-up" clothes, and Paul with the ubiquitous Brownie camera. But at least one little bird had flown the nest - more bedroom space for Pete and Paul, of course, even though Joyce always referred to the middle bedroom as "her" room!

The following year, Mum and Dad celebrated their silver wedding anniversary. Their children presented them with a scroll, seen here. But Mum kept many of their congratulatory cards and these are to be found in Appendix F.

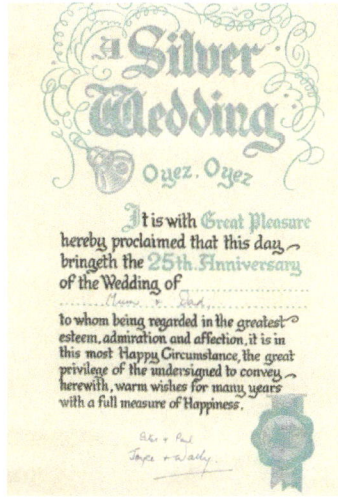

So Joyce had left the family home. We have fewer photos from the times that follow, but here are some which show that we still had family holidays. On one occasion we hired a "camping coach" at Wells in Somerset - a converted railway carriage in fact. Pete recently found the colour photo of us inside the coach, bottle of gin on the floor and playing "Lexicon". Pete and Paul cycled there on their beloved hand-made *Leach Marathon* bikes. These were bought for us at great expense by Mum and Dad as we recall that they cost £36 each and they had to be paid for on instalments at 2/6 per week. That's 12½p in new money, which was a lot for those days.

There are photos of Mum and Dad in the garden and again on the beach - once more, note the formality of wearing a jacket and tie, even if Dad dozed off in the deckchair!

Pete and Paul continued the fishing trips, often with Dad, as in the photo here of the famous gravel pits of South Ockendon. They also began a taste for outdoor adventures and the pictures show them abseiling at Harrison's Rocks near Tunbridge Wells.

So... one down, two more to go. Joyce and Wally went off to set up their own home. Peter and Paul were still at the Grammar School, but were before long off to their own higher education. We never forget that to make this possible, Mum and Dad made many sacrifices, most notably that Mum cleaned the primary school we used to attend for many years. Paul went on to live the heady days of Liverpool in the early 1960s, and Mum and Dad must have thought "phew - space in the house at last" but as we'll see later, he did come back for a while!

In 1967, Paul married Ann McGivern in Cwmbran, South Wales, and here are a few photos of the wedding. On the way, Mum and Dad stayed at Chepstow and there are a couple of photographs which, as we can see, usher in the new age (at least for Dad) of colour photography - well, with one less mouth to feed...

With Paul out of the way (!), Pete also went on to higher education at Hendon College, where he met Jennifer Dade. There are some pictures here of Pete at that time and of him with Jen. Then in 1968 he and Jen got married in Lincolnshire (the picture of Pete in the garden is taken at Jen's family home in Sutton St Edmund). There are some photos of the event, complete with the order of service.

By this time Paul and Ann had seen the arrival of Laura, not the first grandchild, as Joyce and Wally already had Keith and Ann. But this is the end of one era and the start of another, so it's where we leave this section....

12. Travels

We have seen that family holidays were restricted to seaside boarding houses, or a "camping coach". Those were the days when foreign travel was restricted to the rich. Air travel was expensive by any measure of finances, and car travel abroad was not a common event - not that we had a car! In common with the majority of the population, Mum had never been abroad in her life, and of course as we know, Dad's travels were courtesy of the war effort.

But times were changing. There had been some fairly tough days when money was in short supply, and most of the family effort was spent in helping the three children through their education. But now, birds were fleeing the nest, and travel was becoming easier and cheaper. For Mum and Dad a new era opened up.

From a modest start with a trip in 1965 to Northern Ireland (no foreign food to cope with - unless you count white pudding and soda bread!), documented in both black and white, and, later colour, they eventually moved on to holidays in Spain, Portugal and the Channel Islands. A stimulus for this was when Paul and family spent some months on a teacher exchange in Altea on the Costa Blanca. Paul remembers how difficult it was for him to persuade his father that it was a good idea! Eventually they went out to visit the family in the villa they also swapped, and they never looked back.

By this time, grandchildren had arrived, but this aspect is dealt with in greater detail in another section. Here we will concentrate on Mum and Dad's adventures. We'll explain each journey on the pages which follow, and include as an Appendix some gallery pages for each one with an added supply of those dreaded holiday snaps! We'll deal later with some of the many UK trips they made. To begin with, a few examples of what to expect...

This first picture of Mum in an orange grove in Altea is significant, as she never forgot that moment: so many years she had served oranges and lemons in the shop, she said she could not believe that she was actually picking a fresh fruit from the tree!

Nor did she ever think she would be paddling in Torremolinos or in Lloret del Mar, as below.

And the trips were not confine to Spain; they loved Portugal and its fishing boats.

Those were the days of Visitors' Passports, and one of these has survived:

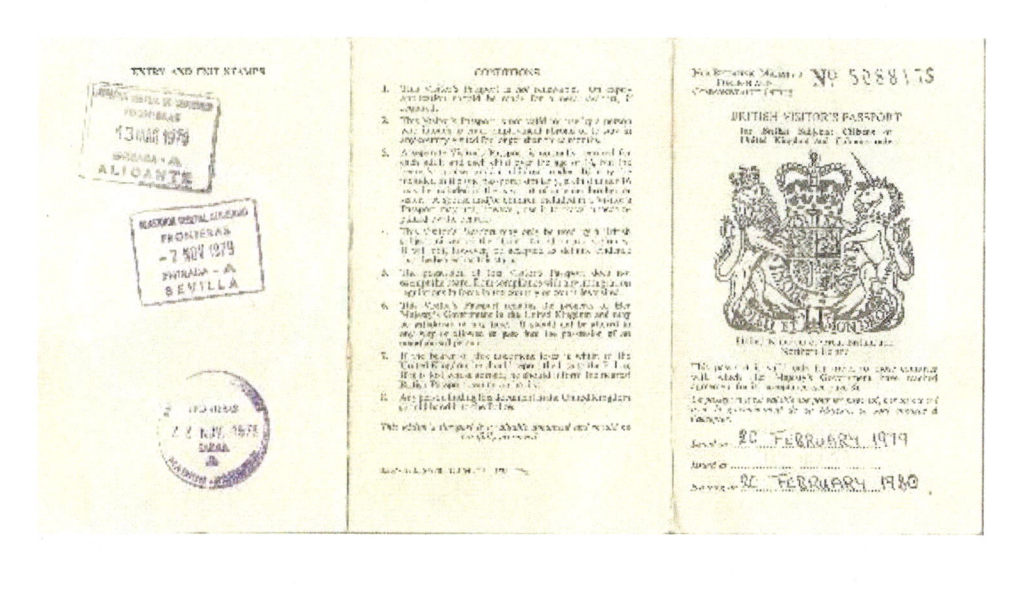

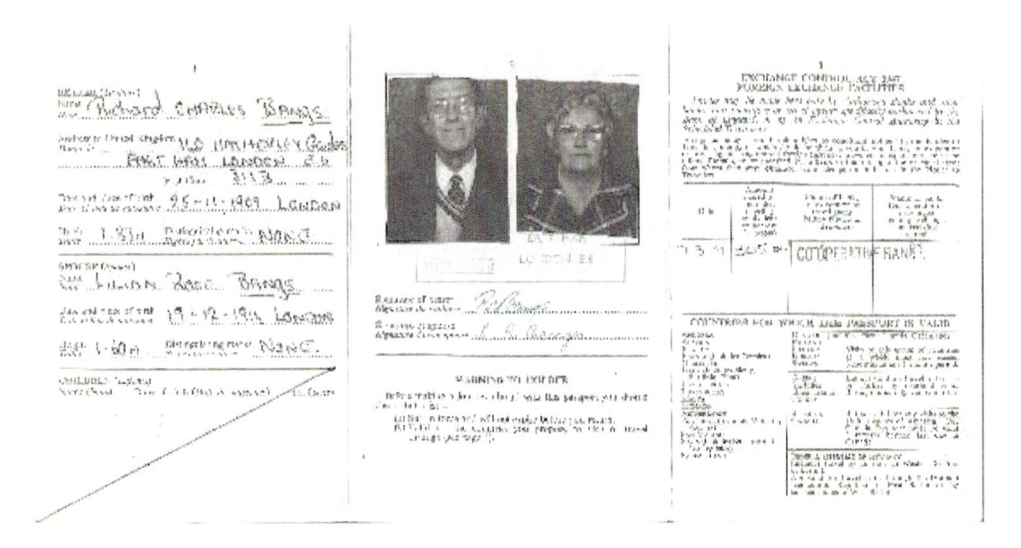

They both delighted in these travels, and we think that these were really golden years for them.

We can follow their travels by simply viewing a selection of the (very) many photos Dad took on these occasions. We'll look at them by destinations, beginning with those nearer to home. In each case sample photos will be added, but many others will be found in Appendix G.

Portrush. The holiday which Mum and Dad took to Portrush in Northern Ireland, was, we think, their first ever flight. They visited many local places, including the famous basalt formations of the Giant's Causeway.

Ireland. They went on a tour around Ireland in August 1970 with Pete and Jen.

Exmouth. To Exmouth with Joyce and Wally and the young grandchildren, Keith and Ann.

Scotland. The trip to Dunoon and Argyll in Scotland was a coach trip which Mum and Dad undertook in June 1976 with their friends, our "Uncle" Harry and "Aunt" Lil Thurling. The trip took in typical Scottish scenery such as Loch Lomond and Dunoon.

Wales. In 1975 they made a trip to North Wales and stayed in Llandudno and visited other local landmarks, including going up the Great Orme headland.

Lake District. In August 1969 Mum and Dad went on a coach trip to the Lake District with its beautiful landscapes of hills, lakes and coast.

Guernsey. They took a trip to Guernsey in the Channel Islands in the late 1970s.

Altea. Mum and Dad's first trip abroad together was in March 1979 to visit Paul and family in Spain, on the Costa Blanca. They stayed in the villa in Playa del Albir, but made quite a few trips, including for a weekend in Valencia on the occasion of the famous "Fallas" fiesta, with its flower processions, burning of wooden statues and fireworks.

Lloret del Mar. Mum and Dad went to Lloret del Mar in September of 1982. During their stay there they also visited the Catalan capital, Barcelona and its cathedral.

Portugal. Portugal was the venue for two holidays which Mum and Dad took in the 1980s. We know that they really enjoyed both trips.

Andalucía. Mum and Dad made several trips to Spain, beginning in the same year as their first visit to Altea - they really got the bug! They made trips to Benalmádena and Torremolinos, and visited the wonderful Moorish Palace of the Alhambra in Granada, the caves at Nerja and Ronda, amongst other places.

Paris. Mum and Dad went to Paris on the occasion of their Golden Wedding anniversary. That was in December 1984, but the trip was in 1985, as we, the children, bought it for them as their anniversary present from us to be taken when the weather got better. They visited Paris' attractions, as well as Versailles.

Other visits.

There were many other trips, at home and a few short visits abroad. In the Appendix we've included just some of the many photos taken on those trips. Mum and Dad certainly got around a bit, considering they never had a car! Places involved include York, Lichfield, Bath, Buckingham Palace, Lincolnshire, Winchester, Milton Abbas, Essex, Burleigh House, Chatsworth, Blenheim Palace, Norfolk, Woolwich, Greenwich, Eastbourne, Southend, Derby, Spalding, and Windsor.

13. The last years together

We have seen how Mum and Dad shared their lives - bringing up the children, surviving the war, getting rid of the children. We've also seen how they began to enjoy travels together which they could only have dreamed about when they were younger.

But life doesn't stop when the kids fly the nest, and we have more stories we can witness with photos and other documents of Mum and Dad's time together. Most of these, inevitably, are focused on family events such as weddings, but these four snaps date from just after Christmas 1963.

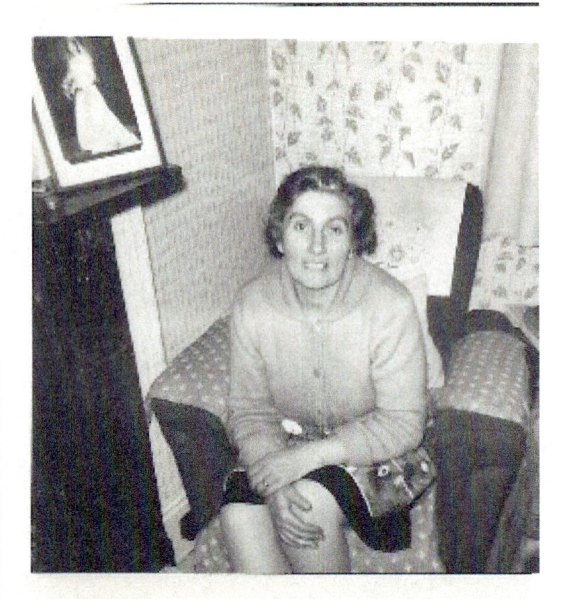

Returning to Dad for a moment, there are some lovely photos here of him with all his siblings, and one of them also with spouses. From left to right in the fuller picture, the "cast list" is: Dad; Uncle Sid; Uncle Reg; Aunt Ruby; Aunt Rose; Mum; Auntie Jean; Auntie Peggy; Auntie Ivy; Uncle Ern; Uncle Bill; and Uncle Wally. Since this is the full set, identifying those in the other pictures will be easy.

Amongst Mum's effects we found one birthday card from Dad which must have meant a lot to her to have kept so carefully. Here it is:

Huggers, kissers, budget-breakers,

Hairpin-experts, washers, bakers,

Buyers, spenders, bargain-snatchers,

Duster-offers, squabble-patchers —

Alongside this we have placed Dad's bus pass and a "business card" which we can never remember being used.

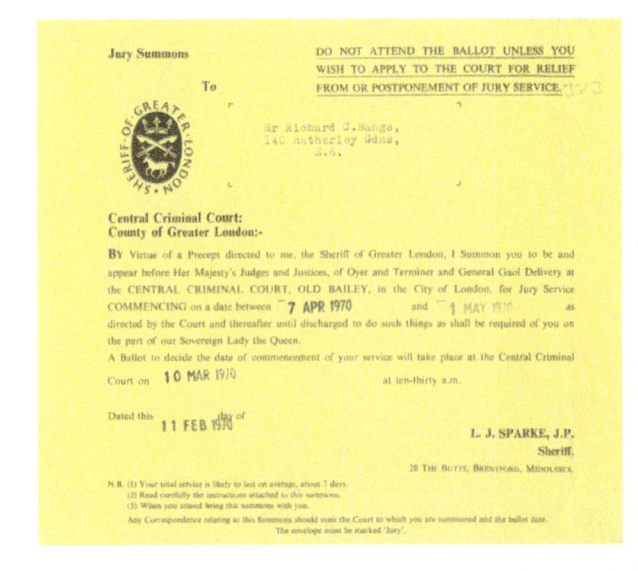

Dad continued to work for the Council, punctuated on one occasion by having to perform Jury Service. He served on a very long fraud case which lasted for 30 days, after which he received a letter of future exemption for life. The letters relating to this are shown here.

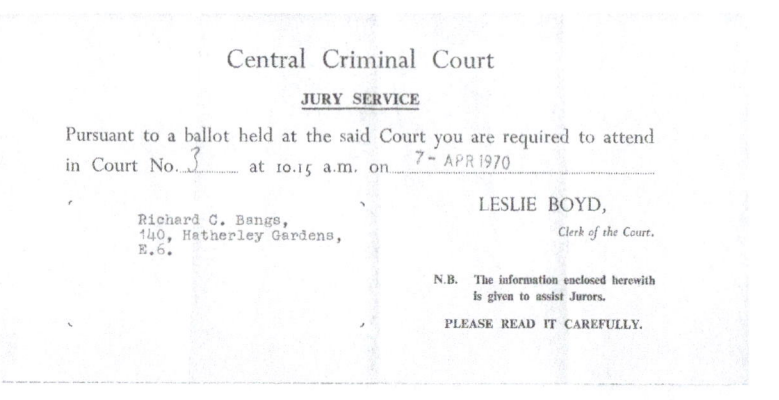

His National Insurance card was kept:

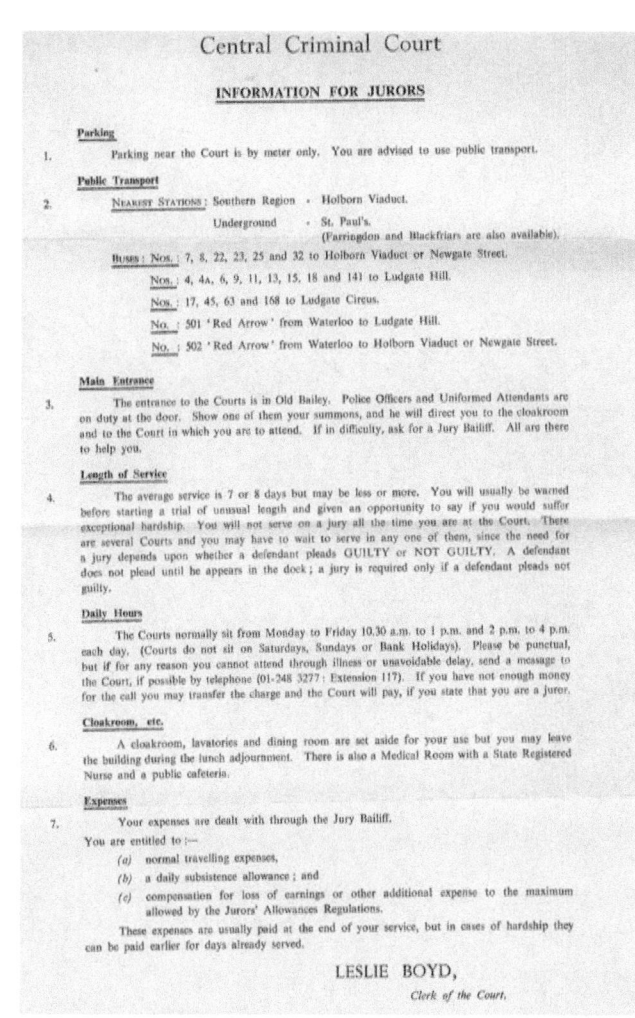

And this is the only photo we have of him at work. (Note the period telephone, the pot of glue, and the jars of red and blue ink!).

On one visit to Pete in Derby, Mum and Dad took the opportunity to visit their old friends and neighbours, the Edgingtons. Mr. Edgington had been a policeman who served in the Metropolitan Police during the war and after.

They enjoyed visits to their children (more on them later) such as the times they stayed with Pete and Jen in Derby, to enjoy Pete's large garden, and to visit Jen's parents on their farm, where it appears from the photos below that they were recruited as cheap labour for fruit picking!

1974 was a very eventful year for both Mum and Dad. Firstly, it was the year in which they both retired from working for Newham Borough Council. Dad had been a local government officer there since before the war, and Mum worked as a school cleaner at Brampton School. Naturally they had planned for their retirement, which worked out quite neatly, as Dad could retire at the normal age of 65, and Mum at 60, cleverly having five years age difference between them.

They made arrangements for their two pensions, the state retirement pension and their "superannuation" pension based on many years of contributions through their salary. The amounts of the latter were based on a final year salary calculation, something which is fast disappearing.

Even though they had planned, the final amounts must have come as rather a surprise to them. Dad's initial state pension was £16.45 per week. Hardly a fortune by today's standards, but acceptable. As for the superannuation, Dad received a "lump sum" and a monthly income. Mum actually ceased work when they went to Derby in late June to help out when Kate was born. She postponed receiving her occupational pension for a few months, until her 60th birthday. This meant she would receive her full pension entitlement. It was typical of Dad's thoughtfulness that in making his own pension arrangements he opted to provide a continuing pension for Mum after his death, even though this was at the expense of a lower pension while he was alive.

Here are two documents about their retirement.

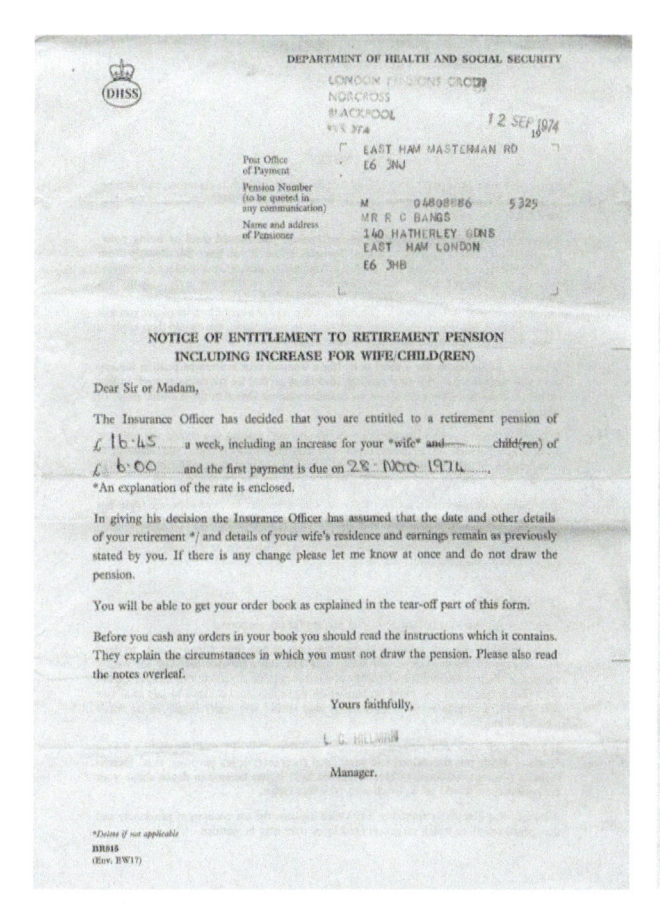

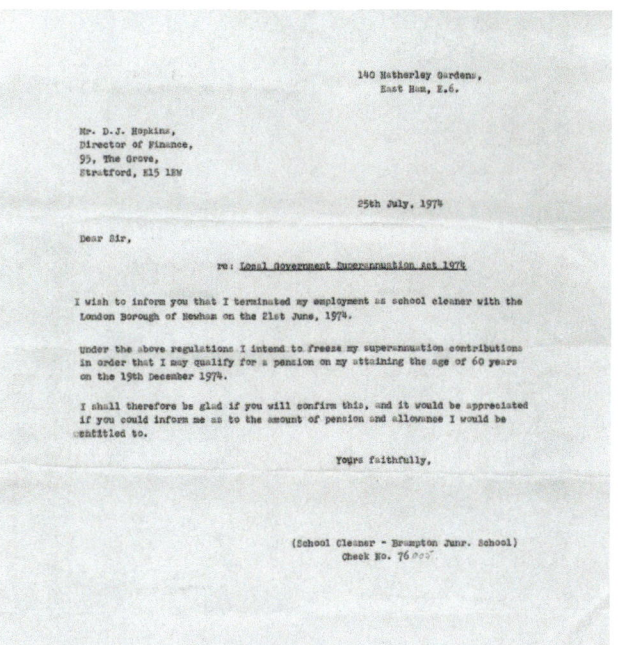

1974 was also the year in which they celebrated their 40th wedding anniversary. Here we have a few photos of the party held at Joyce and Wally's house, Mum dressed in appropriate colours!

They continued to get out and about, especially visiting us and our growing families, but also on their own account, such as the visits which we mentioned earlier, in successive years to the Chelsea Flower show in 1975 and 1976. The photos which Dad took then are in the Appendix, but in this one, if you look carefully, you will see Mum with Uncle Albert and Aunt Bet.

We can also see a photo which celebrates Joyce's 40th birthday.

Life went on quite peaceably for Mum and Dad and we have mentioned their continuing travels. Sadly, in 1978, Mum lost her mother Lilian Bourne, our grandmother, to cancer.

The next big landmark celebration was Mum and Dad's Golden Wedding Anniversary in 1984. Celebrations included a family meal in a restaurant and a party at 140. In the selection of photos you can see Mum, trade-mark tears in eyes at times, and Dad, at both these events. As a family we gave them a present, once they had worked out the set of clues in a sequence of envelopes they had to open, of a trip to Paris, photos of which are in the Appendix. They also kept a restaurant receipt and information about duty-free. Being near Christmas of course, we also have a couple of photos from around the table that year.

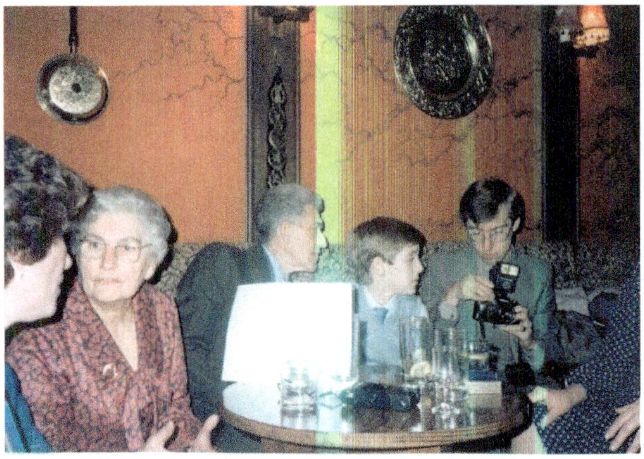

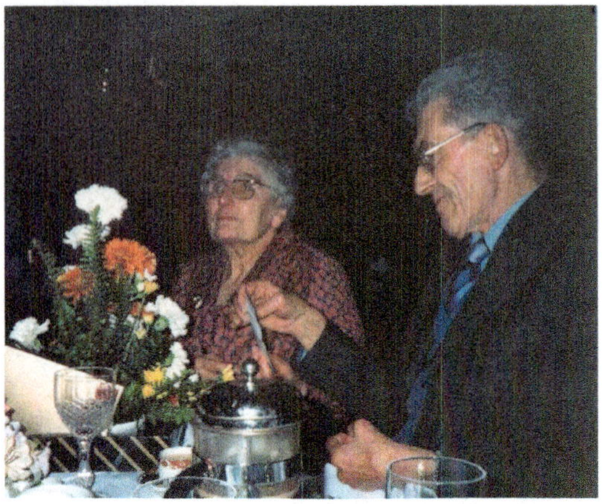

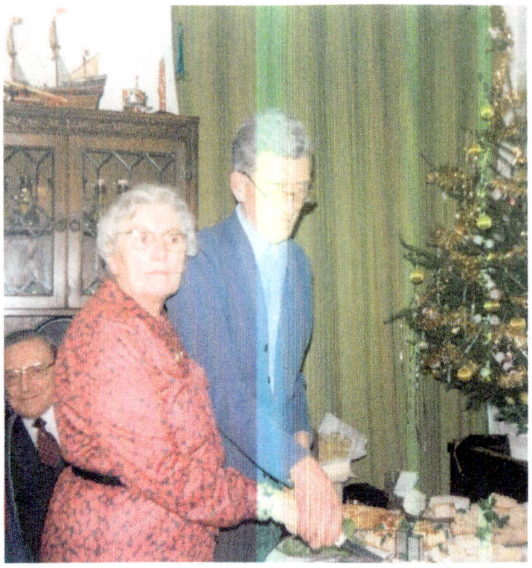

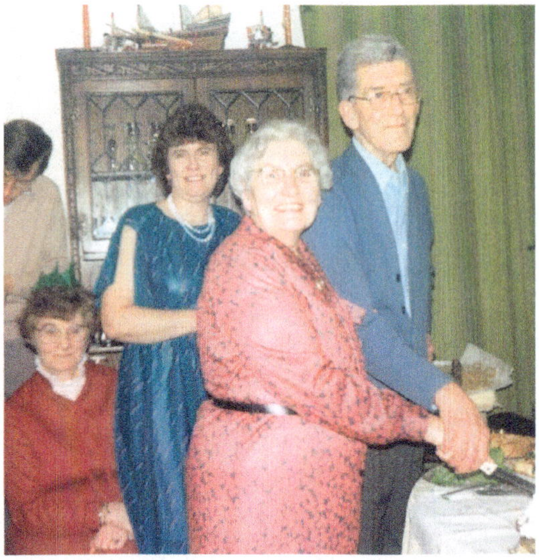

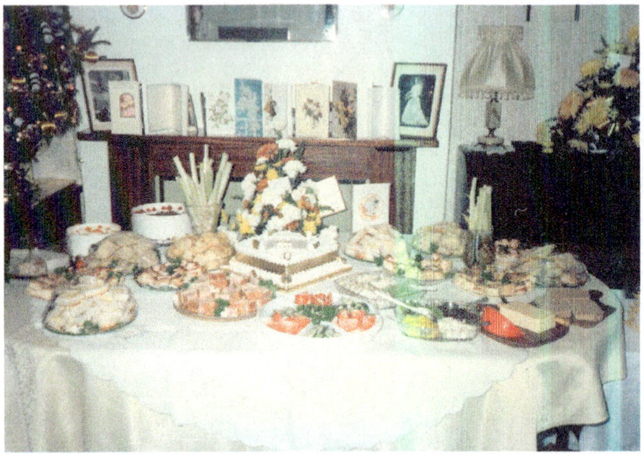

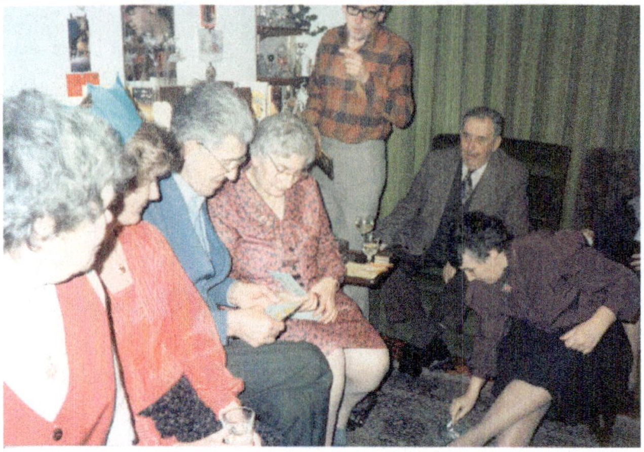

Dick Bangs & Lily Bourne – Their story

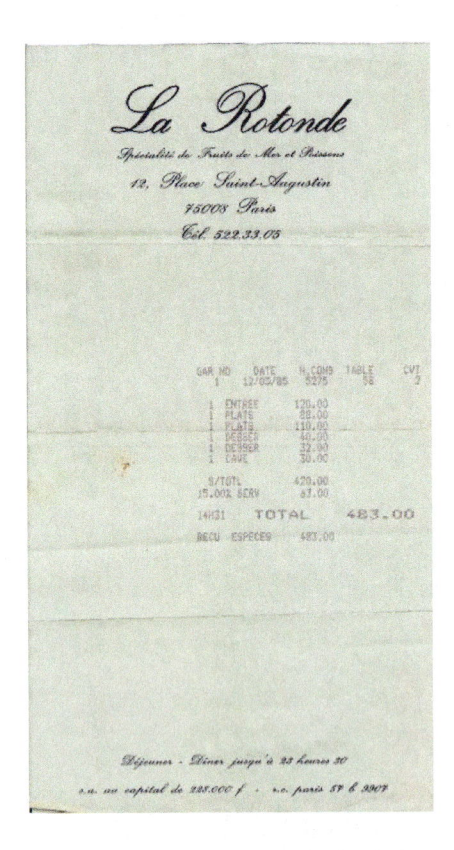

One of the major pleasures enjoyed by Mum and Dad was the simple one of being with their grandchildren. Dad always liked children anyway, and it gave him an immense feeling of joy to be with the younger ones.

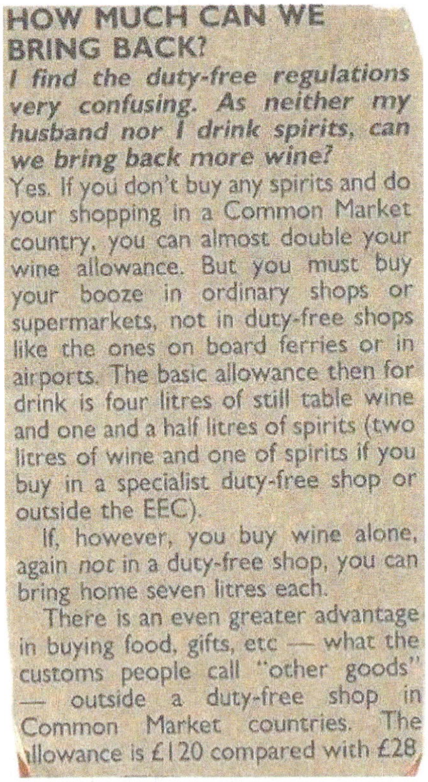

But the years were to take their toll. Sadly, the enjoyment of retirement together did not last for as long as Mum and Dad would have wished. Dad's health suffered, due to circulation problems (probably not helped by his refusal to totally give up smoking), and he became less mobile. Dad died, after some years of suffering these problems, of a leaking aortic aneurysm, in Newham General Hospital on the 13th August 1991. At the time, Mum was being cared for in turn by the three of us, as she had had a fall getting on to a bus, which immobilised her due to a very nasty leg wound. Some documents relating to Dad's decease are to be found in Appendix H, but we will move on to see how Mum coped with life without her beloved Dick.

14. Life without Dad

Mum inevitably could not see a way forward at first without her beloved Dick by her side. But as we all know, time can heal, even if memories never fade. Dad was so often in her thoughts over all her remaining years - we recall how she would cut the first bloom of his favourite rose from the garden and place it on the mantelpiece. She so often remarked how Dad would have been proud of this or that - Paul gaining his doctorate, great-grandchildren being born and so on. Indeed this was sometimes her first, rather than an after-thought.

But Mum was, as ever, resolute and strong-willed in her determination to make the best of any situation. Although supported by those around her, she maintained her independence and led her own life as far as she was able to, until health and time dictated otherwise.

She liked nothing more than contact with her children, grandchildren and great-grandchildren, and we shall see more of them shortly. They were her constant delight and she never tired of hearing of their news even when they were unable to visit her. The mantelpiece and shelves groaned under the weight of the photo frames supplied on a regular basis. And the family was always close to her, as well. One tradition which began in a small way was her collection of souvenir spoons. It eventually became a regular feature of our travels as we all brought back a spoon from our various journeys to add to the collection, which was displayed in a series of racks on the wall - here is a photo of them for you to admire.

But Mum did not in any way retire into her shell like some superannuated tortoise. In many ways she blossomed. Nor was travel over for her. She went to Extremadura in central Spain with Pete, Paul and Jen, and with Jen she visited Ireland to see the location of the Ballykissangel TV series she so liked. She also visited The Netherlands with Joyce and Wally for *Floriade* in 1992 and at the age of 80 took the Eurostar to Paris.

Let's begin with something which Mum started while Dad was still with us. In a small way she began to make cakes and decorate them with icing for various family events. It rapidly became clear that she had a real talent for this art, and cake projects followed one after another - Christmas, baptisms, birthdays and even wedding cakes were produced, with such artistry that at times it is hard to believe that the decorations are made of little else than sugar. Take as an example this spray of orchids. No, not a real bouquet, but Mum's artistry in sugar. To improve on her skills, Mum, along with Auntie Florrie, joined the Sugarcraft Guild and attended classes. The souvenir spoon of the Guild is shown on the right.

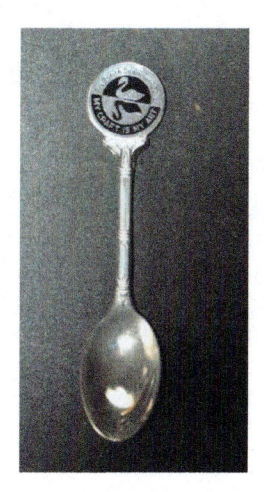

In this photograph, both ladies are at their class:

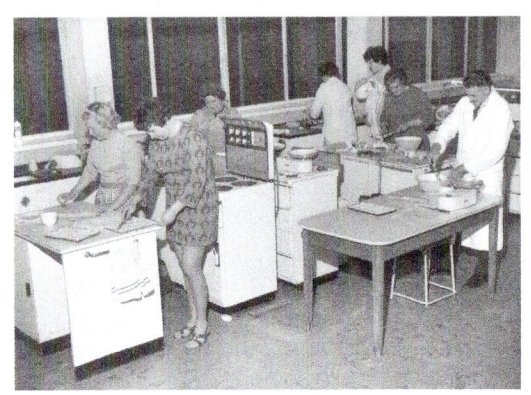

And in the other photo, Mum is seeking inspiration at a national cake show in Telford.

We will show just one example of Mum's incredible work here. This is the wedding cake for grand-daughter Anne. Other examples are to be found in Appendix I. These will illustrate Mum's remarkable talent, which was only cut short when arthritis meant she was unable to control the fine hand work necessary for making items such as flowers.

More trips

Mum's travels and outings didn't stop after Dad passed away. The family went with her for a good many celebration meals. You can see us all at the famous Angel pub in Rotherhithe, in a photo which includes the waiter who was flirting with Mum - no, honestly! Mum laughed just like in this photo.

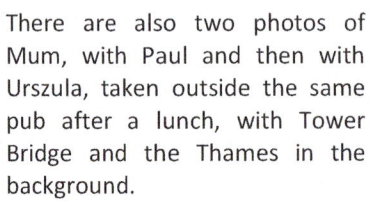

There are also two photos of Mum, with Paul and then with Urszula, taken outside the same pub after a lunch, with Tower Bridge and the Thames in the background.

There were grandchildren's weddings (and Paul's wedding in Warsaw), and a visit to see the Garter Ceremony from inside Windsor Castle, arranged by Paul's wife Ann. There were grandchildren's weddings and for some of these events cine film has survived. In 1992 Joyce and Wally took Mum to Amsterdam for the Floriade Festival. As you can see, the weather was rather chilly, to judge by Mum's clothes!

And here we are having dinner in an old school room converted into a restaurant.

It was no surprise to those of us who knew Mum, that when the tax man decided that he had been over-deducting for some time and gave Mum a rebate, her first instinct was to spend it not on herself, but on providing enjoyment for others. So, with our logistic help, she set up a lunch for the extended family which all who were present remember to this day as an enjoyable and unforgettable experience. Here are a few photos of the occasion to give a flavour of the day. Needless to say, although Mum may look to be close to tears, it's through emotion, not sadness!

Mum travelled to Warsaw in Poland for Paul's marriage to his second wife Urszula. But overseas travel was less of an option for her from now on.

Party time

As she reached her 80th birthday, a celebration was organised at Joyce and Wally's house, and here are two photos from the occasion.

And here she is at Joyce and Wally's Ruby Wedding anniversary party.

And at her own 85th birthday:

When it came to celebrating the landmark of Mum's 90th birthday, we decided to stage a similar lunch to the one which we had so enjoyed with Mum a few years before, so the same restaurant was booked and preparations made. Once more the day was a perfect one - Mum fighting back her emotional tears most of the time.

After the meal, we all watched a slide presentation of Mum's life accompanied by commentaries from the great grandchildren. Here is a selection of photos of that great occasion, and in Appendix J you can see a gallery of the many cards Mum received to celebrate her birthday.

The tables laid up before the guests arrived.

The moment Mum arrived and saw the many guests.

Top table: from left, Urszula (hiding!), Joyce, Mum, Wally, Pete and Jen, with the back of Andy's head.

On this table, from the left, Anne Arnold, Ron, Rita, Andrew and Kate, and opposite them their spouses, Andy, Dora, Les, Margaret and Dennis.

Again, left to right, Tom, Lachlan, Laura, Esther, Holly, Katharine, Lynda, Keith, Urszula, Joyce, Trevor, Emma, Matthew (hiding), Murdo, Jim, Sophie and Helen.

And the same table from the other end: Ann, Trevor, Emma, Matthew, Murdo, Jim, Sophie, Helen, Tom, Esther, Holly, Lynda and Keith.

Keith, Lynda, Laura and Lachlan.

Ann and Helen "catching up".

Andy, Dora, Les, Margaret, Dennis, Anne, Ron, Rita, Andrew and Kate.

Urszula, Margaret and Jen.

Kate and Anne Arnold.

Mum with Joyce.

One cake that Mum didn't make!

Mum with Joyce and Wally.

In 2007, even though Mum's mobility was declining, she was still game for adventures and invited the whole family to a holiday near Corfe Castle in Dorset, where a farmyard complex was rented. We spent a wonderful week there, and in spite of not being able to take too many steps from the wheelchair, Mum greatly enjoyed herself - watching us enjoy ourselves, which is something that always gave her pleasure. Whilst we couldn't get her all the way up to the cliffs to enjoy the wonderful views of Old Harry Rocks, she could get down to the beach at Knoll and on to the pier at Swanage and to the shore at Lulworth Cove. She also enjoyed Abbotsbury Swannery. Some photos shown here will give a flavour of the lovely time we had with Mum.

One day Mum was watching the television and saw the London Eye - the huge wheel on the banks of the Thames, and said "I would like to go on that" which she duly did, as you can see here in the photos.

Enjoying the next generations

Nothing gave Mum greater pleasure than being with her extended family, especially the grandchildren and great-grandchildren. And she continued to get around a bit – with help, of course. Here are some photos of events and encounters in her later years.

Four generations with Mum holding Emma.

Mum again with Emma.

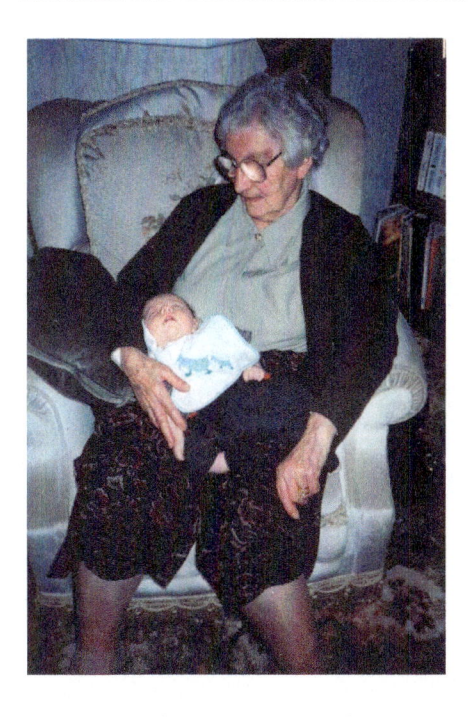

This time with a very tiny Matthew, and on the right at his Christening.

Mum with new-born Katharine.

And this time with very little Holly.

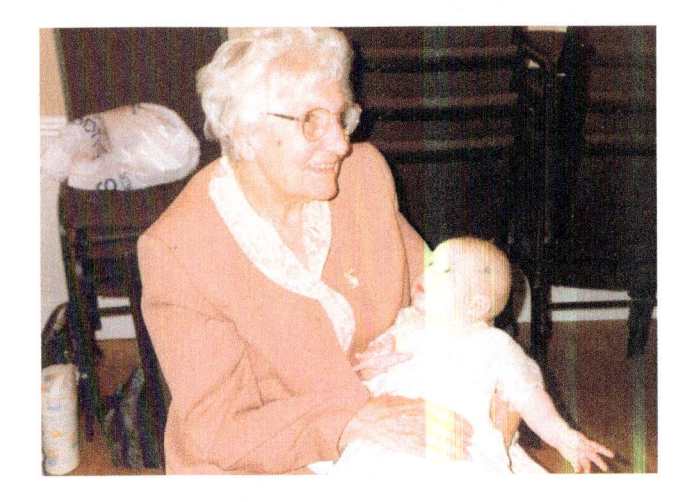

A happy Mum with Holly at her Christening.

And with Holly and Katharine at Holly's first birthday.

Mum at Helen's wedding reception.

Mum with newborn Lachlan.

Here with Esther at her First Communion.

And here she is with tiny Charlotte.

And here are two pictures of Mum at Kate's wedding.

Pensive, again at Kate's wedding.

At Andrew's wedding.

Mum on her 94th birthday.

A visit from niece Margaret and Ron.

Two of the many occasions in Pete's garden.

Mum mowing Pete's grass in 1988.

Here and following, three pictures taken at Pete's 60th birthday.

Here Mum is thinking she won't risk the stepping stones in Dovedale on New Year's Day!

Mum at Joyce's 70th birthday.

Mum loved the Ballykissangel TV series and here she is "on set" - or at least in the village in Ireland where it was filmed, where she went with Jen in 1998, and in Powerscourt Gardens.

This is a photo of Mum at Joyce and Wally's Golden Wedding anniversary lunch.

Mum loved to go on days out, and here is an itinerary prepared by Joyce and Wally for her birthday present, taking in a show. She also loved watching the ballet and was thrilled when Paul took her to Covent Garden to see the Kirov company perform Swan Lake.

Failing health and final years

Mum's health and mobility steadily declined over the years. But one thing was clear - what she wanted most of all was her independence and to be able to stay in the house where she had lived since 1939. With thrice daily visits from a string of carers provided by Newham Council Social Services and a lot of family support, Mum was able to do that for some time. Certainly for much longer than if she had had to fend totally for herself. But the time began to approach when we knew that Mum was beginning to be at risk in her home. It was not easy to convince her that she needed to be in a safer environment, but after some hospital events which included falls, and early attempts to seek sheltered accommodation for her - met with an abrupt rebuttal on her part - we did manage to persuade her that she had to begin a new episode in her life. Thus it was that Mum, on the 18th April 2009, moved into a care home in Romford, Ebury Court, carefully (and as it turned out, wisely) chosen by us after viewing a range of other providers. Mum did not know what to expect from such a home, and was pleasantly surprised - she was probably thinking of a dormitory and hospital type environment.

Ebury Court provided her with an excellent, caring, well run and appropriate environment. After her initial reticence, Mum positively blossomed there. As one of the managers pointed out, she didn't just accept being there, she embraced it. The wide range of activities in which she enthusiastically plunged often meant that we had trouble finding a free time on her part when we might visit her! Below, we include a few photographs to illustrate her days at Ebury Court. You can see Mum, in a sequence of photos explaining with obvious delight how she did her Tai Chi classes (in popularity second only to Derek and his Music and Movement, a highlight of the week), her visit to Buckingham Palace, which fulfilled a long-term dream for her, and the summer fête. She also had visits from a good number of family members, in between her pub lunches, theatre outings and church services. All in all she was having a ball!

The spoon 'necklace' that Mum is wearing is a Norwegian wedding spoon carved by Pete (one of his hobbies). He had brought it to show Mum when it was finished, as it was one of the things that she remembered even though her short-term memory was failing.

Sadly, it was not to last as long as we would have liked. Her health, in spite of the excellent care and the superb food she received, declined in a few months. Mum died, in no pain and very peacefully, on the 3rd September 2009. Her certificate of death is seen here. Our sadness was tempered by the knowledge that in her last months she had experienced an enhanced quality of life far better than we could have imagined possible.

Mum was cremated at South Essex Crematorium on the 14th September, when we held not a funeral, nor a wake, but a celebration of Mum's life. You can see the order of service in the images below, followed by the address which we three dedicated to Mum's life. We wonder what Mum would have thought had she realised that her funeral cost well over 200 times that of her great grandfather Samuel! The receipt is also seen below, and a gallery of the sympathy cards which were sent to the funeral is to be found at Appendix K.

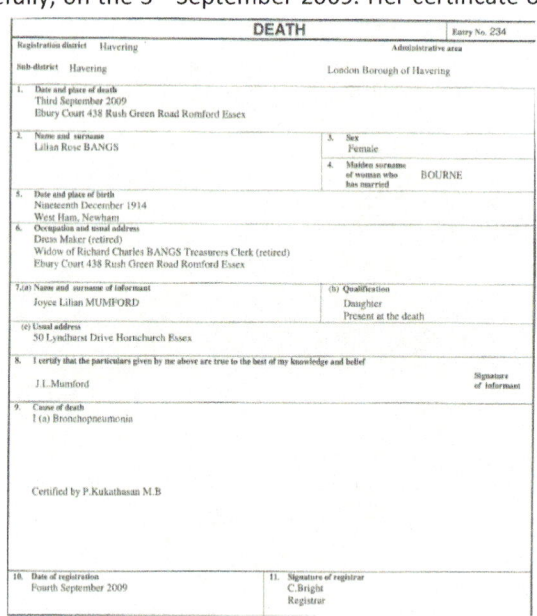

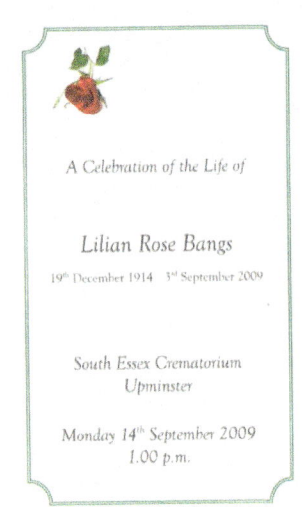

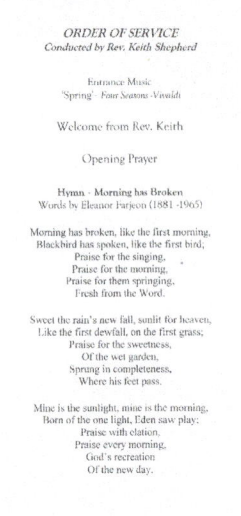

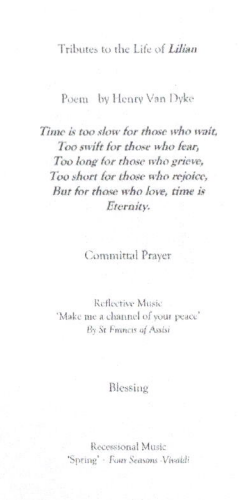

Good afternoon, *and thank you everyone, from all of us, for coming here today, some of you from a long distance indeed. We are here today to celebrate the life of a very special lady, and to say our goodbyes.*

Well who was she? Lilian, Lily, Lil, Aunt Lil, Auntie, Liw, Mum, Nan, Nanny, Great Nanny. Even Mrs Bangs! And what would she have said about today? Well, we could venture a few ideas…. "All these people, just to see me?" or "Who's looking after the children?" or "Have you all got seats?" or "I'll go and put the kettle on". OK, perhaps just a joke, but for us, who knew Mum, it tells us so much about her life, a life characterised by the word "service". Let's think for a while about what that means and how it applies to Mum.

Let's start by going back in time. Where did Mum come from? Thanks to the incredible efforts of her cousin Andrew Peckett, we know that she is from Fenland stock on one side of the family, and from rural Bedfordshire on another. If we go back, as we can, to the sixteenth century, and look through the occupations of many of her (and our) ancestors, we can see a thread of "service" running through time. We can see boot makers, toll collectors, schoolteachers, farriers, dress makers, servants, Reform League politicians, brewery fireman, engine drivers. What marks out their occupations is the concept of helping and serving others. Mum clearly inherited this trait in her genes. So let's look at some of the major milestones in her life and how it is that Mum became the caring person she was…. Pay attention, questions may be asked later! – you're not dealing with three retired teachers for nothing!

Like most good things she started from very small beginnings – in Mum's case literally so. At birth, in 1914, she weighed in at just 3 pounds and was washed in olive oil, wrapped in muslin and placed in a large jug. This was then put into a drawer and surrounded with cotton wool. A forerunner of a premature baby incubator, no doubt. It certainly did its job. At the end of her life she seemed to be shrinking towards the same weight, but in between, everything about Mum was big-hearted.

By the time she was thirteen she was gathering swimming certificates – one even for a quarter mile swim. She was also an active member of her school netball team, although we can't show you her medal, because she lost it in West Ham Park and felt the loss all her life! Devoted to her parents and her younger brother Albert she had a happy childhood. We are fortunate in having quite a few photos of them all in her early years – on both formal and informal occasions. Some of them are posed photos taken in a studio, but more than a few show Mum as a very pretty bridesmaid – always with a ribbon in her long curly hair, squatting on the floor in front of whichever aunt or other relative was the bride. If, as we hope, you come to the reception afterwards, you'll be able to see many of these photos and more.

Mum excelled at school – so much so that her teacher visited home to try and persuade her father – our granddad – to let her take the scholarship, as it was then known, and stay on at school beyond the age of fourteen. Sadly that was not to be, because in those days "girls didn't need to study" and she left school and began helping out in the family greengrocer shop – again the concept of service to the fore. Our grandmother had the vision to see that this was not our Mum's destiny, and via the contacts of one of the shop customers, Mum was able to get a job training to be a dressmaker. The skills she learned then never left her, and she made many of our clothes right through our childhood. Perhaps her 'piece de resistance' was when she made not just Joyce's wedding dress, but the bridesmaids' dresses for all six of the bridesmaids.

We don't know much detail about Mum's teenage years. There were certainly boyfriends and suitors – hardly surprising when you see what a beauty she was at that age - a real stunner. What we do know is that our father came on the scene and they soon started 'courting', as they called it. Mum told us how Dad used to meet her out of work, waiting on the pavement opposite. Her work colleagues would look out for him, and tell her when he had arrived. By all accounts they thought he was 'dishy' too. Often on these occasions they would go for tea – sometimes in a Lyons Corner House – then on to a show in the West End. The Palladium was a frequent venue.

By the standards of the day their romance was fairly swift. By the time she was 19 they were engaged, and got married soon after Mum's twentieth birthday. Since she was under the legal age of consent at that time she had to have the written permission of her father to wed at that age.

Following the customs of the day, Mum gave up her dressmaking job and became a full-time housewife. She and Dad set up home in a flat – well, half a house really – in Stratford. They had frequent excursions into Kent – often on a Sunday – where they would get off at a train station somewhere and walk in the countryside to another station, before returning home.

After fifteen months our sister, Joyce, came along, so Mum added family service to her CV, and by the time Joyce was 3 they moved to 140 Hatherley Gardens, which was to be Mum's home for 70 years, until she moved to Ebury Court in April of this year. Soon after they arrived at Hatherley Gardens war broke out. To escape the danger from bombing, Mum was evacuated to live with friends in Barnet, and this lasted for quite a while. Dad was drafted into the army, and though he served much of the war in this country, in 1944 he was posted to India – just after Paul was born. Mum was left to look after "little Topsey" (Joyce) and "baby Paul". The separation lasted for over a year – and on his return Paul cried at the site of this unknown man! While Dad was in India, Mum and Joyce spent much of the time evacuated once more - this time to live with one of her aunts in remote Norfolk. She corresponded regularly with Dad in India – and we still have all his wonderfully personal letters to her from that period. That separation must have been really hard to bear. But let's not forget that Mum was also rather feisty when she wanted to be. Dad's letters show us that she insisted on taking the risk of going from the safety of evacuation in rural Norfolk to ensure that Joyce could be a bridesmaid at Dad's brother Bill's wedding in London.

I came along in 1946 and Mum continued to devote herself to being a housewife and mother – and what a good one she was too! Mum used her dressmaking skills to make all three of us clothes (and the dresses were just for Joyce – we two did have 'proper' boys' clothes!!), and we remember the regular punctual lunches for when Dad came home from his work at the Town Hall at 1 o'clock.

Having had her own educational ambitions frustrated, Mum was determined that the same would not happen to us. She encouraged all three of us in our turn to work hard and seize whatever opportunities arose. Joyce moved on from Primary School to East Ham Girls Grammar School, and we both went on to the Boys' Grammar. Times were not easy – sweets had only come off ration in 1956 (try explaining the concept of rationing to the new generation!)– and Mum took a job as a school cleaner to ensure that finance was not to be an obstacle to our progress. This proved very much the case as Joyce moved from Grammar School to Teacher Training College in Exmouth. We all have many memories of our earlier years. The encouragement that Mum gave us is legendary. It's well known that Joyce did not inherit Mum's prowess at needlework and cake-decorating, but did follow the talent that she had for singing and playing the piano. There were instances when practising the piano was a chore, but no way would Mum sign the book until the practice had been completed, and this was something to be grateful for in later life.

If any of us had a problem she listened – not giving advice unless asked for. Just by a few words or a look, the problem could be put into perspective. We think, (hope), that these qualities have been passed on to the future generations.

Mum never did a bad deed or speak ill of anyone – although we boys remember her shouting up the stairs "If you two don't go to sleep, I'll come up there and bang your heads together!" Frightened the neighbours, but we knew she would never carry out the threat. Mum was not only our Mum but also a great friend.

We boys also went on to higher education – Paul to Liverpool University and me to Hendon College of Technology - all the time encouraged by Mum to do our best. We all three embarked on careers in teaching, and moved on with our own lives too, getting married and presenting Mum with 6 wonderful grandchildren, who are all here today. All the time Mum kept on working as a school cleaner, only retiring in 1974 – 22 years more of service – when she went up to Derby to help out when Kate, her youngest grandchild was born.

Once their three children were 'off hand', and Dad retired too, Mum and Dad branched out and were able to take more regular holidays – firstly in this country and then abroad – to Ireland, the Channel Irelands, and then, after being persuaded, with some difficulty, to visit Paul and family when they lived on the Costa Blanca, to Spain and Portugal. In between these holidays they visited us all regularly, and nothing pleased them more than relaxing with their grandchildren, and watching them grow up. Mum was always interested in whatever they were doing, and always ready to listen to any of them. You only had to look at Mum's face to see the sparkle in her eyes whenever the children were mentioned.

During this period in her life Mum found the time to develop the creative skills that had been somewhat repressed earlier in her life. It all started when she decorated the cake for Pete and Jen's wedding. Thrilled though they were with it, she gradually learned more advanced skills. These developed over the years as she made and decorated cake after cake for successive family weddings, birthdays and other events. Some of the flowers that she made to decorate her cakes were so real it was hard to believe that they were made of icing sugar! Mum only stopped when arthritis in her hands restricted their mobility.

In 1991 Mum's world fell apart when our Dad died quite suddenly. It set her back more than a little, but gradually she adjusted to her new life without him. She learned that life, while different, could still have its enjoyable moments – not least as her grandchildren presented her with successive great-grandchildren - ten at the last count, or a full football team if we include Kate's stepdaughter Chloe! The shelves and mantelpieces at 140 Hatherley – already well stocked with wedding photos of children and grandchildren - now began almost to sag under the weight of all the extra picture frames. Her photo gallery was her pride and joy, and remarked upon by anyone who visited her.

Mum's mobility deteriorated in later years, but she faced life not so much with resignation as with determination and she never complained. After so many years of serving others, she found it difficult to be at the receiving end of so much help from her dedicated team of carers. They did a great job in keeping her in the home that she loved so much and for so long. Eventually, as her general health declined, the time came for her to accept that she couldn't continue to live on her own.

The day of Mum's transfer from hospital to her new home at Ebury Court was awaited with a mixture of trepidation and uncertainty – but only by us. Mum arrived in her usual positive frame of mind, "Is all this just for me?", and in those all too short months at her new home, she positively blossomed. In the words of Beverley, the manager, whilst others "accepted life" there, Mum "embraced it". Whether it was pub lunches, Tai Chi, "Music and Movement with Derek" and, above all the visit to Buckingham Palace, (fulfilling a life-long desire), Mum loved all the events and met them with head-on enthusiasm, and made new friends. These last months have been a source of great joy, not just for Mum but for us as we saw her regain that sparkle in her eyes, and for that we will always be grateful to each and every one of the Ebury Court staff, whose care and professionalism was, clearly, matched with kindness and love towards our dear mother. We are so pleased to see Ebury Court represented here today.

So now it seems we've got to the "thank you" bit. Apart from once again thanking all of you for being here, and for the affection you have all shown Mum over the years, the three of us want to pay tribute to all our extended families for the love, affection, help and consideration shown to Mum over the many years, but especially to our spouses, Wally, Ann, Urszula and Jen. We want to make a special mention of the amazing dedication shown by Wally, who has done so much to make Mum's life more enjoyable for so many years. And thanks, too, to all our children, their spouses and their children, who have grown up to love and respect their Nanny or great Nanny. It's surely no coincidence that they all of them, without exception, had such affection for her... we wonder where they got that from!

And then, who else is left to thank? Just our Mum, who gave us everything, not just our own lives, but so much of her own. Thank you, Mum, and God bless you.

Mum's death is not, however, the end of the story. For one thing, we, though obviously biased in our opinions, know that Mum was the kindest person you could hope to meet, always interested in putting the welfare of others above her own. We know that this opinion is shared by the very many people whose lives she touched and were better as a result. That is why, as a tribute to Mum, and to form part of her legacy to the world, we have created this work.

Mum did not leave so much in material terms, but her bequest is far greater than that, and apart from the obvious debts which we owe her, there is a whole world in which she created so much affection and love, that what we are recording here hardly does her life justice - but it's an attempt we hope you will appreciate.

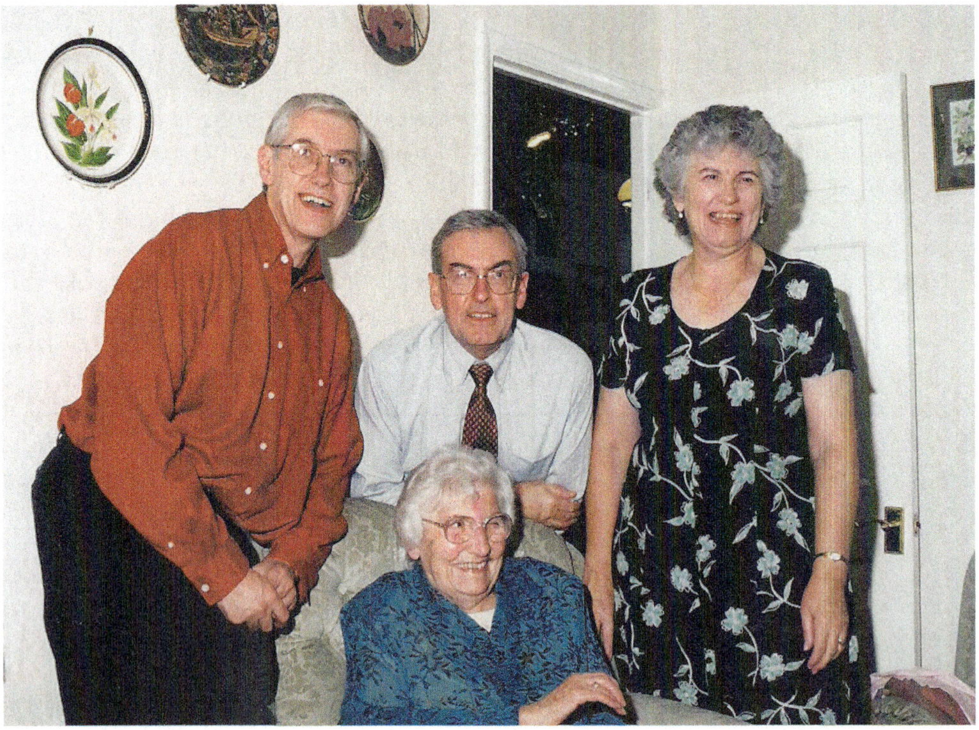

Blank Page

Why have we left a blank page? Because this is a reminder for you, the reader, whichever member of the family you are, to not forget to add your own life, your own memories, your own photos, to an account which has no end …. Those who come after you will thank you for it!

APPENDIX A
Mum's 21st Birthday Cards.

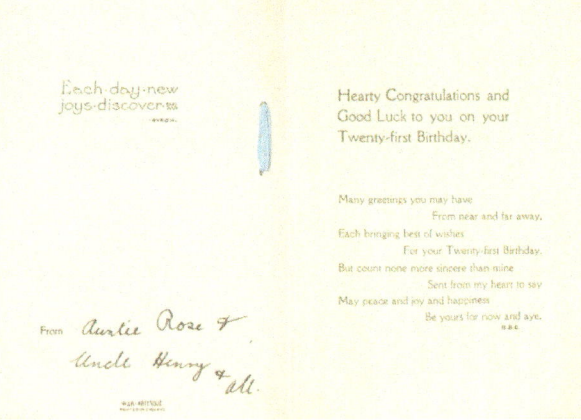

The above card is from Aunt Rose and Uncle Henry - Aunt Rose was Mum's aunt on the Peckett side, sister to our Nanny Bourne.

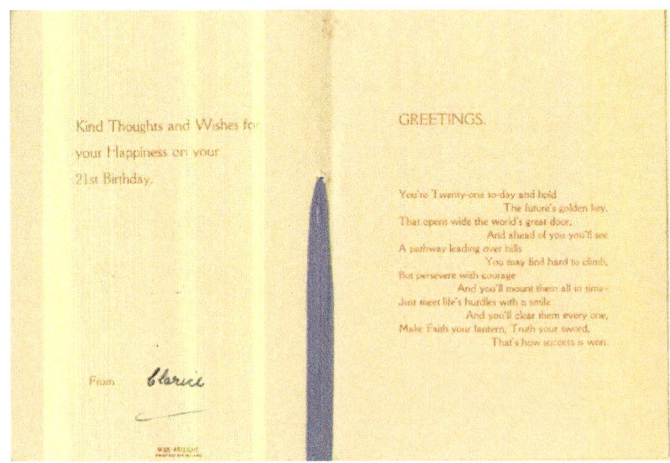

We have no idea who Clarice was, but could have been a work colleague of Mum's.

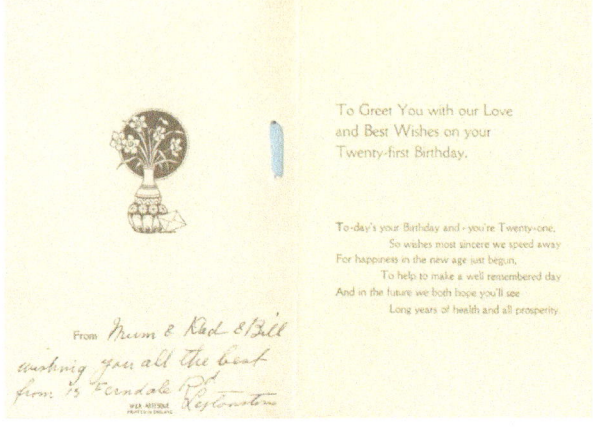

This card has a similar design to the one shown earlier. It's from Dad's parents and his brother Bill, who lived in Ferndale Road, Leytonstone.

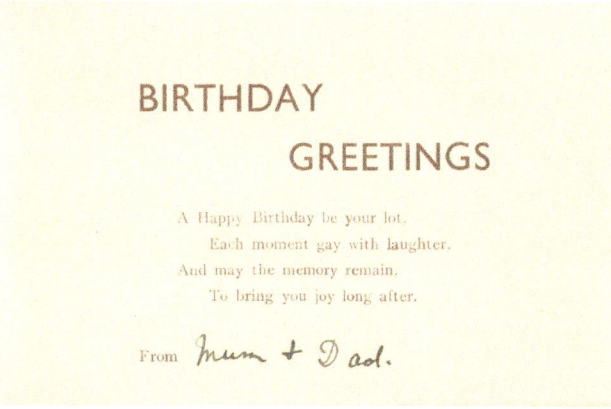

This beautiful, old-fashioned card is from Mum's parents, our Nan and Grandad Bourne.

Another beautiful card in the old "postcard" style, from someone we don't know, called Hetty. The one below is from a Mr and Mrs Hocking, whom we don't know. Notice that it is addressed to Mrs Bangs - Mum had been married just a few months.

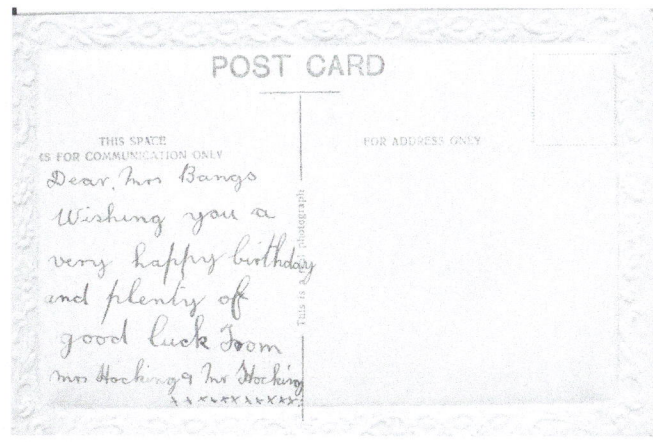

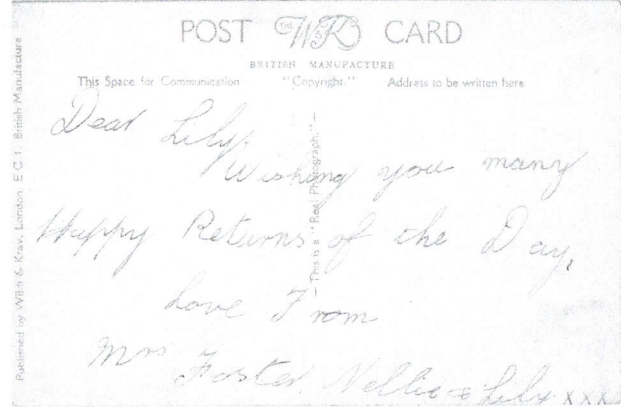

The Fosters were neighbours and friends.

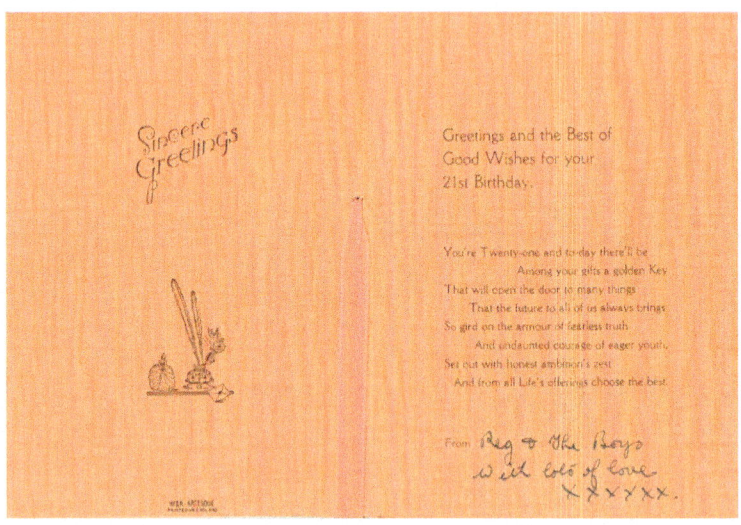

We're not sure who this Reg could be.

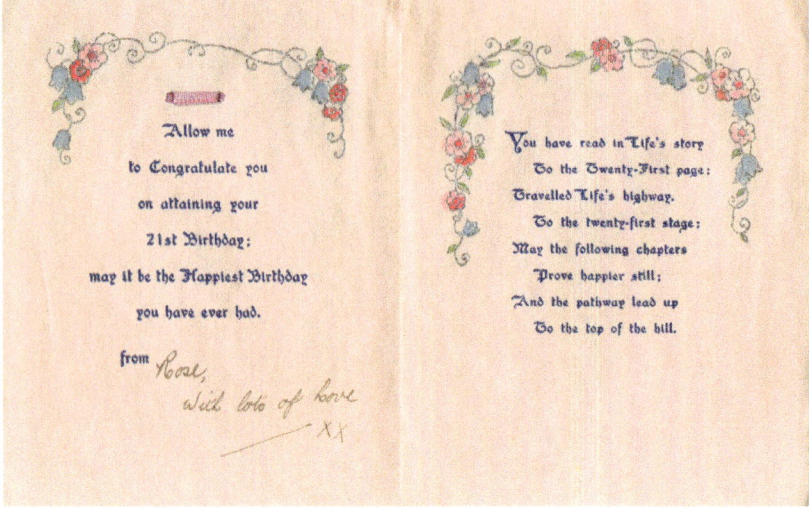

This last one will be from Dad's sister Rose.

APPENDIX B
House receipts

As might be expected, Mum and Dad received many wedding gifts, and these were often treasured over the years. Always on Mum's dressing table was this magnificent Walther Sohne 1930s "Nymphen" Art Deco glass set:

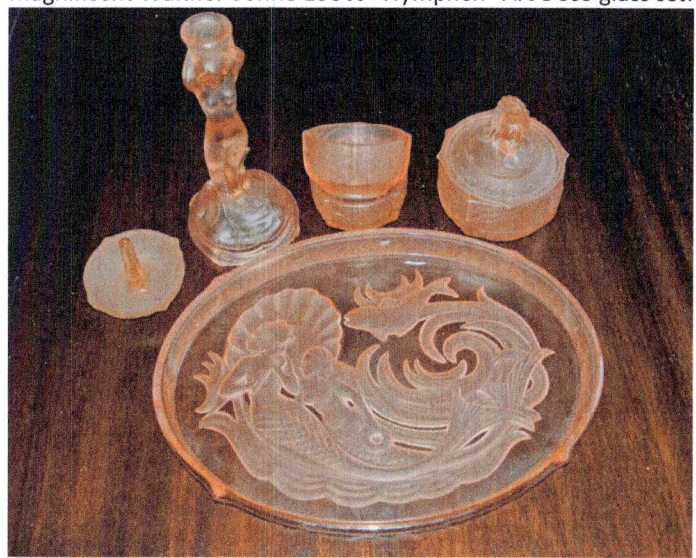

Another treasured item is this wonderful and quite rare 1930s Japanese Art Deco coffee set by Chikaramachi:

There follow some of the more interesting receipts for items Mum and Dad purchased when setting up house. The prices are interesting, and you have to calculate on 1930s wages, and in fact many of the items were quite costly. But there is also a simple bill for some groceries - check those prices! In some cases we can see that the amounts were paid in full, usually by cash - it was not a plastic age, then. There are receipts also made out to our Nan - these seem to be for payment of a sewing machine, though the shop is a clothes shop.

See if you can spot the odd one out. There's one receipt, dated a little later, which shows preparation for a certain event. What could that be?

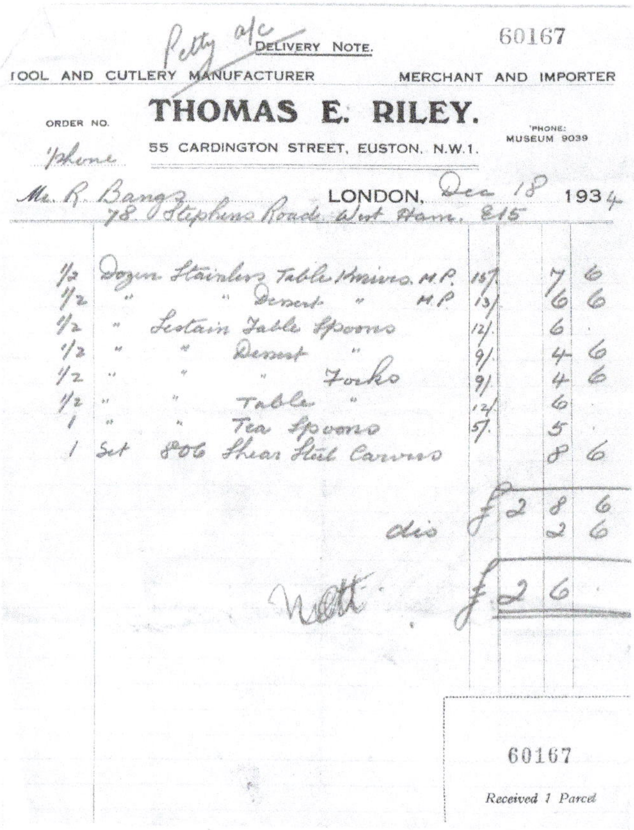

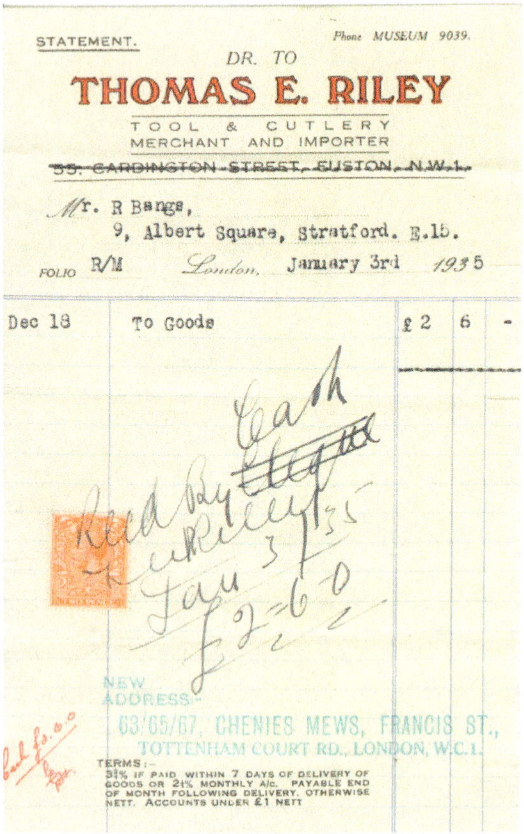

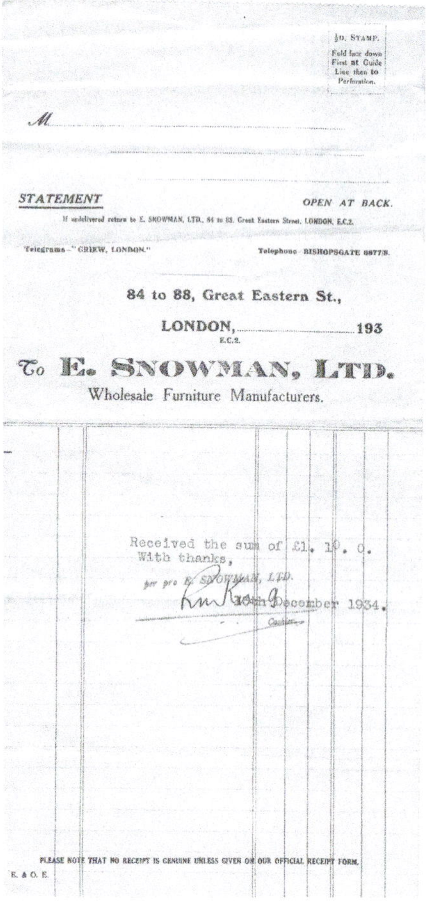

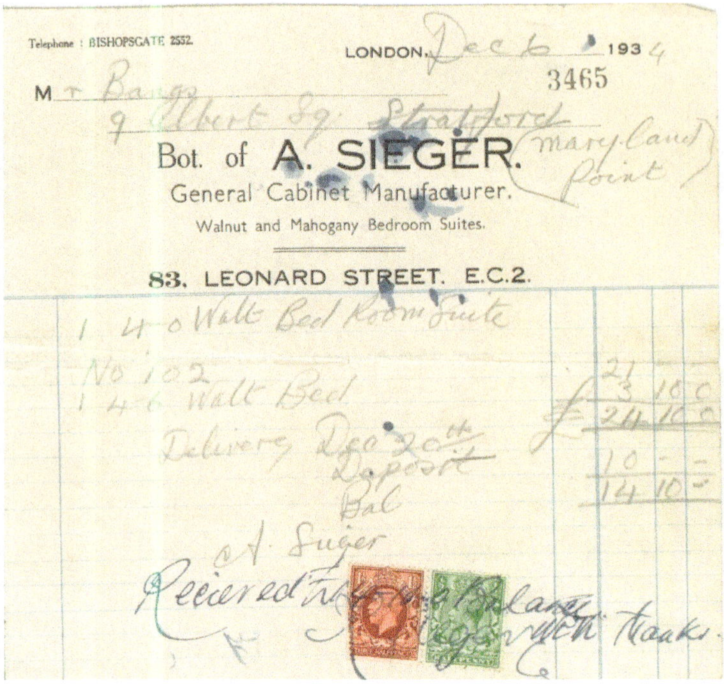

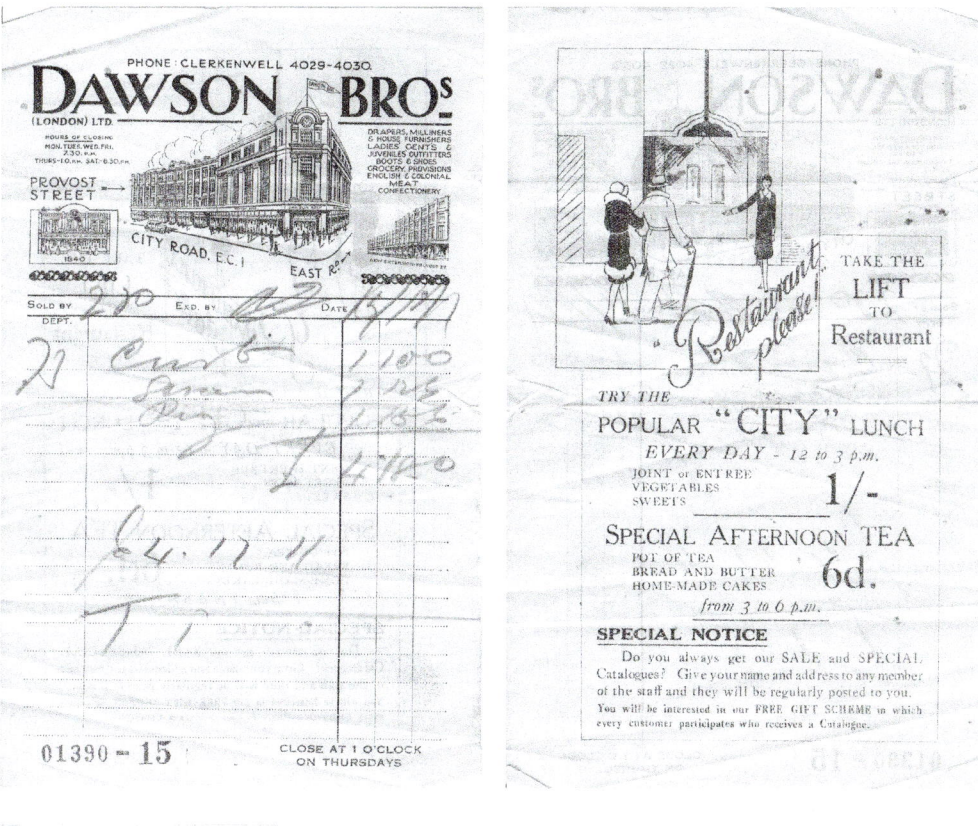

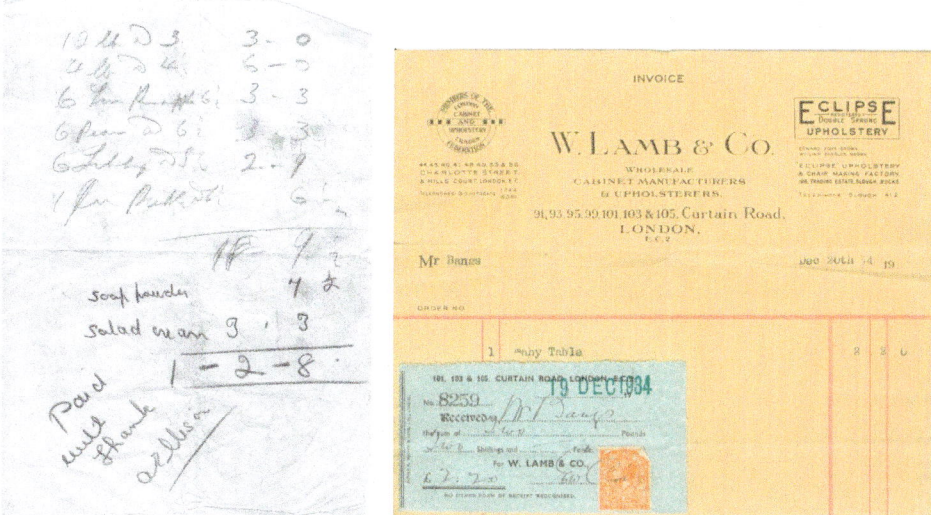

There is an unusual link between one of the receipts and events which occurred much later. This refers to the receipt from Boardman's in Stratford, and the fact that both Paul and Peter had a Saturday job in that very shop in the 1960s. Strange to imagine now, that the shop floor we trod had echoed once to the sound of Mum and Dad's feet! We never gave it a thought at the time. Another point to note is the 1930s designs of some of the printed forms, as well as the fact that receipts in those days above a certain amount needed a postage stamp over which a signature was placed - the original "stamp" duty.

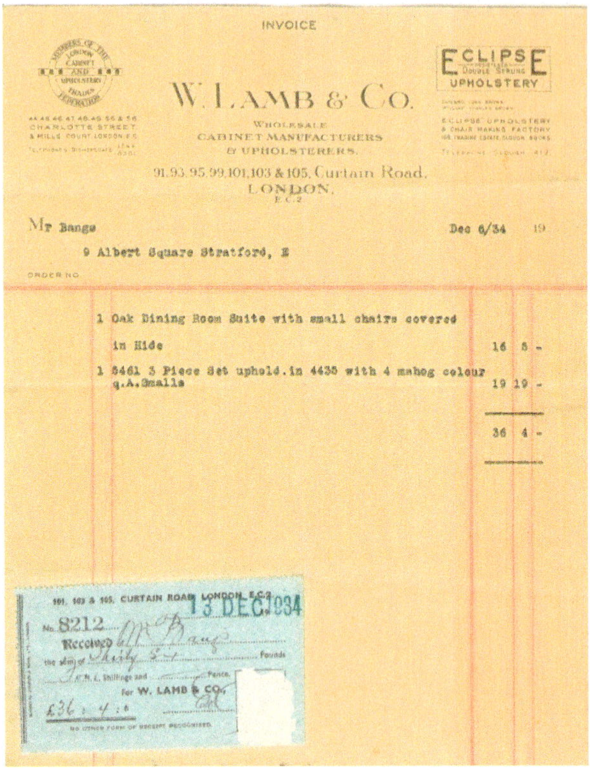

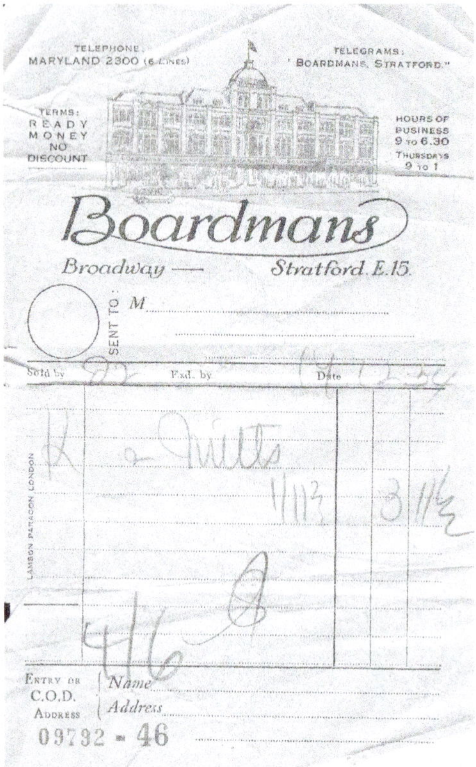

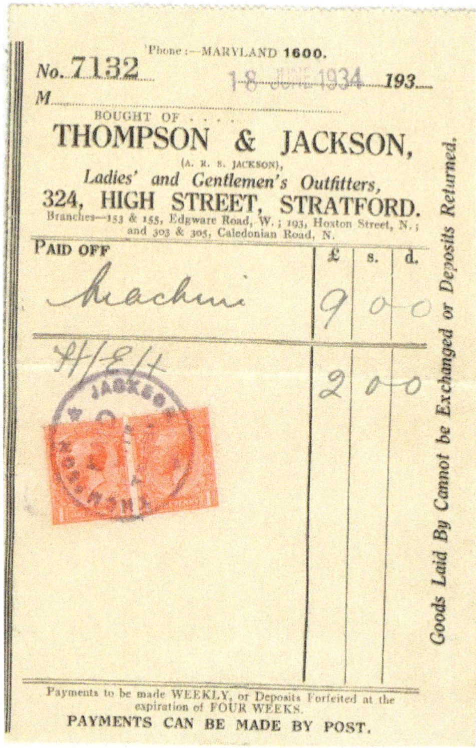

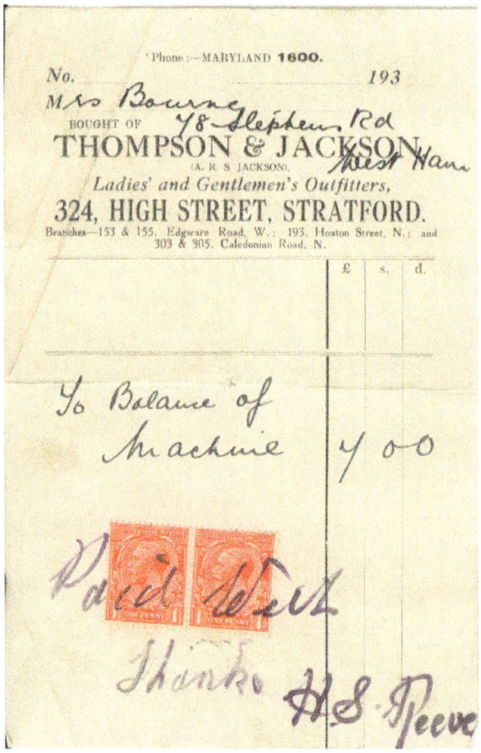

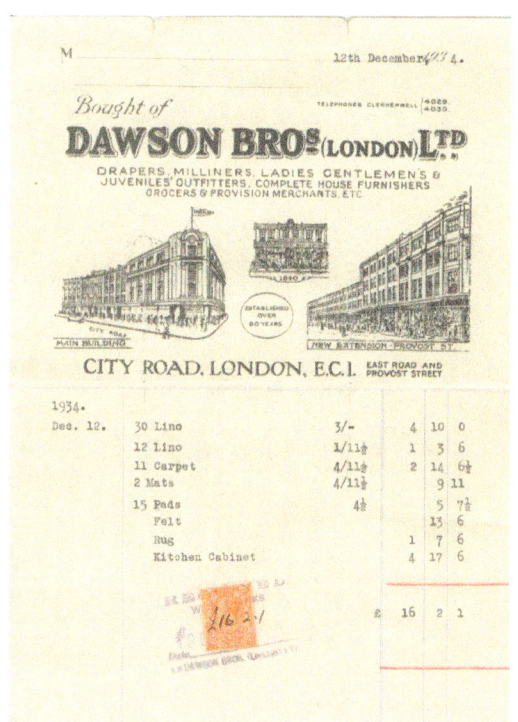

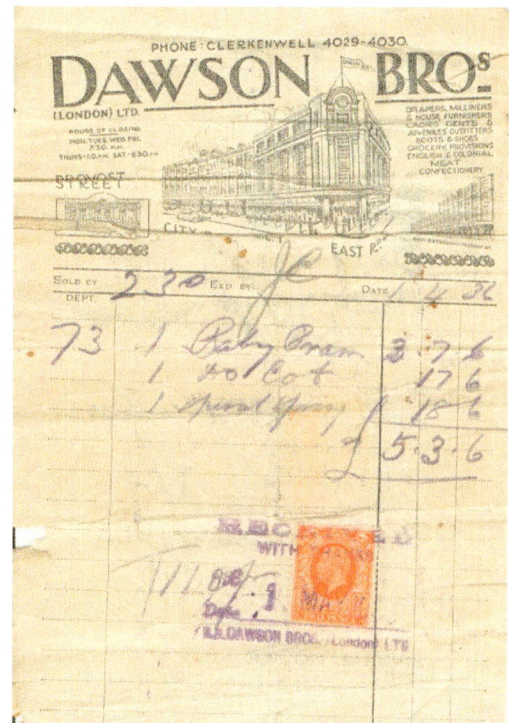

We've also included here the receipt for the family piano. The interesting thing here is not just the huge sum of money for those days - £48.6s (although it was a superb Monington and Weston upright grand - see the photo with our Nan sitting next to it) - but the fact that it was paid for during the war. Where that money came from, even if it was paid by "payments" (presumably means instalments) is a mystery.

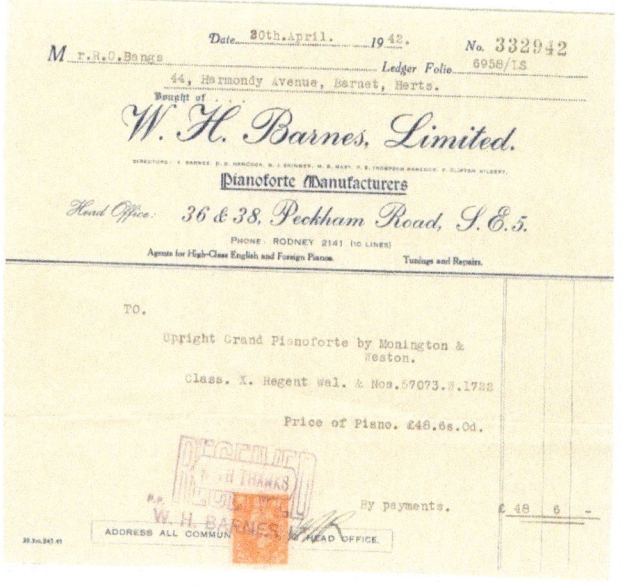

APPENDIX C

Dad's Army Pay Book

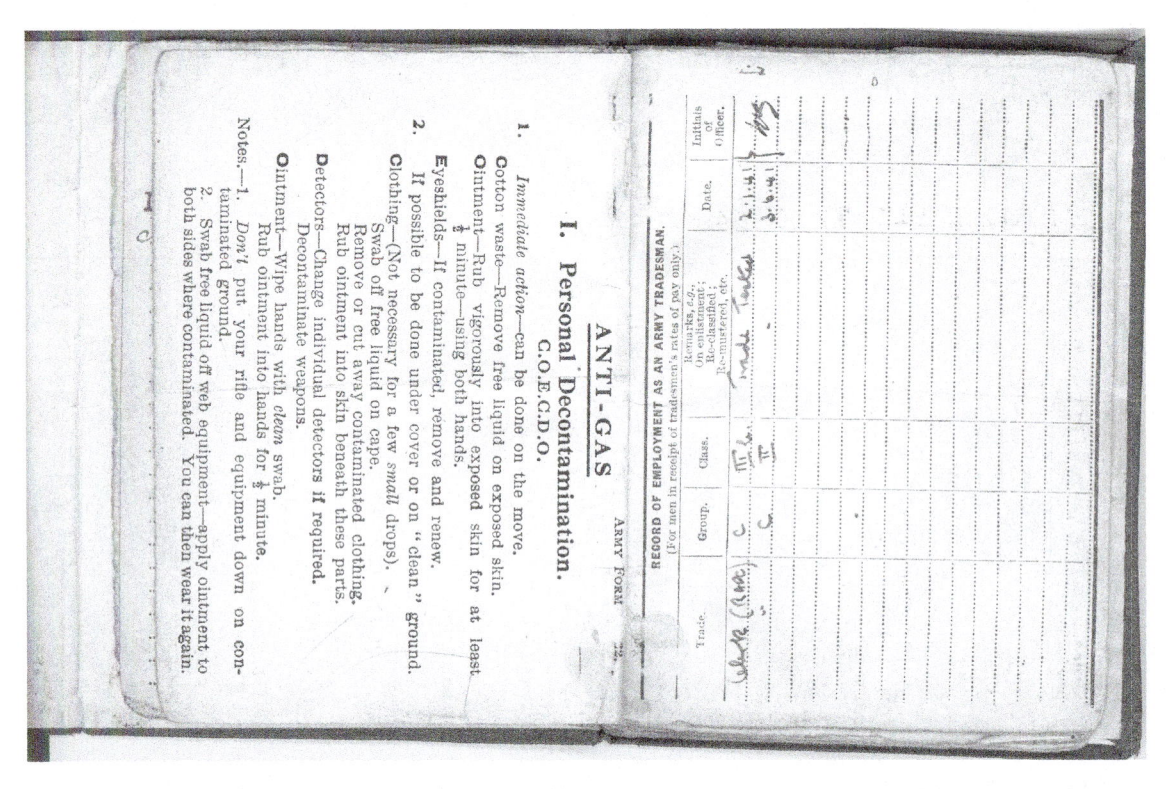

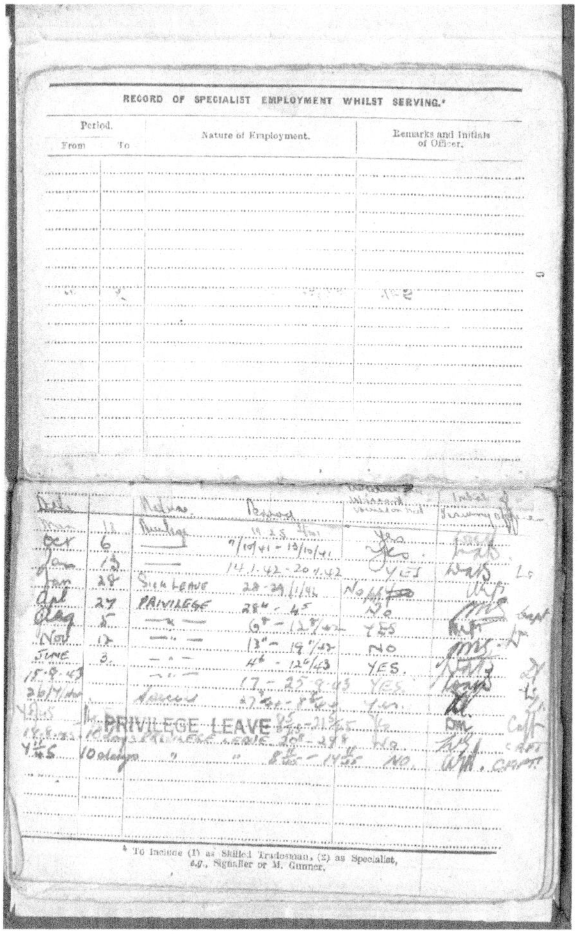

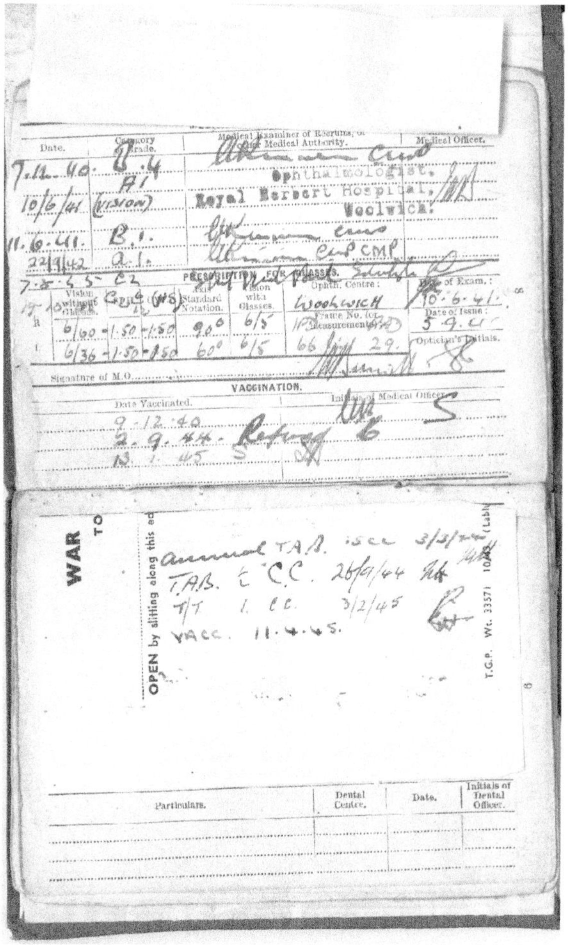

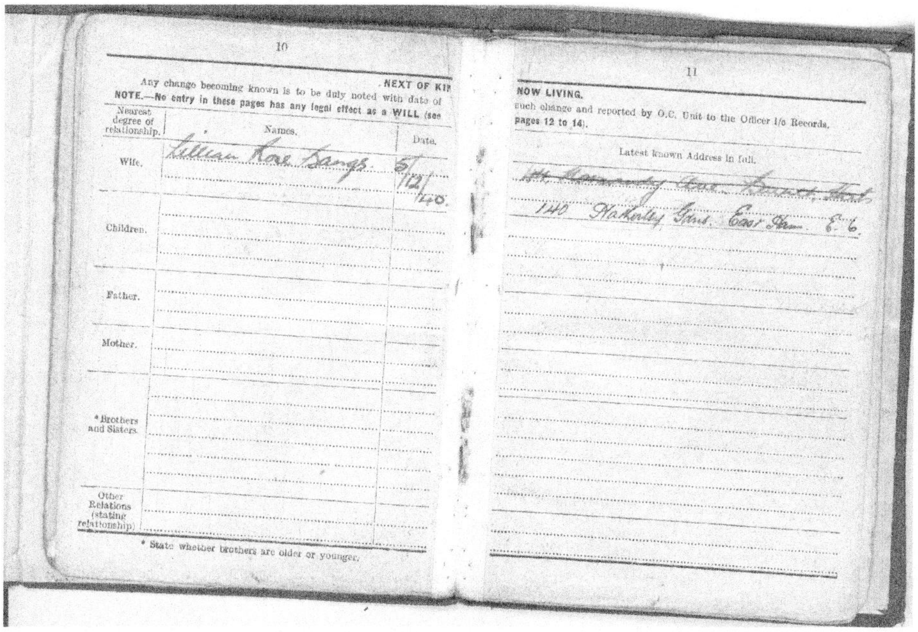

SOLDIERS' WILLS.

1. The soldier should always be careful to insert particulars of his relatives on pages 10 and 11 but it must be clearly understood that the entry of a name on those pages has not the legal effect of a Will and does not have any influence on the distribution of a soldier's estate. Unless a soldier duly makes a Will, his estate has to be distributed in accordance with the laws of Intestacy and the person whom he might intend to benefit may receive little or no share in the distribution.

2. The Soldier's Will should be made out either on the separate Form provided for that purpose, or on one of the Forms contained in this Book, or on a separate sheet of paper, and unless he is on active service or under orders for active service, the testator must be of the age of 21 years, with the exception that a Scotsman can always dispose of movable property (as distinguished from heritable property—see paragraph 10) when of the age of 14 years or over.

3. The bequests in the Will may be varied according to the circumstances and wishes of each Soldier; but the form of attestation and the general outline of the Will, as shown in the following Forms, are to be carefully followed.

4. The Will must be signed by the testator with his name (or, if he cannot write, with his mark), in the presence of two witnesses, who must be present together; and the Will must be acknowledged and attested in the presence of all three, and dated.

5. A person to whom money, etc., is left by the Will, or the husband or wife of such a person, should not be an attesting witness, for the gift would not be good, but he or she may be appointed an executor.

6. In English law a Will may be revoked by the marriage of the testator, and therefore a new Will ought to be made after marriage if desired. By the law of Scotland, the Channel Islands and the Isle of Man, the rights of the widow or children to some part of the estate cannot be defeated by a Will.

7. If any alteration is made in the writing of a Will, the signatures of the testator and the witnesses ought to be made in the margin or other part of the Will, opposite to or near such alteration, or at the foot or end of, or opposite to, a memorandum referring to such alteration and written at the end or some other part of the Will.

8. But an alteration or addition may be made by a *Codicil* (that is to say, by an addition to the Will), executed and witnessed in the same way as the Will.

9. When on active service in the field, or when he has been placed under orders for active service, a soldier of English, Guernsey or Manx domicile is privileged to make his Will in writing without the attesting witnesses (*see* pages 19 and 20), or to declare the same by word of mouth in the presence of witnesses, and if the testator is of English domicile he can dispose of all his property, of whatever kind.

10. A soldier of Scottish, Jersey or Guernsey domicile can make a written Will without witnesses *at any time*, provided that it is entirely in his own handwriting and dated and signed by him at the foot of the document. A soldier of Scottish domicile can dispose by Will of movable property, at any time, when of the age of 14 years or over, but heritable property situated in Scotland cannot be disposed of by Will by a soldier under 21 years of age, unless he is at the time on active service in the field or under orders for active service. Heritable property includes land and houses and rights in and to the same; movable property includes money, stocks, shares and certificates of money value, jewellery and other personal articles.

11. When any of the forms of Will on pages 15 to 20 have been completed by the soldier, it is in his interests to have the Will placed in safe custody, and Officers i/c Records have special facilities for doing this. The soldier should therefore, on completing either of the Will forms, ask the Officer Commanding the Company, etc., to extract the Will from Army Book 64, and to arrange its despatch to the Officer i/c Records concerned, the counterfoil slip being completed by the Officer who extracts the Will.

Page 16

(g) Date. Signed this (g) .... day of .... 19......

(h) Signature of soldier. (h) :..............

(i) Insert full name of soldier making Will. Signed and acknowledged by the said (i) ....

the same having been previously read over to him as and for his last Will, in the presence of us, present at the same time, who, in his presence, at his request, and in the presence of each other, have hereunto subscribed our names as Witnesses.*

(j) Witnesses to sign here. (j) ....

(k) Add addresses in full (k) ....

(j) ....

(k) ....

* N.B.—Witnesses must *NOT* be persons intended to benefit under the Will, or husbands or wives of such persons.

Page 17

Army Form B. 2089.

ON COMPLETION TO BE DESPATCHED TO OFFICER IN CHARGE RECORDS BY O.O. UNIT.

FORM OF WILL to be used by a soldier desirous of leaving legacies to some one or more persons, and the residue to another or others.

(See page 15 for FORM OF WILL leaving everything to one person.)

(a) Signature of soldier in full. I, (a) ....

(b) Rank and army number. (b) ....

(c) Regiment. (c) ....

hereby revoke all Wills heretofore made by me at any time, and declare this to be my last Will and Testament.

(d) Name and address of Executor. I appoint (d) ....

to be the Executor of this my Will.

After payment of my just Debts and Funeral Expenses I give to my (e) ....

(e) Insert "friend," or, if a relative, in what degree.

Page 18

(f) Full name and address of person. (f) ....

(g) State articles or money (g) .... intended to be given. and I give to my (e) ....

(f) ....

(g) ....

All the rest of my Estate and Effects, and everything that I can give or dispose of, I give and bequeath absolutely to my (e) ....

(f) ....

(h) Date. Signed this (h) .... day of .... 19......

(i) Signature of soldier. (i) ....

(j) Full name of soldier making Will. Signed and acknowledged by the said (j) ....

the same having been previously read over to him as and for his last Will, in the presence of us, present at the same time, who, in his presence, at his request, and in the presence of each other, have hereunto subscribed our names as Witnesses.*

(k) Witnesses to sign here. (k) ....

(l) Add addresses in full. (l) ....

(k) ....

(l) ....

* See footnote, page 16.

Page 19

SOLELY FOR USE ON ACTIVE SERVICE. The Will on page 20 must NOT be used until you have been placed under orders for Active Service.

SHORT FORM OF WILL.

(Write Will on next page.)

If a soldier on active service, or under orders for active service, wishes to make a short Will, he may do so on the next page. It must be entirely in his own handwriting and must be signed by him and dated. The full names and addresses of the persons whom he desires to benefit, and the sum of money or the articles of property which he desires to leave to them, must be clearly stated. **The mere entry of the name of an intended legatee on the next page without any mention of what the legatee is to receive is of no legal value.**

The following is a specimen of a Will leaving all to one person :—

In the event of my death I give the whole of my property and effects to my mother, Mrs. Mary Bull, 999, High Street, Aldershot.

(Signature) GEORGE BULL,
Fusilier, No. 1973, Royal Fusrs.

Date 5th August, 1914.

The following is a specimen of a Will leaving legacies to more than one person :—

In the event of my death I give £10 to my friend, Miss Rose Smith, of No. 1, High Street, London, and I give £5 to my sister, Miss Maud Bull, 999, High Street, Aldershot, and I give the remaining part of my property to my mother, Mrs. Mary Bull, 999, High Street, Aldershot.

(Signature) GEORGE BULL,
Fusilier, No. 1973, Royal Fusrs.

Date 5th August, 1914.

Soldiers are, however, recommended to make a formal Will before embarkation on A.F. B. 2089, or one of the forms of formal Will provided on p. 15 and p. 17, and to hand it to their Commanding Officer for transmission to the Record Office for safe custody.

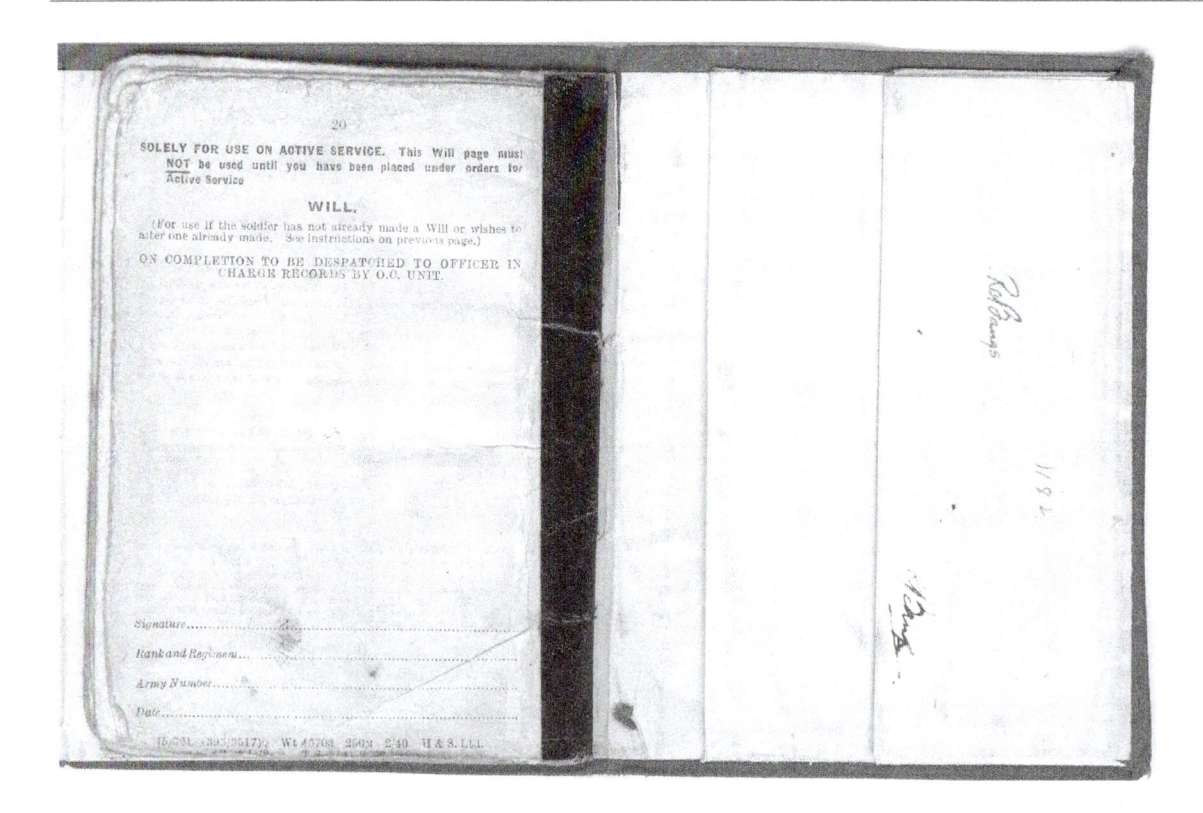

APPENDIX D
Dad's Army Release documents

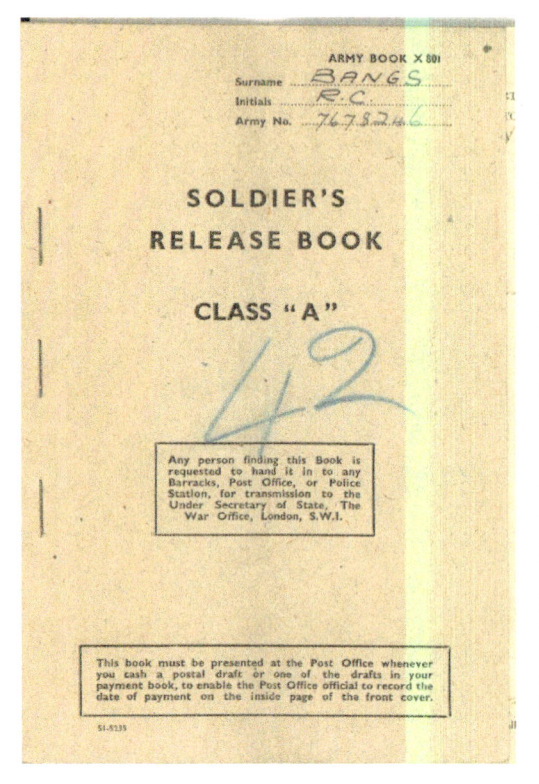

HOSPITAL TREATMENT DURING FURLOUGH

If you need hospital treatment before the end of your release leave you should show this book to your doctor and if he is of opinion that such treatment is necessary he will advise you as to the steps to be taken to obtain that treatment. You should show this Release Book to the hospital authorities when admitted to or attending hospital for treatment.

For the information of the doctor.
Inpatient treatment would normally be given at the nearest military or civil Emergency Medical Scheme hospital where the treatment required can be given. If you are in doubt as to the location of the nearest suitable hospital the Hospital Officer for the district in which the patient resides can give you the required information and he will also be in a position to advise as to the nearest military or E.M.S. hospital where any massage, X-ray examination or other out-patient treatment can be obtained.

Dental Treatment. If you need dental treatment of an emergency nature, *e.g.*, for relief of pain or acute infection, during your leave, you should report to the nearest Army Dental Centre or military hospital. If you live over two miles from any such institution you may obtain such treatment from a civilian dental practitioner to whom you will show this Book and whose attention will be drawn to instructions below. The cost of any other form of treatment or of supply of dentures will NOT be met by W.D. unless prior sanction has been given by the War Office or the Deputy Director of Dental Service of the Command in which you live.

For the information of Practitioner. A soldier, or member (other than an officer) of the A.T.S. or of a V.A.D. may be given treatment of an emergency nature as above at Army expense up to the end of his leave. Cost of treatment given after leave expires will not be met by W.D. but will be the patient's liability.

The practitioner should claim for payment on Army Form O. 1607 which should be sent to the Asst. Director of Medical Services of the area in which the patient is living. Payment will be made for emergency treatment only, and at the rates admissible under the N.H. Ins. Act (Dental Benefit Regulations).

PART IV

TO BE COMPLETED BY DOCTOR PROVIDING TREATMENT WHO SHOULD ALSO DETACH THE FORM AND SEND IT TO THE INSURANCE COMMITTEE (IN NORTHERN IRELAND) TO THE MINISTRY OF LABOUR, PALACE GROUNDS, ARMAGH, NORTHERN IRELAND) FOR THE AREA IN WHICH THE INSURED PERSON IS STAYING.

* The individual named overleaf who was not on my list immediately before serving in H.M. Forces is accepted as from to-day as a temporary / permanent* resident.

* The individual named overleaf who states that he was on my list immediately before serving in H.M. Forces has to-day applied to me for treatment.

* Delete where not applicable.

Date.......................... Signature..........................

| If doctor is to supply drugs he should enter DR here .... | If doctor claims mileage he should enter mileage distance here .... |

PAGE THIRTEEN
A.F. X 201/3
M.P.B. 281/3

CLAIM FOR DISABILITY PENSION—OTHER RANKS—MEN

THIS FORM is to be used only if you claim to be suffering from a disability attributable to or aggravated by WAR SERVICE. You may complete it any time WITHIN SIX MONTHS after the date you ceased to draw service pay.*

When completed, the Form should be sent to the Officer-in-Charge Records, whose address is shown on your Reserve Certificate. Any pension granted on this application will commence on the day following the date of Release.

* After six months from the cessation of service pay, any claim to pension must be made on a different form, to be obtained from the nearest office of the MINISTRY OF PENSIONS, the address of which can be obtained at the local Post Office.

1. Surname .... 2. Army No. ....
   (Block Letters)
3. Christian Name/s ....
4. Present Rank .... 5. Regt. or Corps ....
6. Have you served in the Armed Forces before the present War and been discharged? ("Yes" or "No") ....
   If "Yes," give particulars below:—

Former Regt., Corps or Ship, etc.	Army or Official Number	Date of Discharge	Cause of Discharge	Particulars of Pension (if any) for Disablement or Service

7. Give particulars of your wife and children now under 16 years of age for whom you received family allowances at any time during service:—
   (a) Wife—Full Christian Name/s ....
       and Name before Marriage ....
   (b) Wife's Present Address ....
   (c) Date of Marriage ....
   (d) Children:—
       Full Christian Name/s (and Surname where different from your own) and dates of birth.
       1. ....
          Date of birth ....
       2. ....
          Date of birth ....
       3. ....
          Date of birth ....

8. Give particulars of any child born after Release. Name/s ....
   Date/s of birth ....

RELEASE LEAVE CERTIFICATE

Army Form X 202/A

Army No. 7678246 Present Rank PRIVATE
Surname (Block Letters) BANGS
Christian Name/s RICHARD CHARLES
Unit, Regt. or Corps 34 BATT. ROYAL ARMY PAY CORPS
Date of Last enlistment
Calling up for military service 2.12.1940
(a) Trade on enlistment LEDGER CLERK
(c) Service Trade CLERK RAPC
(b) Trade courses and trade tests passed CLERK RAPC GROUP C CLASSES III II
Military Conduct Ex
Testimonial: Excellent clerk of great intelligence and steady application, punctual, loyal, reliable.

Place FOOTS CRAY, SIDCUP, KENT.   Date 12/12/45
Signature of Soldier R C Bangs

stamps: R.A. (FIELD) PAY OFFICE FOOTS CRAY, SIDCUP, KENT; 27 FEB 1946; 17 DEC 1945 EAST HAM; AB6462

PARTICULARS OF CLAIM

The following questions should be answered with care. The answers will assist in the enquiries to be made of official records. Incomplete answers may delay the consideration of your claim.

Question	Answer
9. What is the disability for which you claim pension? If a wound or injury, state when and where received, and part of the body injured.	(Write your answer on back of form.)
10. Give the names of the hospitals or other places at which you received treatment during service for this disability, and the dates as nearly as you can.	

If you claim solely in respect of a wound or injury, you need not answer any of the following questions, but the claim form must be signed and dated (see below).

Question	Answer
11. (a) When did you first suffer from the disability?	(a)
(b) If before your war service, when did you first notice the effects of war service on it?	(b)
12. State what particular incidents or conditions of service you consider caused or worsened the disability.	
13. (a) With what unit were you then serving?	(a)
(b) Where were you then stationed?	(b)
(c) What was the precise nature of your duties at the time?	(c)
14. If you suffered from the disability before joining the Forces, give the name and address of any doctor, hospital, etc., from whom you received treatment. Give approximate dates.	
15. Have you been treated for the above or any other complaint since Release? If so, state nature of complaint and name and address of doctor or hospital with first and last dates of attendance.	

Signature.................... Date ....
Any person knowingly making a false statement will be liable to prosecution.
Address ....

Address (if different from above) to which you desire the result of your claim to be sent....................

Witness to Signature.................... Date ....
(Any householder)
Address of Witness....................

Second Signature of Applicant....................
(For record purposes)

R.A.P.C. RECORDS Record Office Stamp

DEC 194_
5/b, DORSET SQUARE
LONDON,
N.W.1

If you send this card by post do not fail to enclose your address.

ARMY FORM W5258

RECORD OF SERVICE

No. 7678246 Rank. l/c Name (in block letters) BANGS R.C.

Served in Regts/Corps as follows:

	Regt./Corps	From	To	Assn. joined with date	Remarks by Assn. (if any)
a	RAPC	2.12.40	19.2.46		
b					
c					
d					

Date 1 DEC 1945

Record Officer

For NOTES see reverse.

FOR YOUR GUIDANCE

WHAT TO DO ON LEAVING THE SERVICE, AND HOW TO DO IT

ISSUED BY THE WAR OFFICE AND THE MINISTRY OF LABOUR AND NATIONAL SERVICE

INTRODUCTION

The purpose of this pamphlet is to help you in the change over from Service to Civilian life. It contains information on a number of Service and other matters which will be of importance to you in the period immediately following your release from the Forces.

If you were in a job before joining up, it explains what steps you must take to safeguard your rights to reinstatement, or if you have no job to return to it tells you how to set about getting one.

CONTENTS

1. Release Leave and your Uniform.
2. Matters for your Immediate Attention.
3. Resettlement in Civil Life.
4. National Insurance and Pensions.
5. Northern Ireland.
6. Eire.

1 RELEASE LEAVE AND YOUR UNIFORM

While you are on release leave your position is just the same as if you were on leave from your unit, except that you may take up civilian employment straight away and need not wait until the end of your leave, and that for health and pensions insurance purposes you are treated as a civilian from the date your leave begins. If you want reinstatement with your old employer you must apply promptly.

You are being allowed to take away with you certain articles of uniform. Keep them. In case of an unforeseen National Emergency you may be recalled to the Colours and you will need them. It is particularly necessary for officers to keep their outfit in good order. In the event of their being called up the Government will not give another outfit allowance.

2 MATTERS FOR YOUR IMMEDIATE ATTENTION

Change of Address.—It is very important during your release leave for you to keep your Record Office and your Regimental Paymaster informed of any change in your address or in your family affairs such as births, deaths, marriages, etc. If you don't, your right to pay and allowances, etc., may be affected, or letters may go astray, and you may lose money. In addition, you are legally liable to tell your Record Office of these changes even after expiration of your release leave, and until you are formally discharged.

Note down the address of your Record Office and Pay Office here before you forget.

Officer i/c Records ....(Unit)

......................(Place)

Regimental Paymaster ....(Unit)

......................(Place)

The previous remarks refer to officers as well as other ranks,

except that officers should send notice of any such change to:—

The Under-Secretary of State for War,
The War Office,
London, S.W.1.

Pay Matters.—When you received your advance of pay at the Pay Section of the Dispersal Centre, they gave you a leaflet of information and instruction about the settlement of your account and the payment of any other money credits which may be due to you. Please read this leaflet with the greatest care and carry out any instructions it gives you and any instructions you may receive from the Paymaster later on. This will ensure that you will receive your leave payments and final settlement of your pay account by the due date.

Your post-war credit, if you have served in the ranks since January 1st, 1942, and your gratuity, will be paid to you in the form of deposits in the Post Office Savings Bank. You will be wise to leave them there, unless you need the money at once, until there is a larger choice of things to buy and you can be sure of getting value for what you spend. Deposits in the Post Office Savings Bank earn interest at $2\frac{1}{2}\%$ per annum.

Precaution.—As a safeguard against fraud when you are cashing postal drafts at the Post Office, you will be asked to produce your release book as an identity certificate.

Beware of the man who tries to persuade you to put your money into some attractive sounding scheme. Do not part with your savings to anyone without the most careful enquiry by an independent and reliable adviser.

Ration Book and Identity Card.—Many essential goods, in particular food and clothing, are still rationed and you must, therefore, have a ration book in order to get your share. You can obtain this and an identity card from your local National Registration Office (the police station will give you the address) taking your release book with you and your temporary ration card.

Your clothing coupons will consist of:—

(a) A clothing book containing the proportion of coupons appropriate to the period of the rationing year; and, possibly,

(b) A number of additional coupons to assist in setting you up in civil life.

Parliamentary Registration.—Your name will be automatically removed from a Service Register compiled to a qualifying date later than the date of your release and will be automatically included in the Civilian Residence Register for the constituency containing the address on your identity card on the qualifying date.

Medical attention during furlough.—Read carefully the full instructions given on page 12 of your release book.

Malaria.—If you have served in a malarious country you should inform your doctor. This is important even though you may now be quite fit and even though you have never had an attack of malaria. The first attack may actually occur in this country, the disease having been checked by the suppressive treatment you have received overseas or having been brought out by return to a cold climate. The early treatment and recognition of the disease is a matter of great importance to your health. Go to your doctor early, tell him the facts of your case and keep by you any copy of notes on treatment which you may have received. Malaria is a rare disease in Great Britain and if you look after your health you are helping to prevent its being introduced into the country.

Venereal Disease.—If you have ever suffered from any form of this disease be sure that you have completed the treatment and observations recommended by your medical officer; the observation period for gonorrhoea is a minimum of three months and for syphilis two years. Remember that disappearance of signs and symptoms does not mean that you are cured. If you are not really cured you may transmit your disease to others, particularly your wife and children, so for their sakes as well as your own, make sure. If you are in the least doubt go to your own doctor or to one of the many treatment centres situated in most of the larger towns where you will receive advice free and in confidence.

Travelling Concessions.—Personnel on release leave will be eligible for such railway concession fares as are in force for Service personnel (including concession fares granted to wives and dependent children) only up to and including the date of expiry of their release and foreign service leave.

To obtain railway concession fares, officers and other ranks must produce at the Railway Booking Office their release leave certificates or release certificates as evidence that their leave has not expired.

Concession fare tickets, where such are in force, will be obtainable by wives and dependent children, on production of the normal documents, only up to and including the date of expiry of the release and foreign service leave of personnel. Wives holding six month's concession fare certificates should hand this document in at any Railway Station for cancellation as soon as eligibility for railway concession fares ceases.

During the period of release leave concession fare ticket vouchers, *e.g.*, for unaccompanied children, may be obtained on supplying evidence as to eligiblity from any Service Issuing Authority.

3 RESETTLEMENT IN CIVIL LIFE

The Resettlement Advice Offices.—To help you solve the many and varied problems which may arise when you reach home again, there will be a Resettlement Advice Office in every town of any size. If there is not one in your immediate area, go to the nearest Local Office of the Ministry of Labour and National Service which will tell you how to obtain the information and advice you need. It may be that your requirement can only be met by some Government Department or by the Local Authority or by a Voluntary Organisation, and if the Resettlement Advice Officer cannot himself give you all the help you require, he will be able to tell you exactly where you can get it. If you need help from any of the voluntary organisations including Service Associations, the Resettlement Advice Office will be able to give you the address of the particular organisation or association you want. These offices have been set up especially to help you in this way—go to them with your problems whatever they may be and everything possible will be done to assist you.

Employment.—If you want advice or assistance about your civilian employment or possibilities of training, go to the nearest Local Office of the Ministry of Labour and National Service. The staff there will do all they can to help you.

Reinstatement in Former Employment.—If you want to return to your old employer you may have certain legal rights, provided you were in his employment within the four weeks before your war service began, and he was the last person who employed you within that period. Leaflet R.E.L. 2, given to you on release, explains rights under the Reinstatement in Civil Employment Act, 1944, and how to claim them.

You are advised to read the leaflet carefully. You must not wait until your leave ends if you want to preserve your legal rights under the Act. You should make written application to your former employer not later than the fifth Monday after the day you go on leave. You should also be ready to start work not later than the ninth Monday after the day you go on leave. If you are in any doubt about what you should do you can get advice from any Local Office of the Ministry of Labour and National Service.

If you want to return to some earlier employer who has no obligation to you under the Act, you can, of course, ask him to re-employ you, although the Act does not require him to do so.

Interrupted Apprenticeship.—If you were an apprentice or recognised learner in a skilled occupation when you were called up, you will wish to resume your training on your return to civil employment. The Government have arranged a scheme under which you will be assisted to complete your apprenticeship with your former employer (or, if necessary, with some other employer), or by taking a special course at a Government Training Centre or a Technical College. A time allowance will be given in respect of your service in the Forces so that you will not be called upon to serve the whole of the period of apprenticeship which was unexpired when your apprenticeship was interrupted; also, if you served at your trade while in the Forces that period of service will be taken into account. There will be a State grant to enable the employer to pay you an appropriate adult wage, or if you take a course at a Government Training Centre or Technical College you will be paid maintenance allowances.

You should apply to the Local Office of the Ministry of Labour and National Service for particulars of the scheme appropriate to your trade, and for advice upon how to make an application to obtain the benefits of the scheme. The scheme applies both to men and women.

Vocational Training Scheme.—If you need to be trained for a new job or to resume training interrupted by your war service, intensive courses of training are available in a wide variety of occupations (but see above if you were learning a skilled trade). On completion of training you will be accepted fully as a craftsman by both the employers and the trade unions in the particular industry. The training given will be free and you will receive maintenance allowance for yourself and any dependants. If you have to go away from home for training the Ministry of Labour and National Service will help you to find lodgings and in certain circumstances lodging allowances will be paid. The best way of finding out whether this scheme will help you is to read leaflet P.L. 156, or, if you are disabled, leaflet P.L. 162. These leaflets can be obtained from the Resettlement Advice Office or from the Local Office of the Ministry of Labour and National Service in your home area.

Appointments Offices.—The Appointments Offices of the Ministry of Labour and National Service deal with the specialist type of job. If you have professional or higher qualifications which fit you for professional, administrative, managerial or executive posts, or, having had little or no experience, need advice on the prospects of posts of this kind, the Appointments Offices are in touch with the firms and organisations which require your services. You should make enquiries at the Resettlement Advice Office or the Local Office of the Ministry of Labour and National Service, to find out how you might benefit by registering with an Appointments Office. You should ask for leaflet P.L. 102.

If you are looking for employment or training in the nursing profession, your registration will be dealt with by a Nursing Officer of the Appointments Department.

Further Education and Training Scheme.—If you want to find out about the opportunities for training under the Further Education and Training Scheme you should read the leaflet P.L. 120 which you can get from the Resettlement Advice Office, Regional Appointments Office, or Local Office of the Ministry of Labour and National Service in your home area.

Careers.—In order to help you in choosing a career an introductory handbook and a series of pamphlets have been prepared. They set out full information concerning entry to and prospects in various professions. You may have already obtained in the Service a copy of the handbook and pamphlets in which you are interested, but, if not, copies may be obtained from the Resettlement Advice Office, Regional Appointments Office or Local Office of the Ministry of Labour and National Service.

Resettlement Grants.—If you were in a business of your own or in work on your own account before joining the Forces and need assistance to restart (*e.g.*, for fitting up premises, obtaining equipment, tools, initial stocks and so on) you will be able to apply for a grant from the Ministry of Labour and National Service. You can obtain further information about the scheme from the Resettlement Advice Office or the Local Office of the Ministry of Labour and National Service in your home area.

Disabled Persons (Employment) Act.—This Act contains provisions for the vocational training, industrial rehabilitation and employment of those who have suffered disablement and need special help or assistance in their return to civil life. The Act applies to civilians as well as to ex-Service men and women but there is to be a preference for those who have served in the Forces or in certain of the Women's Services or in the Merchant Navy.

If you are disabled you will have had an opportunity of an interview while in Hospital with a representative of the Ministry of Labour and National Service. If you have not and want advice about employment or training, go to any Local Office of the Ministry of Labour and National Service and ask to see the Disablement Rehabilitation Officer.

The Government of Northern Ireland have announced their intention to introduce corresponding legislation. It is intended that the two schemes will work together and registered disabled persons will be able to qualify under either scheme.

4 NATIONAL INSURANCE AND PENSIONS

National Health and Pensions Insurance.—For health and pensions insurance purposes you are being treated as having left the Forces on the day before your leave begins, and as you were compulsorily insured during service, a contribution has been credited to you for each week of your service up to that date. You are, therefore, now entitled to benefits as a civilian and if you take up insurable work you are required to pay contributions as a civilian. The Ministry of National Insurance will inform you of the name of your Approved Society (if any) and your membership number and send you further information about your insurance position generally. If you fall ill and wish to draw sickness benefit, get a medical certificate from your insurance doctor and send it at once to your Approved Society quoting your membership number and your Service number, or if you are not a member of an Approved Society send it to the Ministry of National Insurance. Similarly, send any claim for maternity benefit to your Society or to the Ministry. Hand the contribution card which has been issued to you to your employer when you start work. If you do not work during the ten weeks following the week in which your release leave begins it is not necessary to have your card franked at a Local Office of the Ministry of Labour and National Service. Afterwards, however, if you should find yourself unable to obtain employment you should get the card franked at the Local Office or you will fall into arrears and may suffer loss of benefit. Your insurance during service entitles you to civilian health and pensions benefits for a period of at least 18 months.

The above paragraph does not apply to officers from whose pay insurance deductions have not been made.

Unemployment Insurance.—You have been given a free insurance against unemployment and contributions have been credited to you at the rate of one for each week of paid service. The Unemployment Book issued to you should be completed with your signature and home address and handed to your employer when you start work. On termination of your release leave, hand it in at the Local Office of the Ministry of Labour and National Service when you make a claim for benefit. Full details of the benefits to be claimed and of the conditions governing claims will be found in leaflet U.I.L. 8, which can be obtained from any Local Office of the Ministry of Labour and National Service.

Disability Pensions.—If you consider that you are suffering disablement from a wound, injury or disease caused or made worse by your war service, you may claim a pension. Pension is awarded by the Ministry of Pensions in respect of disablement accepted as attributable to or aggravated by service during the present war. The rate of pension is dependent on the degree of disablement and the rank held in the Forces.

A form of application is included in your release book. This form indicates what information should be furnished and tells you how to lodge your application. If you should lose or mislay the form, you can make application to the Chief Regional Officer, Ministry of Pensions, whose address can be obtained from any Post Office or Resettlement Advice Office in your home area.

5 NORTHERN IRELAND

The counterpart in Northern Ireland of the Ministry of Labour and National Service is the Ministry of Labour for Northern Ireland. References to Local Offices should in relation to Northern Ireland be read as references to Employment Exchanges.

6 EIRE

If you are spending your release leave in Eire, advice as to employment, training, etc., facilities available in the United Kingdom can be obtained from the United Kingdom Liaison Officer for Labour, 16 Upper Mount Street, Dublin. Medical benefit under the National Health Insurance Acts is not available in Eire.

GO TO THE NEAREST RESETTLEMENT ADVICE OFFICE IF YOU ARE IN ANY DIFFICULTY OR NEED ASSISTANCE IN CONNECTION WITH YOUR RETURN TO CIVIL LIFE

Printed by Harrison & Sons, Ltd. (51—1519).

CLASS "A" RELEASES.

PAY, ALLOWANCES, WAR GRATUITY AND POST WAR CREDITS DURING RELEASE AND OVERSEAS LEAVE.

This leaflet should be read carefully. It explains how Warrant Officers and ranks below will receive pay and allowances during Release and Overseas Leave, how War Gratuities and Post War Credits will be made available and contains other useful information regarding family allowance, dependants' allowance, allotment of pay, income duty, etc.

1. Release and Overseas Leave.

Your 56 days' Release Leave begins on the day after you leave the Military Dispersal Unit, and if you have served overseas for six months or more, one day for each complete month of reckonable service overseas will be added to your 56 days' Release Leave.

2. Balance of your pay Account at date of dispersal.

(a) Your pay account will be balanced as soon as it is known you have left the Military Dispersal Unit, and if your account is in credit, the balance due to you will be sent to the address furnished on page 8 of your Release Book, on or about the 14th day of your leave.

(b) Should your pay account be in debt and there is no balance due to you, the Regimental Paymaster will notify you.

(c) If your pay account is not complete and further information has to be obtained from your last unit or elsewhere, the Regimental Paymaster will, if possible, send you a provisional payment. As soon as the information required has been received any credit remaining due will be forwarded.

3. Pay and Allowances during Release and Overseas Leave.

You will be entitled to pay and ration allowance (at the leave rate) for the period of your Release and Overseas Leave. **The advance of pay given to you on the day you leave the Military Dispersal Unit is part of your leave pay and ration allowance.**

The remainder will be sent to you by means of a Payment Order Book, which will reach you on or about the 20th day of your leave. This book will contain three or more payment orders to be cashed on the dates shown on the orders at the post office named on the cover of the book.

Orders will be dated for the 22nd, 36th and 50th days of your Release Leave and every succeeding 14 days to the end of any overseas leave to which you are entitled.

On the back of the Payment Order Book you will find a statement informing you of the period of your Release and Overseas Leave, also how your pay for the period of your leave has been made up.

If, since 8th May, 1945 (or where release takes place after 7th May, 1946, in the preceding 12 months) you have held a paid rank above that which you now hold, you will be granted the pay of that rank for the period of your Release and Overseas Leave.

If your pay account was in debt on the date you left the Military Dispersal Unit, the debt will be deducted from the amount due to you for Release and Overseas Leave. Your pay for the period of leave will not be reduced below 3s. a day because of any such debt, but if a voluntary allotment is being paid on your behalf, payment will continue during your leave and the minimum rate of 3s. a day will be reduced by the daily amount of the voluntary allotment.

Ration allowance will be credited to your pay account in full.

4. Release Book.

When you present at the Post Office the Postal Draft for your balance of pay on dispersal, or the Payment Order Book for leave payments, take your Release Book with you to prove your identity. The Post Office official will stamp one of the rings inside the cover when a Postal Draft or Payment Order is cashed.

YOUR PAYMENT ORDER BOOK REPRESENTS MONEY ; GUARD IT ACCORDINGLY.

You are advised to take great care of your Release Book and Payment Order Book. The loss of one or both will cause you considerable inconvenience, and you may not be able to receive any payments while enquiries are being made and until it is ascertained if the orders have been cashed by someone else.

5. Allowances—Allotments, etc.

If any of the following allowances or other payments are being made on your behalf, they will continue during your Release and Overseas Leave :—

Family Allowance   Voluntary Allotment
    (including allotment of pay)
Dependants' Allowance   Compulsory Stoppage
Special Dependants' Allowance

6. London Allowance.

The addition to family allowance for wives living in London, if already being paid, will continue during your leave ; it will also continue if your family moves out of the London Area. But if your family moves into London **after** you have begun your leave, the addition for living in London will **not** be added to the amount already being paid.

7. Pre-Natal Allowance.

If your wife becomes eligible for pre-natal allowance during your Release and Overseas Leave, she should complete the necessary form, obtainable from any Post Office, and send it to your Regimental Paymaster.

8. Allowance Order Books.

A communication will be sent to your wife or dependant, or any person to whom an allotment or any other payment is being made on your behalf, authorising the Post Office to cash, in advance, in one lump sum the last four weekly payments due.

9. Marriage while on Leave.

If you marry while you are on leave, send your Regimental Paymaster your marriage certificate, or a certified copy which can be obtained from the Registrar, and a letter at the head of which must be shown your Army number, rank, name, regiment or corps, your address, also the reference number shown on the cover of your Payment Order Book. Family allowance from the date of marriage to the date your leave ends will be paid by your Regimental Paymaster.

If, however, dependants' allowance is being paid on your behalf, that allowance must be withdrawn before family allowance can be paid.

10. War Service Grant.

If a War Service Grant is being paid on your behalf, the grant will continue until the end of your leave.

11. War Gratuity and Post War Credits.

Your War Gratuity and Post War Credits will be credited to a Post Office Savings Bank account in your name. The card you signed at the Military Dispersal Unit will enable a P.O.S.B. account to be opened.

Your Regimental Paymaster will notify you, before your leave expires, of the amount placed to the credit of your Post Office Savings Bank account.

12. War Gratuity.

War Gratuity will be credited for the period you have served, since 3rd September, 1939, up to the date you left the Military Dispersal Unit, less any period in the Reserve or any periods of 28 days or more for which Army pay has been forfeited.

13. Post War Credits.

Post War Credits will count from 1st January, 1942, or from the date you joined for service, if later, until the date your Release and Overseas Leave expires, less any period in the Reserve and days for which Army pay has been forfeited.

14. Travelling Expenses.

A payment was made at the Military Dispersal Unit to meet your travelling expenses during the journey to your home.

If your necessary expenditure on account of bus, etc. fares to reach your home exceeds 9d. (ninepence), you may write to your Regimental Paymaster for a refund.

15. Income Duty.

On release you will be taxable under the P.A.Y.E. scheme immediately you take up civil employment. P.A.Y.E. Income Tax deductions are made according to the actual pay earned and will alter with any variations in your earnings.

Any tax due will be deducted by your employer each pay day, the amounts being calculated from Tax Tables by reference to a **code number** allotted according to the Income Tax reliefs and allowances to which you are entitled.

A form will be sent to you by your Regimental Paymaster. In your own interest you should complete this form very carefully and send it AT ONCE to the local Inspector of Taxes, whose address can be obtained at the Post Office. If you do this, the Inspector of Taxes will be able to inform your employer of your code number within a few days of your starting work. You will then receive all reliefs to which you are entitled. If you do not fill in and forward the form, it will result in your being taxed as a single person without reliefs, and if you are a married man, or if you are eligible for higher reliefs, some time may elapse before the tax deductions are reduced.

16. Notification of Change of Address and Correspondence on other subjects.

If you change your address from that given by you on dispersal, send a postcard or letter to your Regimental Paymaster immediately. Please prepare the postcard or letter as follows —

Army Number......................
Reference Number on the cover of your Payment Order Book........................
Rank and Name (in block capitals)..
Regiment or Corps..
" Please note the following change of address to which all communications should be sent : "
   New Address : ....
                     ....
                     ....
Date............................
                                                                 Signature.

A similar notification should be sent to the Regimental Paymaster if your wife changes her address after you are released.

Postcards or letters addressed to the Regimental Paymaster on other subjects should be headed similarly. This will assist considerably towards your receiving an early reply.

The address of your Regimental Paymaster will appear on the front of your Payment Order Book. Otherwise, the address can be obtained from any Post Office, Police Station, Assistance Board Office, or Soldiers', Sailors' and Airmen's Families' Association office.

Pay Form R17 (Revised)   (SO 9965)   Wt. 31452—D. 6677 475M 10/45 H & S Ltd. (SO 8676) **Gp. 393** J. 10272

4

How to Apply to a Reinstatement Committee

8. So long as you are satisfied that it is unreasonable or impracticable for the employer to reinstate you there is nothing to be gained by applying to a Committee. If, however, you have made a legal claim for reinstatement and either the employer denies that you will ever have any right at all, or you consider that he is not doing what is reasonable and practicable, or he has failed altogether to reply, then you should apply to the Reinstatement Committee as follows :—

Ask the Employment Exchange for a form of application, fill it up and let the same office have it back. All this must be done as soon as possible after you first had reason to complain (*see*, however, para. 4 (5) above).

The Committee consists of a chairman, an employers' representative and an employed persons' representative. You will have an opportunity of appearing and of being represented, if you wish, by any association of employed persons, *e.g.*, a Trade Union, of which you were a member when your application was made to the Committee, or any personal friend, or counsel or a solicitor.

There are certain rights of appeal from Reinstatement Committees to the Umpire that will be explained to you, if necessary, at the time.

What can the Reinstatement Committee do?

9. Subject to any appeal, the Reinstatement Committee will decide any dispute that has arisen between you and the employer on a claim for reinstatement.

If they decide that the employer has not carried out his obligation, they may order him to reinstate you and may specify the occupation and terms and conditions. They may also order compensation to be paid you for any loss you may have suffered as the result of the employer's default, *i.e.*, when he has failed to do what is reasonable and practicable.

An employer who fails to obey an order for reinstatement will be liable to heavy penalties under the Act.

Special classes of pre-service employment

10. Special arrangements are being made for the reinstatement of ex-Service men and women who before their war service were in the employment of a Government Department. If you are such a person you should, if you want to be reinstated, apply to the Establishment Officer of the Government Department in which you were employed, addressing your application to the appropriate local office if you were employed in a local, as distinct from a headquarters, office. If you are in any difficulty you should apply to the local office of the Ministry of Labour which will advise you how to proceed. Similarly, if before service in the armed forces, you were employed in the Police Service or the Fire Service, and desire to be reinstated in that employment you should apply, in the case of the Police to the Chief Officer of Police, or in the case of the Fire Service to the Fire Force Commander of the Fire Force Area where you were employed.

Further Information

11. You will appreciate that it has not been possible in this leaflet to give more than a summary, and anyone who wishes to have more detailed particulars of the rights under the Reinstatement in Civil Employment Act can obtain a copy of the Act from H.M. Stationery Office, price 4d., and Employment Exchanges will provide free a leaflet giving a more detailed explanation than this leaflet.

(22522) 15507 542 1,000,000 6/45 K.H.K. Gp. 8/3

LEAFLET FOR MEN AND WOMEN LEAVING THE FORCES

REINSTATEMENT IN CIVIL EMPLOYMENT

Note.—In so far as these explanatory notes interpret the law they are subject to the fact that, in the event of a dispute, an authoritative interpretation can be given only by a Reinstatement Committee, or the Umpire, in relation to particular cases that may come before them (*see* para. 8).

1. If you want to return to your old employer when your war service ends, read this leaflet carefully because a special law has been passed giving certain rights to reinstatement, and these paragraphs explain the rights and show how to claim them. If, however, you want to enter some new employment, either because you prefer a change or because your old employer is no longer able to employ you, the Employment Exchange or other Local Office of the Ministry of Labour will do their best to help you. If your previous employment was in a Government Department, the Police Service or the Fire Service (whether before or since the Service was nationalised), you should note para. 10 of this leaflet.

2. Employers' obligations are limited to what is reasonable and practicable in any particular case and you will notice that these words occur frequently in the leaflet. In some cases, *e.g.*, where several men or women have passed through the same job immediately before going into the Forces, it will never become possible to reinstate all of them. A preference will be given to the senior employees, *see* para. 5. There will be some cases where factories and shops have been destroyed and reinstatement will not be possible. In other cases, for example, where a factory has turned over to war work, or has been closed, or has been damaged, it may be some time before reorganisation will make it reasonable and practicable for you to be reinstated, and you must renew your application at intervals to keep it alive, *see* para. 6. It is left to Reinstatement Committees (*see* para. 8) to decide disputed cases.

Have you these Legal Rights?

3. It is open, of course, to any man or woman leaving the Forces to apply to return to his or her old employer, but, in order to have a *legal claim* to reinstatement you must satisfy the two following conditions :—

(1) You must have started your whole-time service in the Armed Forces (or corresponding Women's Services) after 25th May, 1939; *and*

(2) You must have had an employer within the four weeks before you started your whole-time service in the Forces. (If you had more than one employer in those four weeks, any liability for reinstatement falls on the last employer.)

If you satisfy both these conditions, your old employer has to take you back provided it is reasonable and practicable for him to do so, and provided application is made to him in accordance with the rules explained in the next paragraph.

R.E.L.2. (*Revised*)

2

How to claim the Legal Rights

4. This is what you must do to claim the legal right to reinstatement :—

(1) Forward an application *in writing not later than the fifth Monday* after your last day of whole-time service in the Forces. *If you are granted final leave* (e.g., *resettlement leave or leave pending discharge*) *you must not wait until your leave ends. You must count the fifth Monday from the day you go on leave. If you are not granted such final leave, the period for application begins from the day your full pay ends.* Unless you do this you may lose your legal right to reinstatement (*but see* (2) below). The best way is to use the special form handed to you with this leaflet and to give it or post it to your former employer. If you wish, you can hand the form or post it to an Employment Exchange of the Ministry of Labour and they will then pass it on to your former employer, provided they can get into touch with him. If you should be uncertain about the employer's present address it would be better always to send the application through an Employment Exchange.

(2) If, however, you are prevented by sickness or other reasonable cause from applying within this time limit, you will not lose your legal right provided that you do in fact apply as soon as you possibly can.

(3) At the same time as you forward your application or as soon as possible afterwards, tell your employer in writing on what date you will be ready to start work—the special form has a space for this. *The date you give for starting work must be not later than the ninth Monday after your last day of whole-time service in the Forces. If you are granted final leave you must count the ninth Monday from the day you go on leave.* Unless you do this you may lose any legal right to reinstatement (*but see* (4) below).

(4) If, however, owing to sickness or other reasonable cause, you are not available for work until after this time limit, you will not lose your legal right provided that you do in fact notify the employer immediately you are available for work.

(5) If you do not hear from the employer within about a fortnight, write to him again, and if you still do not get a reply by the date you said you were ready to start work you had better then apply to the Reinstatement Committee (*see* para. 8 below).

(6) Keep a separate note of the date or dates on which you communicate with your employer as above.

What the Employer has to do on getting a Legal Application from You

5. The employer must offer you, if he can, work in your old occupation on terms and conditions not less favourable than what you would have had in that occupation if you had never joined the Forces. If it is not reasonable and practicable for him to do that, he must offer the next best alternative, if any, that is reasonable and practicable.

The employer must offer to start you, if he can, on the day you have notified as the day you are available to start work. He may, however, not be able to employ you as soon as that and, in such a case, he must offer to start you at the first opportunity (if any) when it becomes reasonable and practicable.

3

The employer does not have to reinstate you if that could only be done by dismissing another worker who satisfies all three of the following :—

(1) he was in the employment before you joined the Forces; and
(2) he had been employed longer than you had been; and
(3) his employment was at least as permanent as yours.

He must, however, dismiss a worker who does not satisfy these three conditions if that is the only way in which he can make room for you and there is nothing else that makes it unreasonable or impracticable for him to reinstate you. The employer does not have to create a job that would not otherwise exist solely because you have made a claim for reinstatement.

What to do when you get the Employer's Reply

6. If the employer offers to start you on a certain day you must *begin work* on that day, or you will lose your legal right to reinstatement, unless you were *sick* or had *other good reason* for not then starting work. If you have good reason for not starting work on the day notified by the employer you must write to him at once to explain the reason or you will lose your legal rights; if the reason is a temporary one you must get into touch with him again as soon as you are available.

If the employer says he cannot at present take you back but you think that it would be reasonable and practicable for him to do so; or if the employer offers you work in an occupation different from that in which you were last employed before going into the Forces, and you think that he is under an obligation to offer you work in your old occupation; or if you think that you are entitled to better terms and conditions; then, if the employer does not agree, you should make an application to the Reinstatement Committee for them to decide it (*see* para. 8).

If, after you have started work, you consider that you are being employed in a less favourable occupation than you should be, or in your old occupation but on worse terms and conditions than you should be, and your employer does not agree, you can go on doing the work and this will not stop you applying to the Reinstatement Committee to decide whether you should have something better.

If it is not possible for you to be reinstated for the present and you wish to keep your claim alive, you must *renew your application in writing not* later than 13 weeks after you first made it (*see* para. 4 (6) above) and then, if necessary, at further intervals of not more than 13 weeks.

How Long is the Employer bound to Employ You?

7. Many of those who are taken back into work by their old employers will no doubt be kept on, quite apart from any question of legal obligation. If, however, you have a legal claim and are reinstated by your old employer he is bound to keep you for at least 26 weeks or, in some cases, 52 weeks, from the date of starting work or for so much of that period as is reasonable and practicable. The minimum period of 26 weeks is extended to 52 weeks if you were in the employment of your old employer for 52 weeks or more before you joined the Forces.

You should be kept on in an occupation and on terms and conditions not less favourable than at the start of your reinstatement, or, if that ceases to be reasonable and practicable, then in the next best alternative.

If the employer dismisses you or changes your occupation or terms and conditions for the worse before the minimum period of 26 weeks or 52 weeks has run out, and you think he has acted unreasonably, you should apply to the Reinstatement Committee (*see* para. 8).

REINSTATEMENT IN CIVIL EMPLOYMENT ACT, 1944
APPLICATION TO BE TAKEN INTO EMPLOYMENT

(N.B.—*This form may be completed and signed either by the applicant or by someone acting with his authority.*)

To..

....
(Name and address of former employer)

I have finished a period of war service and I wish to return to my former employment. I therefore make application under the Reinstatement in Civil Employment Act, 1944, to be taken into your employment.

Particulars supplied by applicant (*see* Notes overleaf).

1. Surname of applicant (BLOCK LETTERS) ....
   Christian name(s) (**in full**) ....

2. Address for reply ....

3. Last employment within the four weeks before beginning war service (*see* Note 3).
   (a) Name of employer ....
   (b) Place of employment ....

   (c) Nature of employment ....
   (d) Identifying particulars (Branch, Department, Check No. (if known), etc.) ....

4. Particulars of whole-time war service (*see* Note 4).
   (a) Service entered ....
   (b) Date whole-time war service began ....
   (c) Date this whole-time service ended ....

5. Particulars of certain further whole-time service (*see* Note 5).
   (a) Nature of service ....
   (b) Date of beginning of service ....
   (c) Circumstances in which service was undertaken ....

   (d) Date this service ended ....

6. Notification of availability for employment (*see* Note 6).
   * I can start work on ....
   * I will notify you in writing when I can start work } and I shall be glad to hear from you whether you can offer me employment and, if so, when, and on what terms and conditions.

7. Other remarks (*see* Note 7).

Date of application................................ Signature..
* *Delete whichever is not applicable.*

FOR OFFICIAL USE

For use *only* when application is made at a local office† of the Ministry of Labour and National Service or of the Ministry of Labour for Northern Ireland.

(a) Date of receipt of application ....
(b) Date application forwarded to employer ....

Local Office.. Signature..
Manager.

† Section 2 (4) of the Reinstatement in Civil Employment Act, 1944, provides that application to an employer may be made at an employment exchange or other appointed local office of the Ministry of Labour, and it shall be the duty of the Minister to take such steps as may be practicable to forward it to the former employer. The Minister, however, takes no responsibility for the accuracy of any of the statements made by the applicant, or in respect of any matter in the application affecting the validity of the application. *Any correspondence regarding such matters should be addressed to the applicant and not to the Minister*

R.E.1

NOTES FOR GUIDANCE OF APPLICANT

1. An application under the Act must be in writing and it may be made either direct to the former employer or through a local office of the Ministry of Labour. If made through a local office, it must be made in this form. The application must be made not later than the fifth Monday after the end of war service, unless the applicant was prevented from making it within that period by sickness or other reasonable cause, and the application was made as soon as reasonably may be after the expiration of that period.

If the undertaking in which the applicant was last employed (*see* Note 3) has been taken over by another employer, the application should be addressed to that employer. Applicants who seek reinstatement as merchant seamen should apply to the Shipping Federation Limited (Merchant Navy Reserve Pool) and not to a particular employer. Such applications should be sent to the Superintendent of the appropriate Mercantile Marine Office, or lodged at a local office of the Ministry. Applicants who seek employment under dock labour schemes and who are in doubt as to whom they should apply are advised to lodge their applications at a local office of the Ministry.

2. Valid applications can be made only by the following persons:—

   (a) Male persons who, after 25th May, 1939, enter upon a period of whole-time service in the armed forces of the Crown.

   (b) Female persons who, after 25th May, 1939, enter upon a period of whole-time service in any of the following capacities:—

   Member of Queen Alexandra's Royal Naval Nursing Service or any reserve thereof.
   Member of the Women's Royal Naval Service.
   Woman medical practitioner serving in the Royal Navy or any naval reserve.
   Member of Queen Alexandra's Imperial Military Nursing Service or any reserve thereof.
   Member of the Territorial Army Nursing Service or any reserve thereof.
   Member of the Auxiliary Territorial Service.
   Woman employed with the Royal Army Medical Corps or the Army Dental Corps with relative rank as an officer.
   Member of Princess Mary's Royal Air Force Nursing Service or any reserve thereof.
   Member of the Women's Auxiliary Air Force.
   Woman employed with the Medical Branch or the Dental Branch of the Royal Air Force with relative rank as an officer.
   Member of the Voluntary Aid Detachments employed under the Admiralty, Army Council or Air Council.

   (c) Persons (whether male or female) who, after 10th April, 1941, enter upon a period of whole-time service in consequence of an enrolment notice under the National Service Acts, 1939 to 1942, in the National Fire Service, Police War Reserve or Civil Defence Reserve.

3. **Last employment before beginning war service.**

   Give information about the last employment within the period of four weeks immediately preceding the beginning of war service.

4. **Particulars of whole-time service.**

   Under item 4 (a) state briefly to which of the whole-time services mentioned in Note 2 above the applicant belonged, *e.g.*, R.N., Army, A.T.S., N.F.S., etc. Under item 4 (b) state the date that whole-time service began. If the service was in a civil defence force, the date must be the date of enrolment under the National Service Acts. Under item 4 (c) state the date the applicant went on final leave pending release or discharge. If no such leave was granted, state the date when applicant's whole-time service ended.

5. **Particulars of certain further whole-time service.**

   This section of the application form should be completed *only* if the period of whole-time war service shown in section 4 was followed by a further period of whole-time service of the kind mentioned in Note 2 above, or by whole-time civilian service which the applicant was released or discharged from the forces or women's services to perform, or which was performed by direction or written request of the Ministry of Labour.

6. **Notification of availability for employment.**

   If possible, state when available for work. The date must be not later than the ninth Monday after the end of war service, unless delay arises owing to sickness or other reasonable cause. If there should be such delay, notification of availability should be made as soon as possible. If no date is stated on this application form, the employer should be notified later and within the period allowed.

7. **Other remarks.**

   If the application or the notification of availability for work is delayed owing to sickness or other reasonable cause, the reason should be stated in section 7 overleaf. Any other matters to which the applicant wishes to draw attention can also be stated in section 7 (*e.g.*, special skill, disability, etc.).

Army Form X 202/B.

CERTIFICATE OF TRANSFER to the ARMY RESERVE

Army No. 7678246   Rank PRIVATE

Surname (Block letters) BANGS

Christian Name(s) RICHARD CHARLES

Regt. or Corps ROYAL ARMY PAY CORPS

The transfer of the above-named to the appropriate Class of the Army Reserve (see note below) is confirmed with effect from 20 February 1946.*

*The date to be inserted here will be that following the day on which Release Leave terminates, including any additional leave to which the soldier may be entitled by virtue of service overseas.

Note.—The appropriate Class of the Army Reserve is as follows :—

(i) Royal Army Reserve—in the case of a regular soldier with reserve service to complete;

(ii) Army Reserve, Class Z (T)—in the case of a man of the Territorial Army, including those called up for service under the National Service Acts;

(iii) Army Reserve, Class Z—in the case of all other soldiers not included in (i) or (ii) above.

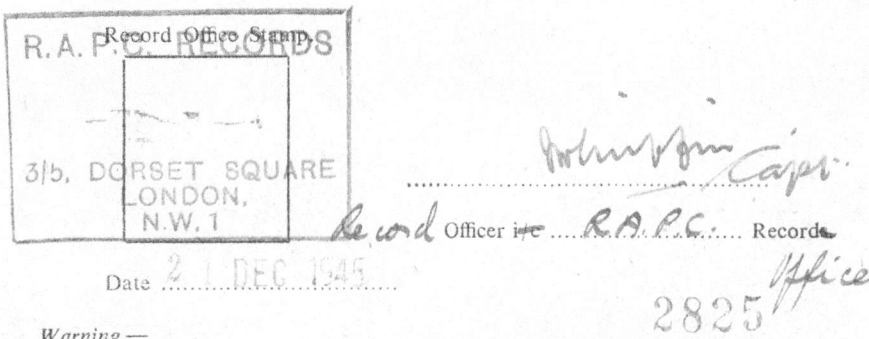

R.A.P.C. RECORDS
3/5, DORSET SQUARE
LONDON, N.W.1

Record Officer i/c R.A.P.C. Records Office

Date 21 DEC 1945

2825

Warning.—

Any alteration of the particulars given in this certificate may render the holder liable to prosecution under the Seamen's and Soldiers' False Characters Act, 1906.

If this certificate is lost or mislaid, no duplicate can be obtained.

Wt. 45088/4735 1000M 2/45 KJL/7396/16 Gp. 38/3.

Army Form B 2072
(Revised 1945)

UNEMPLOYMENT INSURANCE ACTS.

Memorandum for—

(No.) 7678246

(Rank and Name) PTE. BANGS R.C.

(Regiment) ROYAL ARMY PAY CORPS

The Ministry of National Insurance has this day been requested to credit you with the number of contributions to which you are entitled under the Unemployment Insurance Acts, in respect of your Army service. No stamped Unemployment Books are issued by the War Office, but an Unemployment Book will be forwarded to you by the Ministry of National Insurance at an early date, for presentation to your employer if you are proceeding to insurable employment. If you require assistance in obtaining employment, or are unable to obtain employment and wish to claim unemployment benefit you should apply at once (taking your Unemployment Book with you, if you have received it) to the nearest local office of the Ministry of Labour and National Service, which Department acts as agent for the Ministry of National Insurance in this matter.

The credit of Unemployment Insurance contributions is made on the basis of one contribution for each week of approved service. The effect of this is to place you on your return to civil life in the same position in relation to unemployment benefit as if you had been employed as a civilian in insurable employment for the same period. A soldier discharged in consequence of a conviction on any proceedings under the Army Act or by any civil court will not be eligible to receive unemployment benefit during the period of six weeks next after his discharge. No deductions are made from a soldier's pay in respect of Unemployment Insurance while he is serving. The contributions are for benefit purposes only and in no circumstances can any cash payment or allowance be made in lieu of the credit. Further, the credit of these contributions does not in any way relieve the employer or employee from payment of contributions under the Unemployment Insurance Acts for employment in an insurable occupation in civil life, even if such employment occurs during a period of furlough.

It should be understood that the contributions credited in respect of Army service will not be available for benefit in Eire or the Isle of Man or the Channel Islands. They will only be so available in Great Britain or, in certain circumstances, Northern Ireland, as and when you are unemployed there.

6/45 (SO 10055) Wt. 29627—6945 248M 11/45 H & S Ltd. (SO 9418) Gp. 393

APPENDIX E
Rent documents

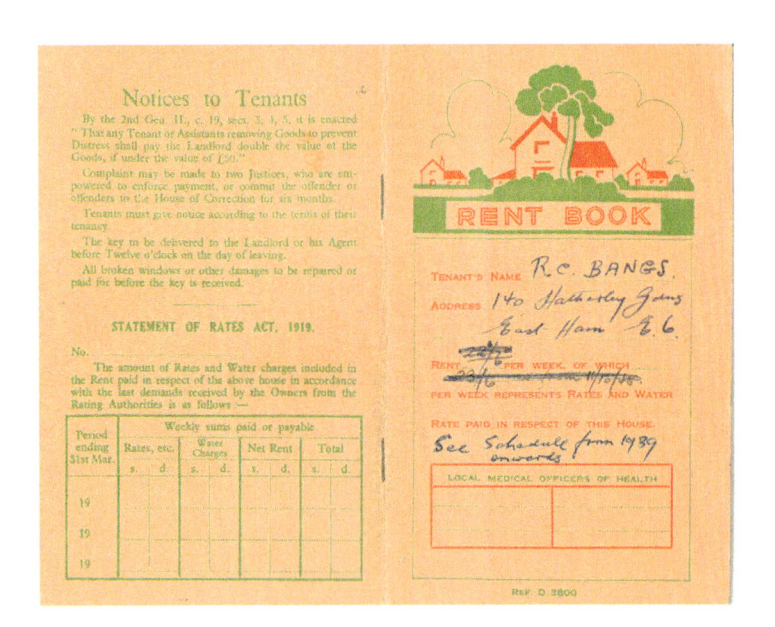

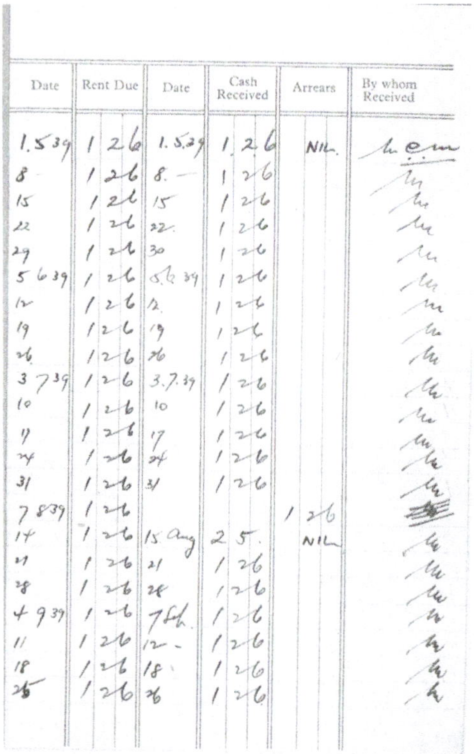

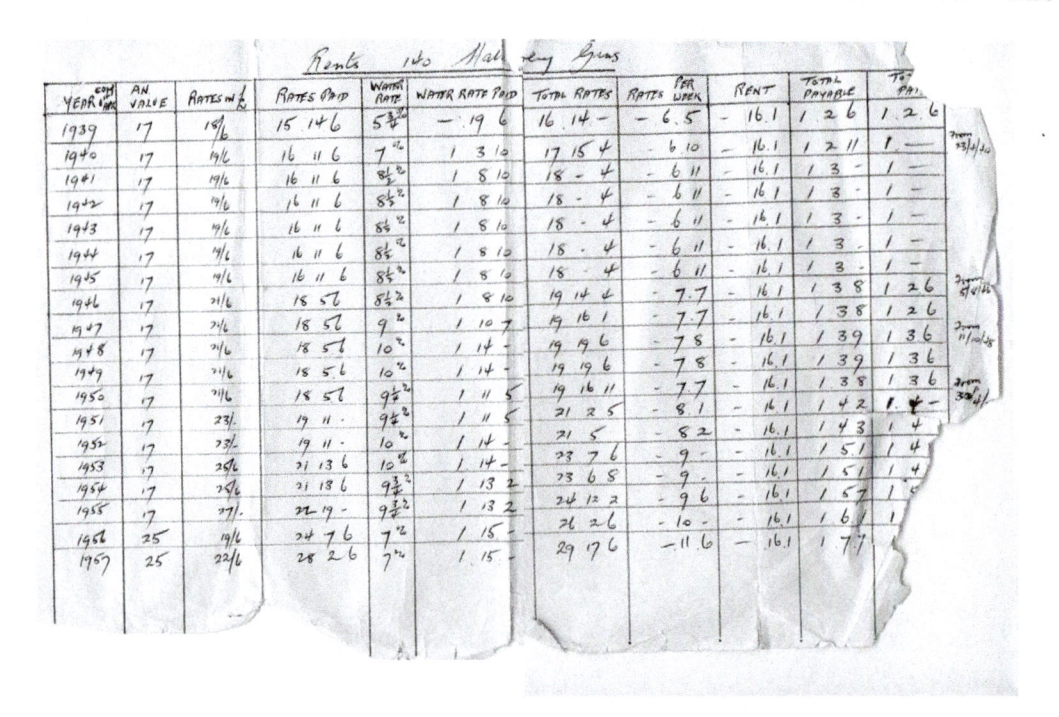

Letter 1 — 10/7/41

16 South View Drive,
E.18.
10/7/41

Dear Mr. Bangs,

I am very sorry indeed that I did not reply to your letter dated 10/2/41. I am afraid that it was just one of those things one ought to have done but has left undone. However, I did get the necessary roof repairs done promptly.

I hope you and your family are keeping fit & well, and that you are finding Army life not too bad.

We are all well here, but my turn for call-up has come. I shall probably go sometime in August.

I shall then unfortunately be unable to attend to my mother's affairs, and my sister Mrs. R. J. MOXOM of "Highlands" 97, Queens Rd, Hertford, Herts will be doing this.

When I hear from you that you have received this letter, I will forward to you a new bank paying-in book for M/c R. J. MOXOM. Barclays Bank, Hertford. The rents should then be paid in at any Barclays branch, commencing at a date which we can arrange later. I hope this will be convenient & that you will be good enough to reply as soon as possible.

I am going into the R.A.F. as a ground-gunner so the Jerries had better beware.

Kind regards to yourself & wife

Yours sincerely,
M. Mitchell

Letter 2 — 9/5/53

16 South View Drive
South Woodford
E.18.
9/5/53

Dear Mr. Bangs,

I am enclosing a notice of increase in rent owing to the increase in rates, last month. No doubt you have been expecting this but I have been so very busy lately that I just have not got round to it.

As I am late in giving you this notice perhaps you will commence paying at the new rate from Monday 18th May 53. Let us hope that one day the rates will go down!

Form F — Rent Act, 1957

R.A.A. (1957).
Waterlow & Sons Limited

FORM F
RENT ACT, 1957
Notice of Election by Landlord as to Internal Decorative Repairs.

[Note:— In the case of a statutory tenancy created under Section 4 of the Requisitioned Houses and Housing (Amendments) Act, 1955, a copy of this notice should be served on the local authority.]

Date 28/8/1957

To Mr. R. C. Bangs

tenant of 140, Hatherley Gardens, East Ham, E.6.

I hereby give you notice that I, Mary Cameron Mitchell, the landlord of the above-mentioned premises, hereby elect to be treated for the purposes of the Rent Act, 1957, as responsible for internal decorative repairs (Note 1).

If you wish to be responsible for these repairs yourself, fill up the form of notice herewith dissenting from my election and send it to me within one month after the service on you of this notice (Note 2).

If you do this, and do not keep the premises in a reasonable state of decorative repair, having due regard to the age, character and locality of the premises, this would entitle me to apply to the county court who could make an order for possession against you if they thought it reasonable to do so.

If you do not do this, the limit to which your rent can be put up will be increased by £ —: 4s. 2d. per week.

Signature of [landlord] (agent authorised to serve this notice) M. Mitchell

Address of landlord Highlands, 97, Queens Road, Hertford, Herts.
[Address of agent 16, Southview Drive, South Woodford, E.18.]

R.A. 1 (1957).
WATERLOW & SONS LIMITED

FORM A

RENT ACT, 1957

Notice of Increase of Rent otherwise than solely on account of Increased Rates or Improvements.

(Note :— In the case of a statutory tenancy created under Section 4 of the Requisitioned Houses and Housing (Amendment) Act, 1955, this notice will have no effect unless a copy is served by the landlord on the local authority not later than three days after the service of this notice on the tenant.)

Date _28th August_ 19_57_.

To _Mr. R. C. Bangs_

tenant of _140, Hatherley Gardens, East Ham, London, E.6._

1. The rent payable by you as tenant of the above-mentioned premises is at present £ _1_ : _7_ s. _6_ d. per week.

2. I am entitled to increase the rent in accordance with the above-mentioned Act (Note 1) to a sum not exceeding the rent limit set out in paragraph 6 below.

3. I hereby give you notice (Note 2) that the rent will be increased as from _2nd. Dec. 1957_ (Note 3) by £ _-_ : _7_ s. _6_ d. per week [~~as from~~ ~~by a further £~~ ~~s.~~ ~~d. per~~] and as from _2nd. June 1958_ by a further £ _-_ : _1_ s. _10_ d. per week (Note 4).]

[4. There is no certificate of disrepair in force at present (Note 5).]

[4. ~~There is a certificate of disrepair in force at present. If the certificate has not been cancelled before the first date for an increase mentioned above, this notice will not increase the rent until the first day on which rent falls due for a rental period commencing after the certificate has been cancelled. This means that you will not have to pay any increase of rent under this notice before that day.~~]

[5. ~~There is at present in force an undertaking to remedy defects given by me more than six months ago, with which I have not yet complied. If I have not complied with the undertaking before the first date for an increase mentioned above, this notice will not increase the rent until the first day on which rent falls due for a rental period commencing after the defects mentioned in the undertaking have been remedied. This means that you will not have to pay any increase of rent under this notice before that day.~~]

6. The rent limit is arrived at by adding together the amounts shown opposite the following items :—
£   s.   d. per week
(a)   2   (Note 6) times £ _33_ : _-_ s. _-_ d. per annum, which is the gross value of the premises for the purposes of the Rent Act, 1957. (Note 7).   _1_   _5_   _4_
(b) Rates borne by landlord (Note 8).   _-_   _11_   _6_
(c) Charge for furniture and/or services as agreed with you or determined by the county court.   _-_
(d) Improvements (Note 9).

Rent Limit £ _1_. _16_. _10_. per week.

Signature of [~~landlord~~] [agent authorised to serve this notice] _M C Mitchell_

[Name of landlord if notice served by agent _Mary Cameron MITCHELL_]

Address of landlord _Highlands, 97, Queens Road, Hertford, Herts._

[Address of agent _16, Southview Drive, South Woodford, London, E.18._

---

16 Southview Drive
E.18
20/3/60

Dear Mr Bangs,

Sorry to have to serve the enclosed notice on you. Can't you do something to get the rates reduced?

I should be obliged if you would sign the copy, date it & return it to me for my records.

Hope you are all flourishing. We are all well here. Kind regards

M C Mitchell

18, Willow Drive,
Little Common
Bexhill-on-Sea, Sussex.

2nd. Dec. 1970.

Dear Mr. Bangs,

My sister and I are considering improving the property at 140, Hatherley Gardens to provide the standard amenities to which the 1969 Housing Act refers.

This would necessitate the supply of hot water to a bath, wash-hand basin and sink and we might consider providing a bathroom for this purpose. If this work was carried out and approved by the Council, the tenancy would then become a regulated tenancy and a new "fair rent" would be assessed by the rent officer.

No doubt you are familiar with the new legislation on this matter but the booklet "House Improvement and Rents – A Guide for Landlords and Tenants" gives detailed information on the subject and this is obtainable from the Local Rent Officer.

I should be obliged if you would let me know if you agree in principle with this suggestion. If so, I would come to London to discuss the alterations with you, with the Council officials and with a reputable builder.

Kind regards,

Yours sincerely,

M C Mitchell

Dear Mr Mitchell

In reply to your letter regarding your proposal to improve the standard amenities of the property, I wish to point out one or two factors that you are no doubt aware of. The cement situation of the amenities now prevailing, and that I installed 15 years ago a hot water system, namely an Ascot Multipoint Heater which serves both sink and bath. Further you will no doubt recall that I put in a new bath a few years ago.

Viewing the situation all problems as far as I am concerned, under the present conditions, having only my wife and I who are involved, we manage quite well on the amenities now prevailing, and I therefore cannot see that the other improvements you are considering would be any advantage to me.

> 18, Willow Drive
> Little Common
> Bexhill-on-Sea
> Sussex
> 28/1/71
>
> Dear Mr Bangs,
>
> Thank you for your reply to my letter regarding improvements to No. 140 Hatherley Gardens. I am sorry that you do not feel that this will be to your advantage but I must take further steps in this matter and for this purpose I have instructed Messrs Hamletts to act for my sister + me. They will be communicating with you in due course.
>
> Kind regards,
> Yours sincerely
> M. C. Mitchell

APPLICATION FOR CERTIFICATE OF FAIR RENT
by landlord under controlled tenancy

To the Rent Officer

Please write in BLOCK LETTERS or type.

1. Address of premises
   140, Hatherley Gardens,
   East Ham, London, E.6.

2. Name of tenant
   Mr. R. C. Bangs.

3. Description of existing premises (including the number of rooms and, if part only of a building, on which floor or floors)
   Freehold dwelling house.
   3 bedrooms, 2 reception rooms, kitchen with bath outside toilet.

4. Brief description of proposed works shown in accompanying plans and specifications
   Removal of existing W.C. and erection of extension to provide bathroom and separate W.C.
   Estimated cost £1152 plus Fees £90......... Total £1242.

5. Note of any accommodation of which tenant has shared use: state whether sharing is with landlord or another tenant.
   None

Details of any services provided by the landlord or a superior landlord
   None.

7. Terms of the tenancy
   If these cannot be stated briefly, a copy of the agreement may be attached.
   a. Date of commencement. Before 1939.
   b. Rent now payable £2. 07½ s d per week exclusive/inclusive of rates
   c. Repairing obligations
      i. of landlord Outside repairs and decorations.
      ii. of tenant   Internal decorations.
   d. Other terms   "

(A separate sheet may be attached if necessary)

8. Any disrepair or defect which the applicant claims is due to the failure of the tenant (including a former tenant under the controlled tenancy) to comply with the terms of the tenancy
   None.

9. Any improvements, including replacements of any fixtures or fittings which have been carried out by the tenant (including a former tenant under the controlled tenancy) otherwise than under the terms of the tenancy
   Introduction of heater to give hot water to sink and bath in kitchen.
   Replacement of bath in kitchen (less £5 paid by landlord.)

Fair rent proposed by the applicant to be specified in the Certificate of Fair Rent
(EXCLUSIVE of rates) £ 6. 50p per week

11. If any services are provided by the landlord or a superior landlord state what amount, if any, of the fair rent proposed in 10 above should be noted in the certificate as fairly attributable to the provision of services
    £ Nil s d per

I hereby apply for a Certificate of Fair Rent specifying a fair rent under a regulated tenancy of the premises named in paragraph 1 above after completion of the works shown in the plans and specifications which accompanied the application for qualification certificate.

I enclose copies of these plans and specifications and a copy of the certificate of provisional approval.

For Self and Joint Owner
Signed M. C. Mitchell
*(Landlord/agent authorised to make this application)

Name and address of landlord

Mr. M.C.T.Mitchell   and   Mrs. J.B.Loxen
18, Willow Drive,   Highlands
Little Common,   27, Wyamtha Road,
Bexhill-on-Sea, Sussex.   Hertford, Herts.
If signed by agent, name and address of agent

Date 7th August 1971.

[Invoice from G. H. Arnold, Carpentry & Joinery, dated 15th June 1972, to Mr. Bangs for supply and fix 12ft. fitted kitchen units, finished in laminate and lined, corner sink unit to match — £185.00; additional item worktop over washing machine — £3.00; total £188.00, less deposit £50.00, amount due £138.00. Paid 21-6-72, G. H. Arnold.]

[Rent Register form, Registration Area: London Borough of Hounslow, Registration No. 7334. Premises: 140, Netherby Gardens, East Kew, W5 3JB. 3 rooms, kitchen, bathroom/WC, W.C. Pedestrian side entrance. Hot water to both LR and sink. Tenant: Richard Charles Bangs. Landlord: H.C.T. Mitchell & Bros, J. Keene, 18, Miller Drive, Bexhill-on-Sea, Sussex, TN39 4JT. Rental period: Weekly. Tenant internal decorations, Landlord external decorations, external repairs and internal structural maintenance. Rent determined by Rent Officer: £6.75 per week exclusive of rates. Effective date: 20th June 1972. Registered 10th July 1975.]

Copy

4 April 1978

Dear Sir

With reference to your letter ref DAH/MM/6 309 dated 30 March 1978, regarding the application by Mr Mitchell for an increase of rent.

I am objecting to the amount of the increase which represents an increase of approx. 30% which I consider excessive.

The only improvement that Mr. Mitchell has made since the last rent was registered in June 1975 was renewing the roof which was normal maintenance as this was in need of repair.

Yours f——

Copy   1st April 1974

Dear Sir

Your Ref DAH/MM/16 309
Rent Act 1968 - 1974

Further to your letter dated 30 March 1978 and my reply dated 4 April 1978 in which I objected to the increase of rent requested by Mr Mitchell.

I am now writing to state that I now wish to withdraw my objection to the increase.

Yours f——

RENT REGISTER (1978)

Registration Area: London Borough of Newham **Registration No:** 12,544

PREMISES: House, 140, Hatherley Gardens, East Ham, E6, 5HH
5 rooms, kitchen, bathroom/LB, W.C. Pedestrian side entrance.
Hot water to bath, LB and sink. **Rateable Value:** £219

TENANCY: Richard Charles Bangs

Landlord: M.C.F. Mitchell, 18, Willow Drive, Bexhill-on-Sea, Sussex
AND Mrs. J.B. Mason, 97, Queens Road, Hertford, Herts.

Tenant internal decorations, landlord external decorations, external repairs and internal structural maintenance.

Services provided by landlord: None
Furniture provided by landlord: None

REGISTRATIONS — Application made by: Landlord
- Application received: 28th March 1978
- Last Registration date: 14th July 1975 / 26th June 1975 / 7324
- Rent Assessed: £8.75 per week
- Registered on: 26th April 1978
- Effective from: 26th June 1978

General and Water rates are borne by the landlord but are recoverable from the tenant.

RENT REGISTER (1981)

Registration Area: London Borough of Newham

PREMISES: House, 140, Hatherley Gardens, East Ham, E6 3HH
5 rooms, kitchen, bathroom/LB, separate wc, pedestrian side access, hot water to bath, LB & sink. **Rateable Value:** £193

TENANCY: Richard Charles Bangs

Landlord: M.C.F. Mitchell & Mrs. J.B. Mason, 18, Willow Drive, Bexhill-on-Sea, Sussex

Agent: Hamletts, 764, Barking Road, Plaistow, E13 9PJ.

Tenant internal decorations, landlord external decorations, external repairs and internal structural maintenance.

Services: None
Furniture: None

REGISTRATION — Application made by: Landlord
- Application received: 26th March 1981
- Last Registration: 28th April 1978 / 13,544
- Rent Assessed: £12.75 per week
- Registered on: 14th July 1981
- Effective from: 14th July 1981

18, Willow Drive,
Bexhill-on-Sea,
East Sussex, TN39 4PX.
22 April 1987

Dear Mr. Bangs,

I write to advise you that on account of changes in rates, the rent payable for 140, Hatherley Gdns., inclusive of rates, will be reduced to £30.84p per week as at 6 April 1987. This is calculated as follows:—

Payable to 31 March 1987. (Advised on 24.4.86) Per week
Rent and Rates   £32.00

Payable from 6 April 1987.
Rent   £19   £19.00
Rates   537.45 (219 @ 245.41)
Water   78.24 (219 @ 21.8 plus £24 standing
                     charge & hose £0.50)
         £615.69   11.84
                                Payable from 6.4.87. £30.84

As the "Fair Rent" is shortly due for revision, I suggest that you leave the monthly Bankers' Order unchanged until the new rent is assessed. Hamletts are attending to this for me.

I regret having to tell you that my sister, the joint owner, who I think you once met, died last September. Her share of the property was left to her son but I shall continue to manage the property.

Kind regards to your wife and yourself
Yours sincerely
M. Mitchell

P.S. Please sign and return the attached duplicate.

HAMLETTS
SURVEYORS & ESTATE AGENTS
INSURANCE AGENTS · VALUERS
764 BARKING ROAD
PLAISTOW · E·13

RENT ACT 1980
NOTICE OF INCREASE OF RENT UNDER REGULATED TENANCY UP TO AMOUNT OF REGISTERED RENT.

Date: ....

To ...Mr R.C. Bangs... Tenant of ...140 Hatherley Gardens...

A rent of £......... per week ...... was registered on .... as the Fair Rent for the above mentioned premises.

Under the Rent Act 1980 the Landlord is entitled to increase the rent for any rental period beginning while the tenancy is a statutory tenancy up to the amount of the registered rent.

We hereby give you notice that your rent will be increased as follows:—

Present rent per	Increase in rent per	New rent per	Date payable
£	£	£	

Signature of Agent authorised to serve this Notice

Name of Landlord if notice served by Agent
....M. Mitchell, J.B. Mason....
Address of Landlord
....18 Willow Drive, Bexhill on Sea, East Sussex TN39 4PX....
Address of Agent
....Hamletts as above....

Letter 1

140 Hatherley Gardens
East Ham
LONDON E6 3HB

P Bailey
Rent Officer
Rent Officer Service
1 New Plaistow Road
Stratford
LONDON E15 3JB

14 May 1991

Dear Mr Bailey

I am writing in response to your letter (Ref. 0038422) of 9 May 1991, informing me of the application for registration of a fair rent for the above property, and would ask you to take into account the following points:

    I naturally appreciate the repairs carried out by the landlord as and when needed, especially those outlined in Section 15, but would point out that these are not improvements, but repairs which are the landlord's responsibility, as stated in Section 11, and which, of course, also represent a protection of the fabric of the property. No actual improvements have been made since the last registration of a Fair Rent.

    Any inspection of the premises will show that we continue to be careful and responsible tenants who keep the house in excellent decorative order and state of repair.

    Market values of similar houses have fallen during the period in question.

Based on the above points, I fail to see the justification for such an exorbitant increase in the rent applicable on this occasion.

I look forward to hearing from you and will supply any further information you might require.

Yours sincerely

Mr R C Bangs (Tenant)

Letter 2

140, Hatherley Gardens
East Ham
London
E6 3HB

Mr M. C. Mitchell
18, Willow Drive
Little Common
Bexhill on Sea
East Sussex
TN39 4PX

14th August, 1991

Dear Mr Mitchell,

I am sorry to have to inform you that my husband, Richard Bangs, died yesterday, 13th August 1991. As his widow and beneficiary I would be grateful if you could arrange for the tenancy to be transferred to my name from that date, as I have right of succession under the Housing Act, 1957.

I look forward to hearing from you and receiving a new tenancy agreement for my signature.

Yours sincerely,

Lilah Bangs

Letter 3

Pannells
Belchamp St. Paul
Sudbury
Suffolk CO10 7BS
Tel: (0787) 277410

5 September 1991

Mrs R.C. Bangs
140, Hatherley Gardens
East Ham
London E6 3HB

Dear Mrs Bangs,

I believe that you have recently heard from my uncle, Mr Matthew Mitchell, in reply to your letter to him dated 14 August 1991 about your tenancy position.

You may be aware that for many years until 1986 the joint owners of 140 Hatherley Gardens were my uncle, Mr Mitchell, and my mother, Mrs Moxon. My mother died in 1986 and I inherited her half-share interest in the property. Since then my uncle has continued to deal with all matters relating to the tenancy and the property.

I regret that I have not been able to meet you personally but I live up in Suffolk and my visits to London involve my travelling to the western side of London and I rarely have occasion to visit the eastern parts of the city.

May I say how sorry I was to learn of the death of your husband. My uncle told me just as I was preparing to go away on my summer holiday, and from which I have just returned. His death must have been a bitter blow to you after such a long married life together. My parents were fortunate enough to spend 56 years of married life together but when my mother died in 1986 my father found it very difficult to adjust for the remaining 2 years of his life. I hope that you will be able to get over the shock of his death and that as the next weeks and months go by you will find that the pain eases and that you can start to think of the happiness and good times you had in years gone by.

So far as the matter of the transfer of the tenancy is concerned, I will be dealing with this in the next week or two and will write to you again as soon as I have had time to attend to it and various other things requiring attention on my recent return from holiday.

I hope that it will be possible for me to come and pay you a visit in the not too distant future in order that I may introduce myself to you and get to know you a little. I will, of course, let you know in advance when I hope to be able to call.

Yours sincerely,

John Moxon

Letter 4

Pannells
Belchamp St. Paul
Sudbury
Suffolk CO10 7BS
Tel: (0787) 277410

23 September 1991

Mrs L.R. Bangs
140, Hatherley Gardens
East Ham
London E6 3HB

Dear Mrs Bangs,

I trust you received my earlier letter to you dated 5 September and I now write to say that I have looked into the question of the transfer of the tenancy.

The position seems to be quite straightforward. As the widow of your late husband, Mr R.C. Bangs, who was the tenant of 140, Hatherley Gardens you have the statutory right of succession to the tenancy and you automatically become the tenant in his place, with all the terms of his statutory tenancy applying to you as the statutory tenant by succession. I do not think there is any question of any new tenancy being created since you have become a statutory tenant by succession pursuant to the provisions of the Rent Act 1977 and Housing Act 1980.

I hope it will be convenient for you, as tenant, to continue to pay the rent to my uncle, Mr Matthew Mitchell, in the same way as your late husband did while he was alive. The rent was, of course, increased on the rent review last July and the new weekly rent is £28.50 per week, exclusive, effective from 14 July 1991 and I understand that you have been making the increased payments since then on a monthly basis, as agreed with my uncle.

I am also now writing to the Rent Registration Department in Newham to inform the Rent Officer of the death of your husband and of the transfer of the tenancy to you as his widow by virtue of your statutory right of succession.

I trust that this makes the position clear to you. No doubt you will seek advice on your position if you feel it necessary to do so and please let me know if there is anything more you require from me in the above connection.

I should be grateful if you would acknowledge safe receipt of this letter.

Yours sincerely,

John Moxon

Dear Mr Mitchell,

I am just catching up with my correspondence and I write to thank you for your condolences on the death of my husband. It will take some time to adjust to being on my own but I have a very good family & they will help me through it.

As you say we have had a very amicable arrangement for 50 years and hope it will continue to be so.

I can assure you that Dick had the same regard for you as you had for him.

Your nephew sent me a very nice letter of condolence and I have his another one this morning stating that the tenancy will continue in my name and he hopes to visit me sometime in the future. He also says I will be paying the rent to you the same as before.

Thanking you once again for your kind thoughts

Yours Sincerely
Lilian Bangs

Dear Mr Moxon   27.9.91

Thank you for your letter of the 23rd September stating my position as tenant of 140 Hatherley Gardens.

I would also like to thank you for your earlier letter on 14 September conveying your condolences on the death of my husband.

Yes it was a bitter blow, after all those years, but I have many happy memories to look back on, and a very good family.

It will take quite a while to adjust to living on my own but as you say the pain will ease as time goes by.

I will be very pleased to see you any time you wish to call, you have only to give me a ring to make sure I am at home, as I shall be visiting my family on & off from time to time.

Thanking you once again.
Yours sincerely
Lilian Bangs

Thank you also for notifying the Rent officer of the change in tenancy
Yours Sincerely
Lilian Bangs

Pannells
Belchamp St. Paul
Sudbury
Suffolk CO10 7BS
Tel: (01787) 277410

Mrs L E Bangs   5th August 1998
140, Hatherley Gardens
West End
London E6 3HB

Dear Mrs Bangs,

What I am about to tell you will no doubt come as a surprise to you, but I hope nothing more than that.

The fact of the matter is that my uncle and I have decided to sell No.140 to a property company with you, as the tenant, remaining in possession. Your position and rights as the tenant will be exactly the same. The only real difference from your point of view, will be that you will be paying your rent to the property company, which will, as the new owner, assume all the landlord's responsibilities.

I am sorry to spring this on you like this but it has all happened very quickly. My uncle and I were advised not to tell you until a legal agreement had been reached because if you had been told sooner and the deal had fallen through you might have felt rather uncomfortable, or worried, and the last thing I or my uncle wanted to do was to put you under any kind of pressure or cause you any concern. The agreement was reached only yesterday between the solicitors and so I can now tell you the full position as it is. The property will change hands on Tuesday 1st September, i.e. in just under 4 weeks' time. My uncle and I will of course continue to keep the building insured until that date.

The property company is called DANRISS PROPERTY CORPORATION LTD and its main office is at 17, Linhope Street, London NW1 6HT. Tel: 0171 724 6647. The person there we have been in contact with is a Mr Perry Field. They will no doubt be contacting you in the near future.

Why has all this happened? My uncle, who is now 89, has for some time been talking about selling the house to someone who would buy it with you as tenant still in possession. Managing a rented property in London is something neither he nor I ever really wanted to have to do. I knew that both he and my mother (before she died) had been hoping that the opportunity might arise to sell it some years ago and then spend some of the money on a few nice things in their old age. But no suitable opportunity ever arose. Then we had all that trouble with the builders last year and the year before and then we were facing more trouble getting the redecorations and plastering done, as well as the expense of a full external re-painting next year. Both my uncle and aunt have not been too well and I have also been under the weather these past few months with 2 eye operations and various other things.

A few weeks ago we received an offer out of the blue from Danriss to buy the house with you remaining as tenant. As it was a reasonable offer from our point of view we, and particularly my uncle, decided to accept it. But, as I say, we were advised not to tell you until an agreement had finally been reached. Personally, I would have preferred to tell you sooner than this.

Having to get a Landlord's Gas Safety Inspection Certificate has nothing to do with the sale. We have got to do it in any event, whether the house is sold or not. And our responsibility continues right up to 1st September. I hope British Gas will be in touch with you very soon.

As to the redecoration and re-plastering, Danriss are well aware of it and I hope they will do it promptly for you. They will be much more efficient about that sort of thing than I or my uncle ever could be.

As to the rent payable up to 1st September 1998, I think the position is as follows:

The total rent which should be paid for the period Monday 30th March 1998 to Monday 24th August 1998 is 21 weeks at £49 per week, which is £1,029.00.
In fact, you have already paid, by Bankers Order, 4 months at £212.33 per month for April, May, June and July: total £849.32.
That means there will only be another £179.68 to pay up to and including Monday 24th August 1998 (£1,029.00 less £849.32).

If you are agreeable, I think the best thing to do would be for you to cancel your Bankers Order now (assuming the July payment has already gone through) and ask your Bank to make a 'one-off' payment to my uncle's Bank of £179.68 on or about 24th August, which will clear the rent account completely so far as we are concerned. Alternatively, if your Bank won't do that for you, then you could perhaps send a cheque to my uncle for £179.68.

Once the sale is completed on 1st September it will be a great load off the minds of both myself and my uncle. It will, of course, mean more to him than to me because I have only been involved over the past 10 years or so, whereas he has had to deal with the letting for 40 to 50 years.

I would like to think that our family has been a reasonably good landlord both to you and to your husband over the past 50 years. You, certainly, have been very good tenants and it is fortunate that both families have got on well together over all those years.

The ending of our present landlord/tenant relationship has come very suddenly but I am sure that Danriss will be fair and reasonable landlords to you.

Although I expect we will be in touch again before the end of this month, I will take this opportunity of wishing both you and all your family all the best for the future and of hoping that you will enjoy several more happy years at No.140 which has been your home for so long.

Yours sincerely,

John Moxon

140 Hatherley Gdns
East Ham
E6 3HB

11.8.98

Dear Mr Moxom,

I am in receipt of your letter regarding the sale of the house & I must say I was not surprised, but having been here for 59 yrs. I thought you could have apprised me of the situation a little earlier.

Having said that, my husband & I and lately myself alone have enjoyed a good relationship as tenant & landlord and have done our best to keep the house well decorated and it's quite a shame that things haven't worked out just recently, as you can imagine how I feel every time I walk into that room.

I hope you have also mentioned the other jobs outstanding namely. the window frame in the lounge which the builder ruined fixing the sill the cistern over the taps & overflows in the tank.

I have send to the bank to stop the standing order for the rent and will be sending to Mr Mitchell cheque for £179·00 in due course.

In closing I do hope your heel is improving and will continue to do so.

My family join in in wishing all the best for the future
Yours Sincerely
L. R. Bangs.

Pannells
Belchamp St. Paul
Sudbury
Suffolk CO10 7BS
Tel: (01787) 277410

22 August 1998

Dear Mrs Bangs,

Thank you very much for your letter of 19th August, received yesterday, enclosing the Gas Safety Certificate and the Invoice. I am very grateful to you for dealing with the cheque for British Gas. I hope the engineer's visit on Wednesday did not cause you too much inconvenience. I have passed on to our solicitors the Certificate. They will be sending it to Searles' solicitors.

I must also thank you for your earlier letter, dated 11th August, which came last week. I can fully understand you feeling that we could have told you about the sale sooner than we did. I felt bad about it, but both the solicitors and Searles strongly advised us not to tell you until a legal contract had been made. What that says about human relationships and person communication I don't know, but I am sorry if you felt a bit upset about it.

All being well, the sale will be completed on 1st September. I have told Mr Field (of Searles) about the outstanding re-decoration works etc. and hop he will deal with them promptly for you. I am sure Searles will be good landlords to you.

My uncle told me he had written to you. I know he is relieved to have the worry and responsibility of the property taken away. Although I am a bit younger than he is, I also feel a great relief!

Wishing you and your family all the best,

Yours Sincerely,
John Moxom.

COPY

140 Hatherley Gdns
East Ham
E6 3HB

10.10.98

Re: 140 Hatherley Gdns E6 3HB

Dear Sir,

My previous landlords of 59 yrs. namely (Mr M.C. Mitchell & Mr J Moxom) informed me that you would be taking over these premises on 1st September 1998. I have had no communication from you at all therefore I will be pleased if you will let me know how when and to whom I should pay my rent and the method of payment

Yours Sincerely

Copy

140 Hatherley Gdns,
East Ham
E6 3AB

2-11-98

Dear Sir,
My previous landlord said he acquainted you with the outstanding repairs that were necessary before you took over.

Namely: The tank in the bathroom is leaking as are several taps for which I would appreciate an early repair as apart from the waste of water I am on a meter.

The window frame in the lounge on which my decoration was destroyed when they put a new sill in.

The wall in the bedroom where the water came in needs plastering & redecorating.

The putty has all fell out in one of the panes in the back door & I am afraid off the security risk

There is a crack in the Bathroom window & one in the kitchen window which the workman did when they put a new sill in

and the post on the gate is rotted stopping the gate from closing and I have refrained from knocking it back in case I damage the wall which doesn't look too safe.

Hoping you will instruct your builders to start the repairs as soon as possible.

Yours sincerely
L. R. Bangs

---

140 Hatherley Gdns
East Ham E6 3AB

3-9-99

Re Registration of Rent

Dear Mr Williams,
I expect you are aware of the change of owner of these premises from 1st September 1998 and in view of the state of the paintwork on the outside of the house he seems to be asking quite a large increase in rent.

There have been no urgent repairs since the change over only repairs pending when taken on.

However I have now received your notice today that you will be inspecting the premises on the 23 Sept and I will be pleased to accommodate you

Yours faithfully
L. R. Bangs (Mrs)

Dear Sir
I am writing to inform you of the overflowing gutter at the back in two places which the workman were to have fixed. also since they painted the house I cannot open a window in the bedrooms and I must have some air through the house. My son has managed downstairs but as we have not a ladder and it has to be done from the out side I trust you will attend to this promptly.

I have telephoned your office for the first time 3 wks ago and then I had no reply. so after a few days away I telephoned again last week and again today twice having been told they would ring me back but no joy I am sure you will not want a repeat of the problem I had before in the back room & I certainly do not so I would like something done very quickly please

140 Hatherley Gardens
East Ham
London
E6 3HB

The Managing Director
Danriss Property Corporation Ltd.
17, Linhope Street,
London, N.W.1 6HT

24 April 2000

Dear Sir or Madam,

RE: The property at the above address.

Our mother, Mrs L Bangs, has requested that we write to you concerning [the management] of her home, which is the property at the above address.

A little while ago, she was contacted by your Mr. Field, who, amongst other [things requested] that she send a letter to yourselves stating her satisfaction with work carried [out on her] property. This letter is to respond to that request, but perhaps not in the way [you] would wish.

Since Danriss took over the property, in September 1997 – the property has [seen a] decline in the standard of maintenance. We hardly need to remind you that [rent was] considerably increased last September and that recently this was made even [higher] due to the situation regarding rent capping. Some internal re-decoration, ma[de necessary by] previous failures of maintenance which led to penetration of rain, were carri[ed out]. However, the external fabric of the building is now in a worse state of repai[r than] since our parents first took on the tenancy of the property in May 1939.

There were various items which our mother had pointed out as in need of at[tention as] urgent. These included:

- Overflowing gutters
- Rotting window sills and window frames
- Cracked stone window ledges
- Rear door rotted, insecure and dangerous
- Rear gate thoroughly rotten
- Need for complete external re-decoration

rendering and painting is extremely slapdash and poor; the rear gate was fitted with huge spaces, and on complaint is little better, workmen arranging to start work at agreed times and then not turning up, with ridiculous excuses. We could go on.

We are sure that if such a low standard of repair were carried out on your own property you would refuse to pay the contractors. Our mother has the right to expect similar standards. It should be pointed out that a tenancy agreement is a contract in law. Our mother has fulfilled her obligations to the full and continues so to do. Your company, as the other party to the contract, is in breach.

The above situation is completely unacceptable. We request that you address these matters a[s] a matter of urgency, as time is now of the essence in this matter. Perhaps a representative from the company could view the property at a mutually agreed time as, to our knowledge, th[e] house has not been inspected since it was taken over. Failing this, we will have no alternative but to take the matter further, and there are many options open to us.

Please reply to our mother at the above address. We look forward to hearing from you.

Yours faithfully

Mrs J Mumford
Dr P R Bangs
Mr P J Bangs

CC: The Senior Rent Officer,
Newham Borough Council

30.5.03

140 Hatherley Gdns
East Ham
E6-3HB

Dear Madam,

I am in receipt of your letter regarding changing my standing order for my rent.

I trust Danriss has also passed on the fact that the rain is coming in my bedroom which I notified them a few weeks ago. Two builders arrived to assess the damage but I have heard nothing since but I did phone Natalie to remind her the day before I received a letter from [Danriss] telling me of the change.

The rain is also coming over the gutter at the back of the house over the dining room. Looking forward to hearing from you re this problem.

Yours
L Bangs

---

140 Hatherley Gdns
East Ham
E6-3HB

21.9.03
TEL. 0208-4710237

Dear Madam,

I wrote to you when you took over the management of my house and explained that the roof was leaking in my bedroom. As I have heard nothing from you since I hope you will get something done about it before the weather sets in as when it rains it seeps further into the ceiling & dampens the wall spoiling my decorations.

This dry weather cannot last much longer so look forward to hearing from you very soon.

Yours
Mrs L. Bangs

Castle Estates
Residential Letting Agents and Property Managers

Mrs L Bangs
140 Hatherley Gardens
East Ham
London
E6 3HB

Castle House
Dawson Road
Mount Farm
Bletchley
Milton Keynes
MK1 1QY
Tel: 0870 839 2727
Fax: 0870 839 2728
www.castle-estates.co.uk

28th April 2008.

Dear Mrs Bangs,

I refer to the above property and your recent report that there is still water coming through the roof in the area of the chimney surround.

Maintenance UK whom are the contractors whom carried out the works to the roof, and advised me that they will be putting up scaffolding in the next couple of days, in order that they can establish where the problem lies.

Should you have any queries please contact me on 0870 839 2774.

Yours Sincerely,

Susan Lander-Brown
Castle Estates

RENT ACT 1977
Section 45(2) as amended by Housing Act 1980 and Rent (Relief from Phasing) Order 1987

Notice of Increase of Rent under Regulated Tenancy where a Fair Rent has been registered and the Increase is *Not* Subject to the Phasing Provisions of Schedule 8 to the Rent Act 1977

Please read the Notes carefully and keep this form

To: Mrs L R Bangs
tenant of 140 Hatherley Gardens, London E6 3HB

1. (a) A rent of **£ 84.00** per week (exclusive of rates) has been [registered by the Rent Officer] [determined by a Rent Assessment Committee] for the above premises and takes effect from 5th May 2008 [This includes Council Tax]

2. Unless:-
(a) a different rent is registered by the Rent Officer or determined by a Rent Assessment Committee, or
(b) the Rent Officer agrees to cancel the registration, or
(c) the rent is registered as variable -
the maximum rent (exclusive of rates) you can be charged from the date in Paragraph 1 is the full registered rent as shown in that paragraph.

3. I hereby give you notice that your rent (exclusive of rates will be increased as follows:-

Present Rent	£ 75.00 per week (£325.00 pcm)
New rent from 1st June 2008.*	£ 84.00 per week (£364.00 pcm)

The date at* must not be earlier than the date in paragraph 1 above nor 4 weeks before the date of service of the Notice.

[It is noted in the rent register that rates in respect of the above premises are borne by me or a superior landlord. I am entitled to add the amount for rates to the rent and to pass on to you future increases in rates without serving a Notice of Increase.]

Signed
On behalf of: Bright House Homes Ltd
Address of Landlord: 7-10 Chandos Street,
London W1H 9HH

[Name and Address of Agent: Touchstone Corporate Property Service Ltd
Castle House, Mount Farm, Bletchley
Milton Keynes MK1 1QY

Date: 6th May 2008

APPENDIX F

Silver Wedding Cards

Dad to Mum

Mum to Dad

From Joyce and Wally

From Nan

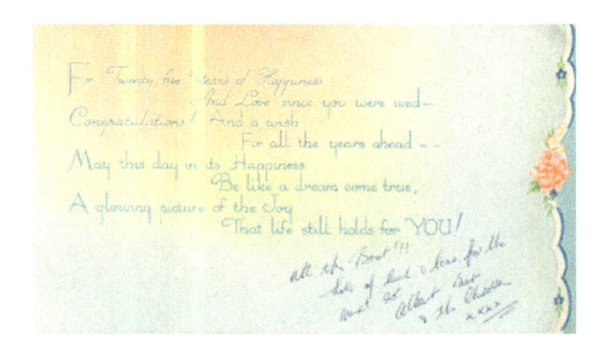

From Uncle Albert and family

From Wally's Mum and Dad

From Aunt Alice and Uncle George

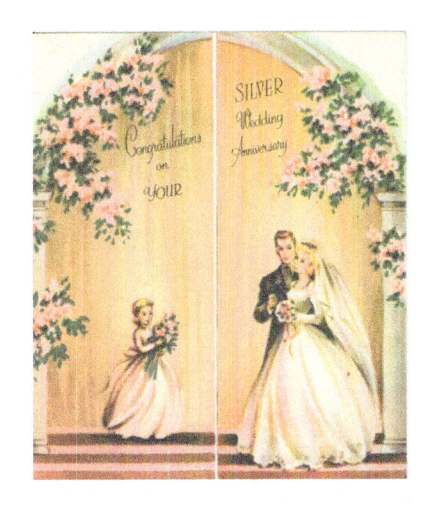

From Auntie Florrie, Uncle Arthur and family

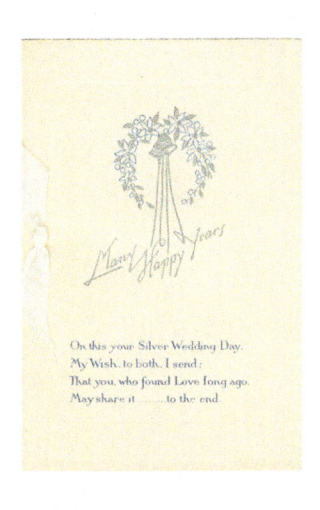

From Aunt Rose and Uncle Henry

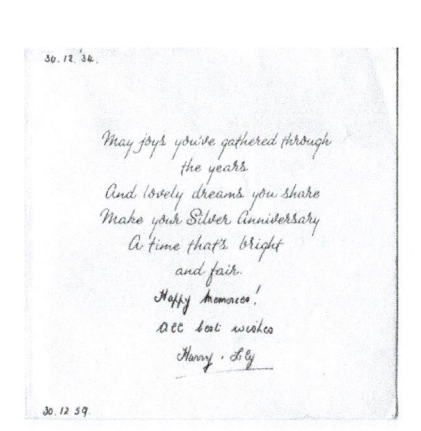

From Uncle Harry and Aunty Lily

From Uncle Jack and Aunty Molly (Auntie Florrie's sister)

From Myrtle, Percy and family (neighbours)

From Nance and Albert

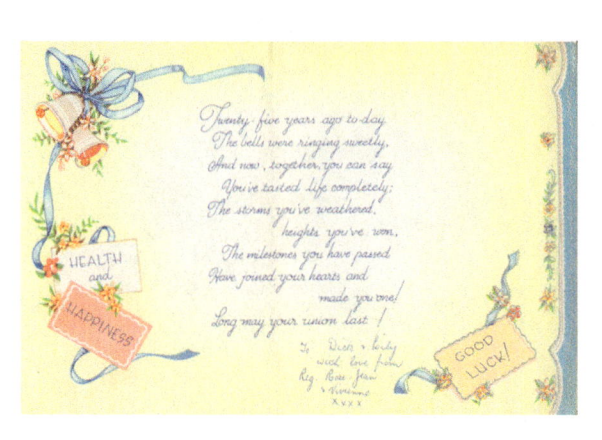

From Uncle Reg, Aunt Rose and family

From Stan, Olive and family
(Wally's cousin)

From Uncle Sid

APPENDIX G

Travels

Portrush, Northern Ireland

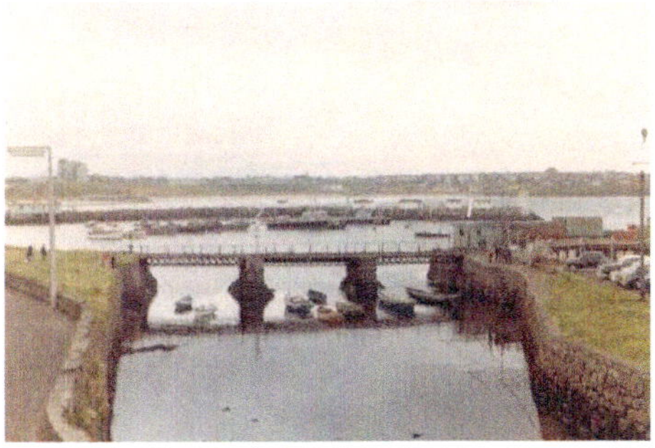

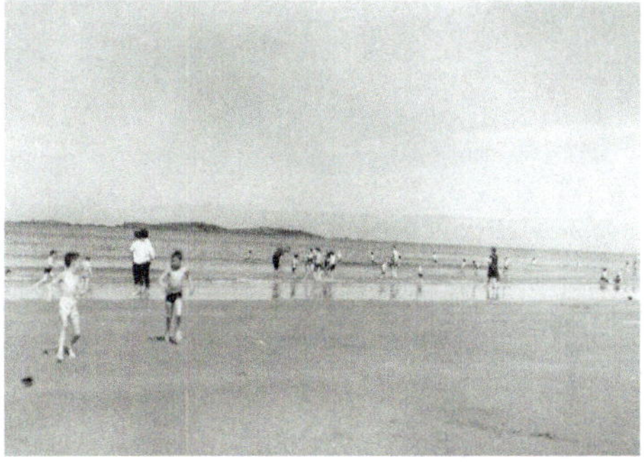

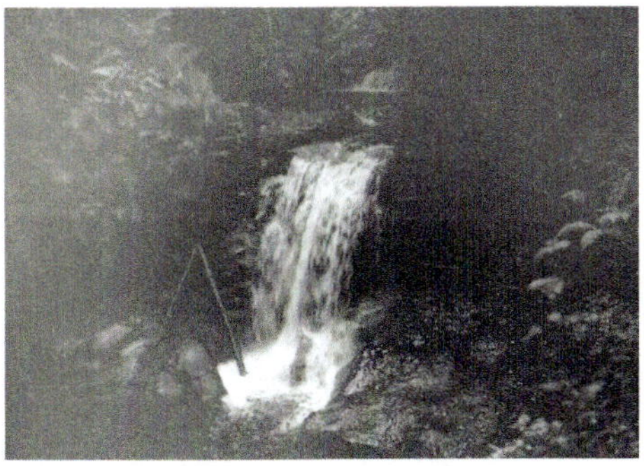

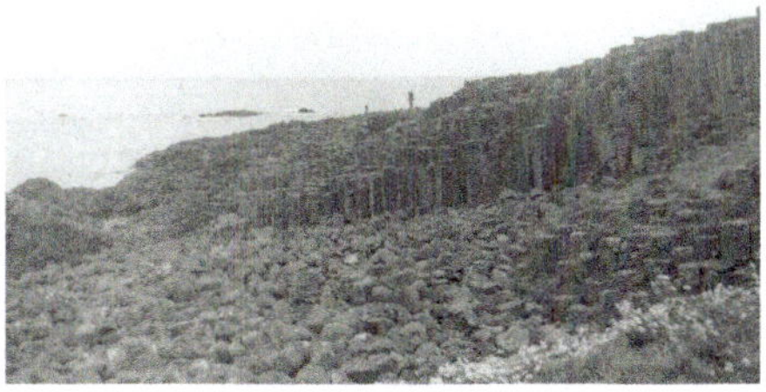

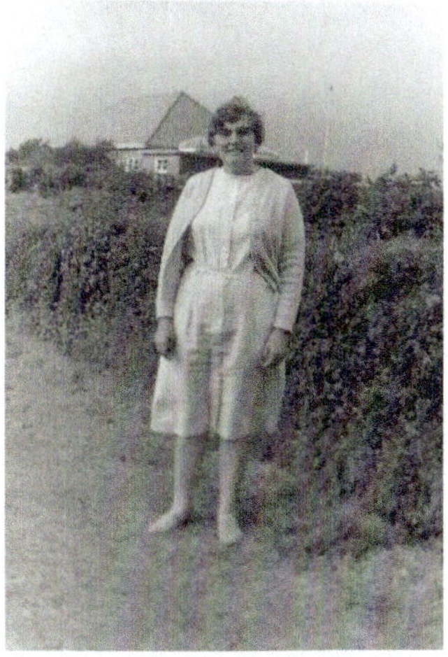

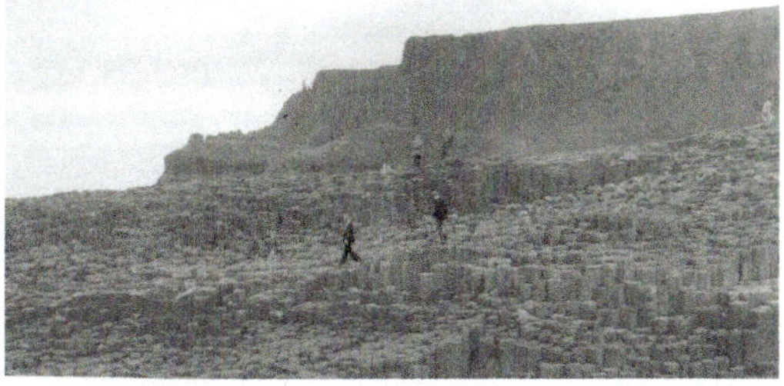

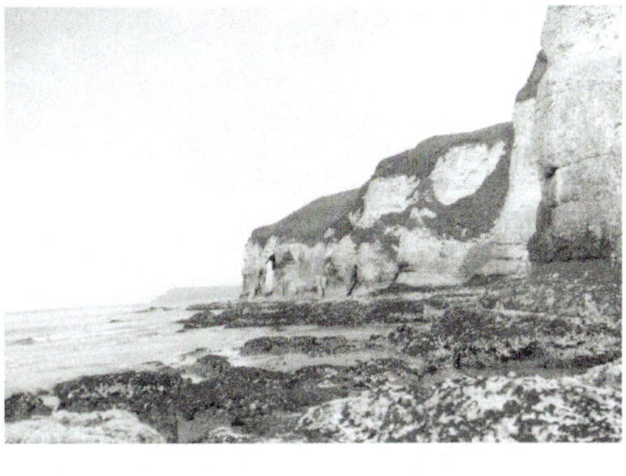

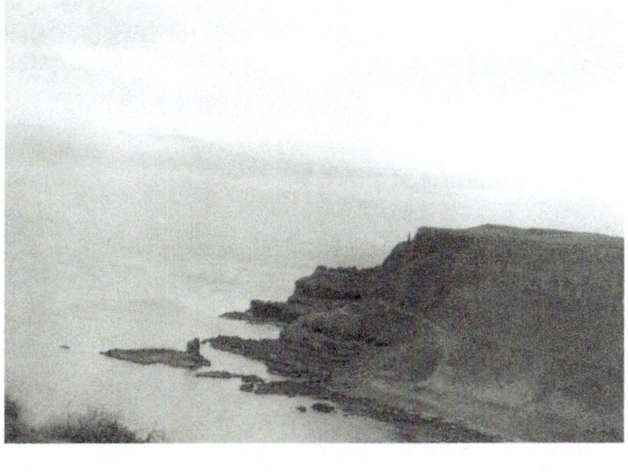

Ireland

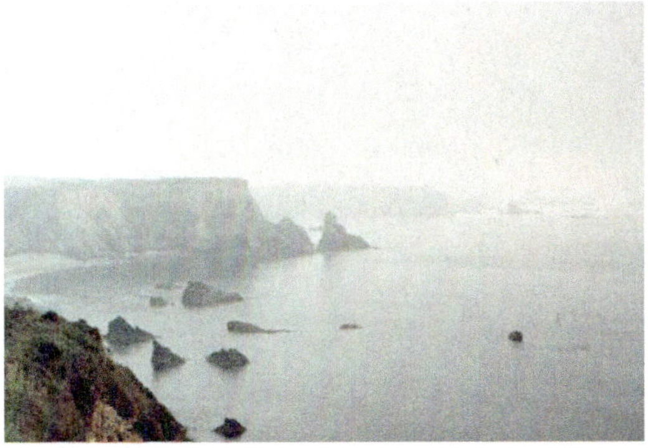

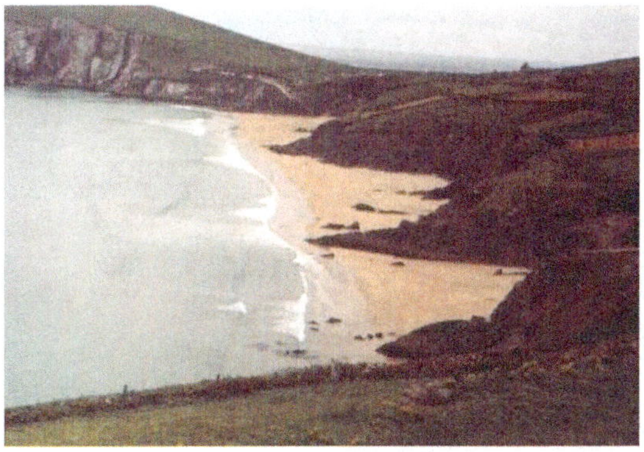

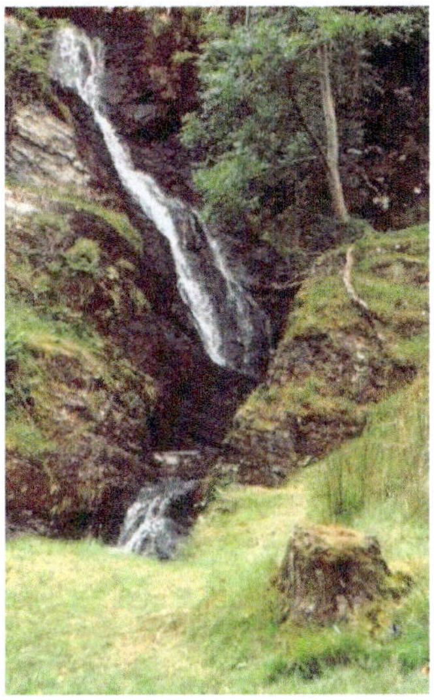

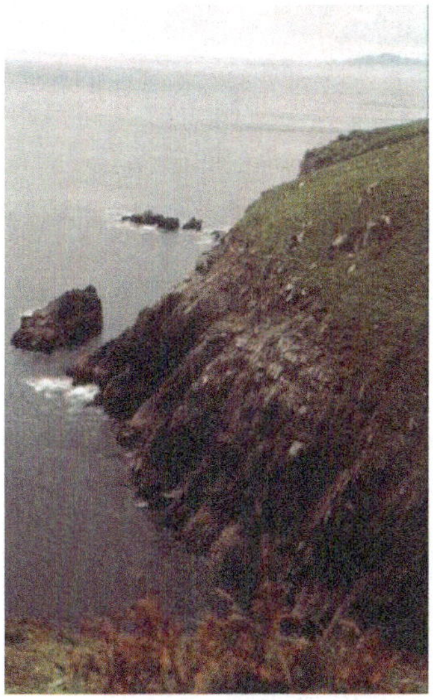

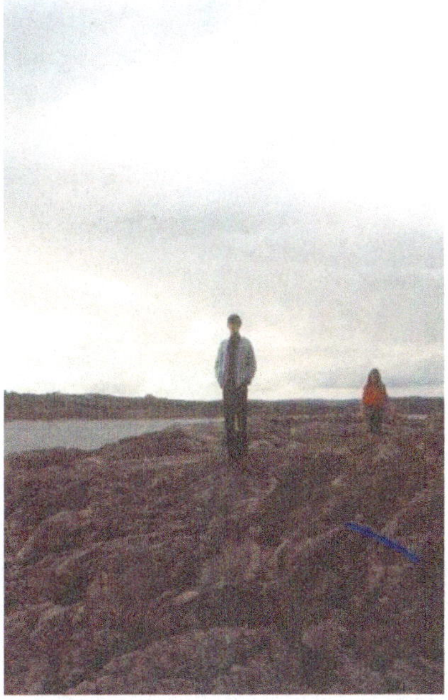

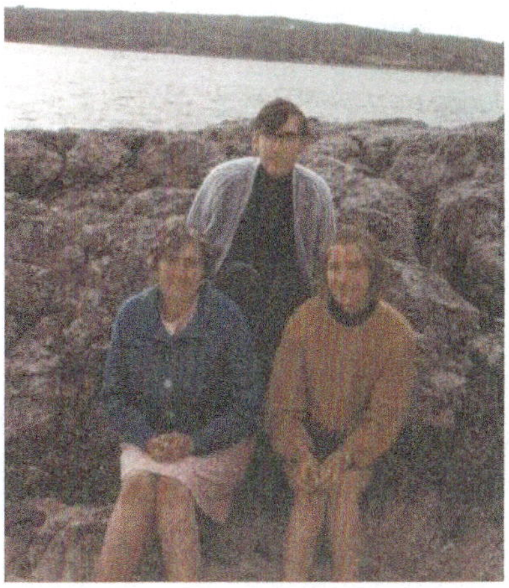

210 Dick Bangs & Lily Bourne – Their story

Dick Bangs & Lily Bourne – Their story

Exmouth

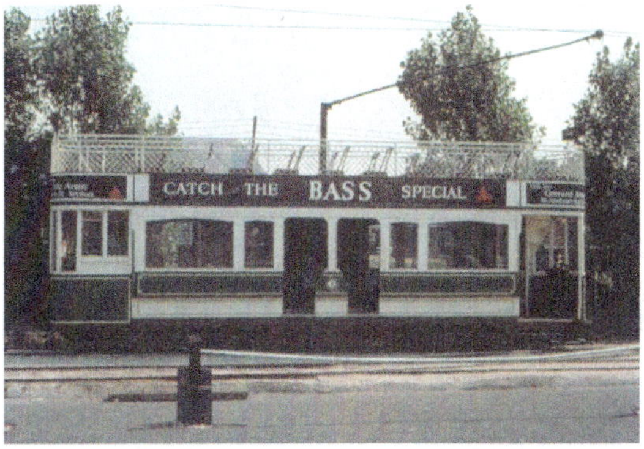
CATCH THE BASS SPECIAL

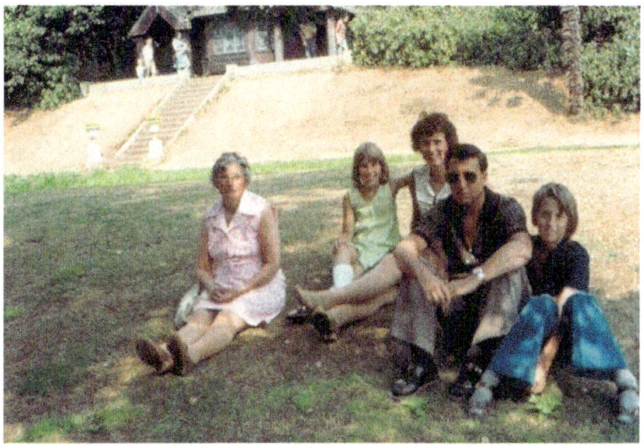

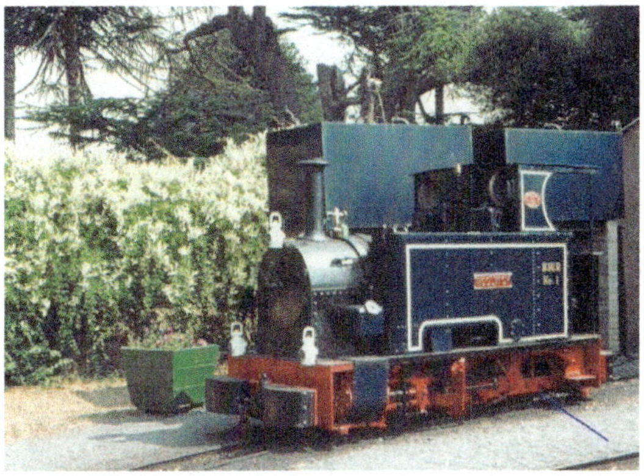

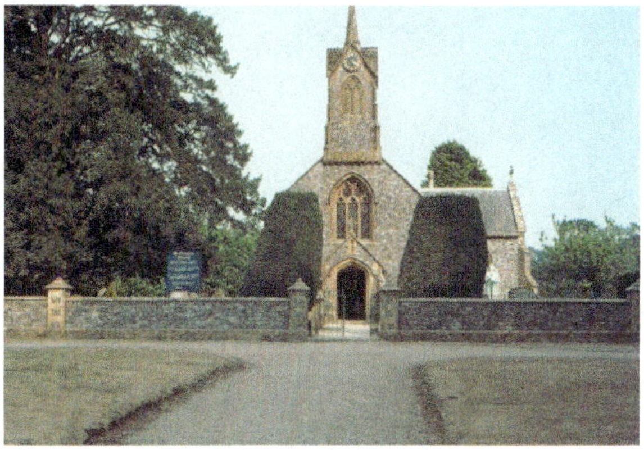

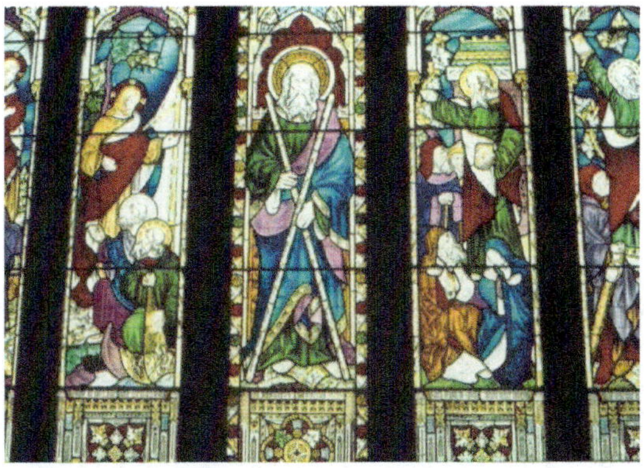

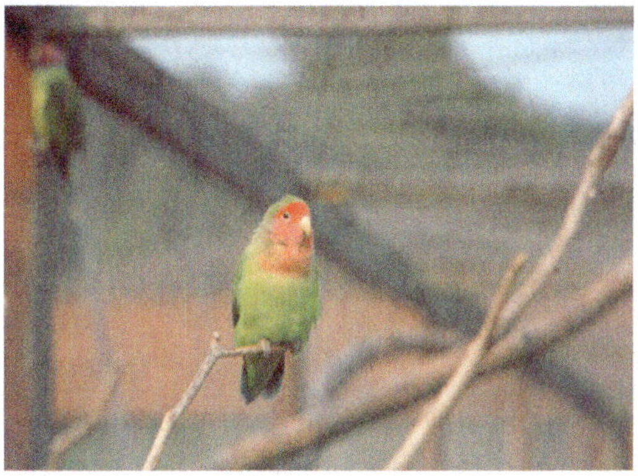

Scotland

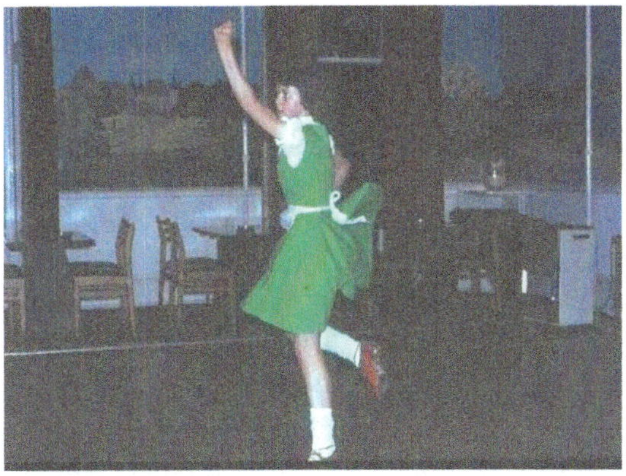

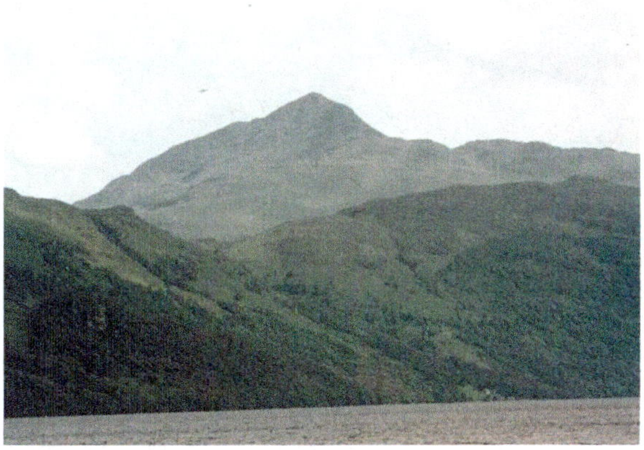

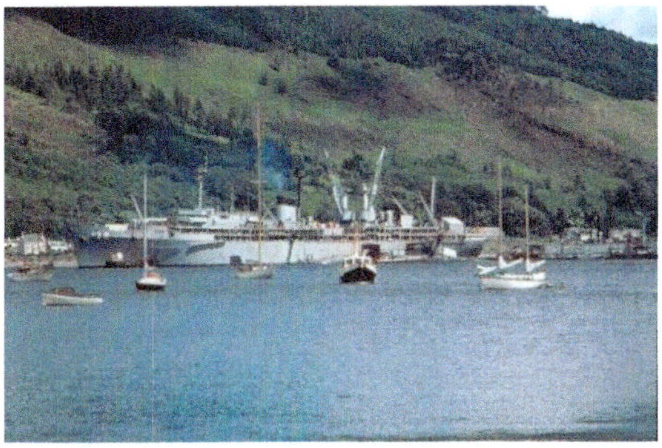

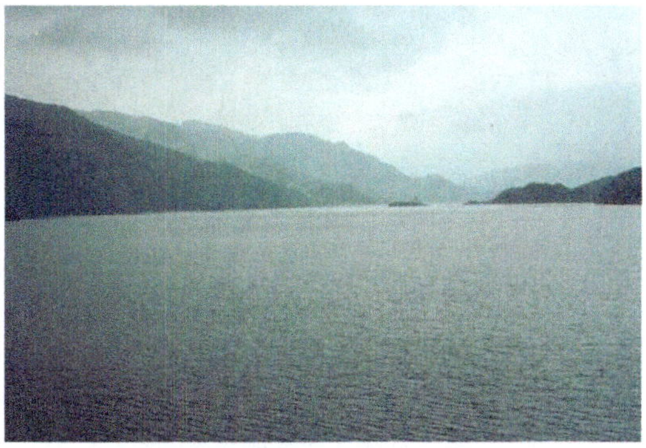

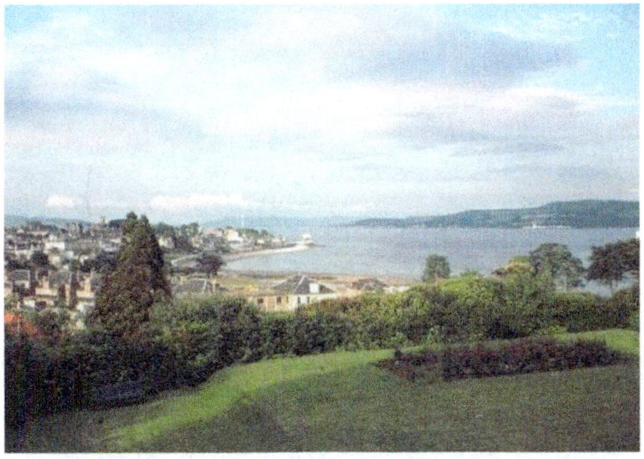

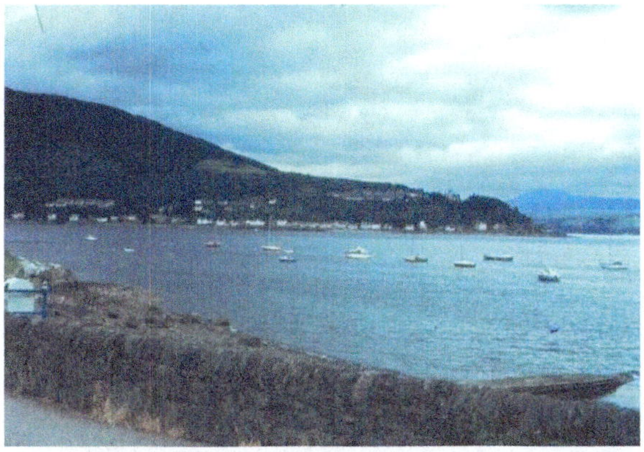

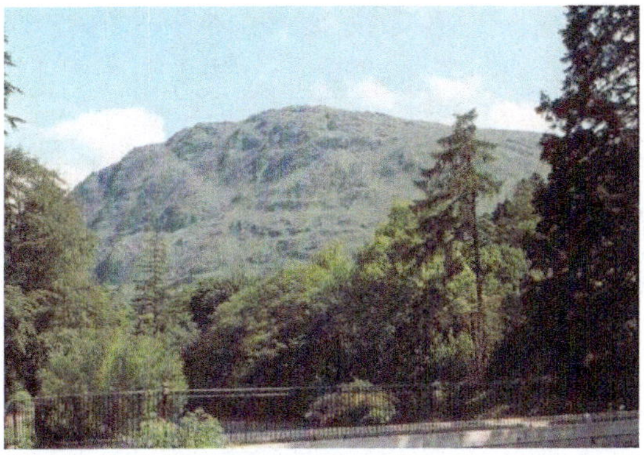

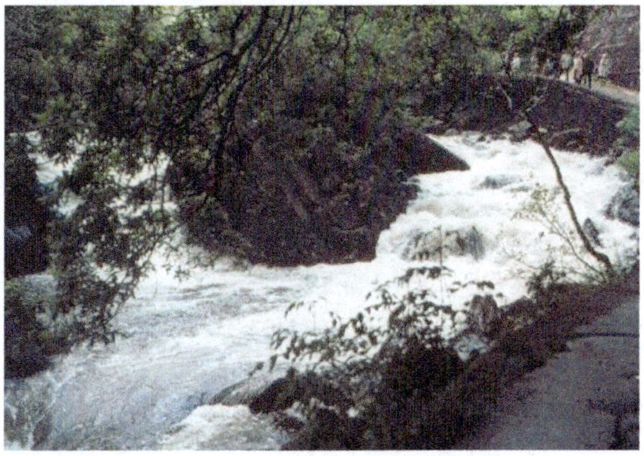

Wales

Dick Bangs & Lily Bourne – Their story

217

Lake District

Dick Bangs & Lily Bourne – Their story

Guernsey

Dick Bangs & Lily Bourne – Their story

Altea

Dick Bangs & Lily Bourne – Their story

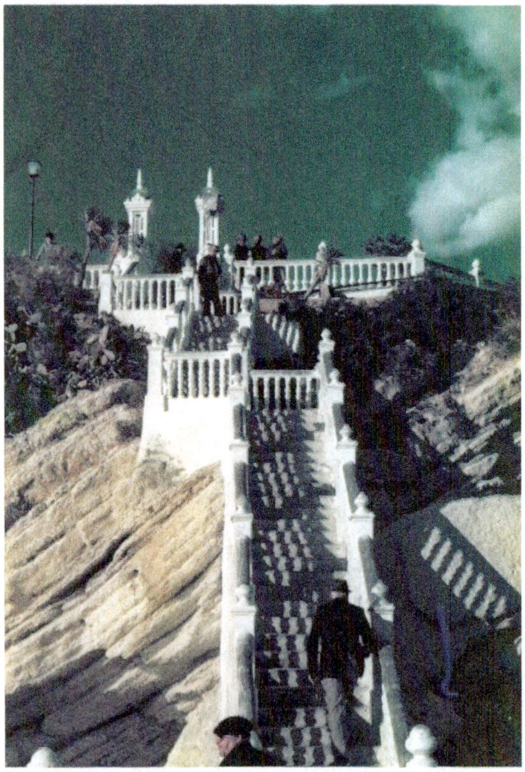

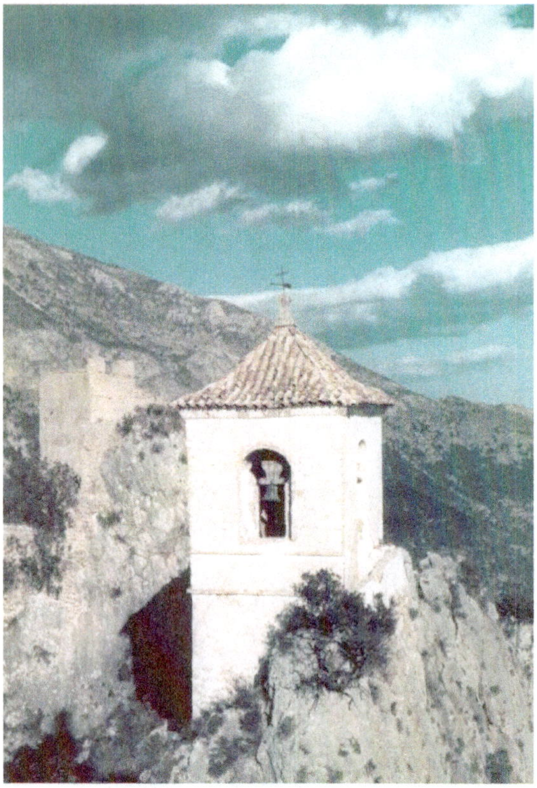

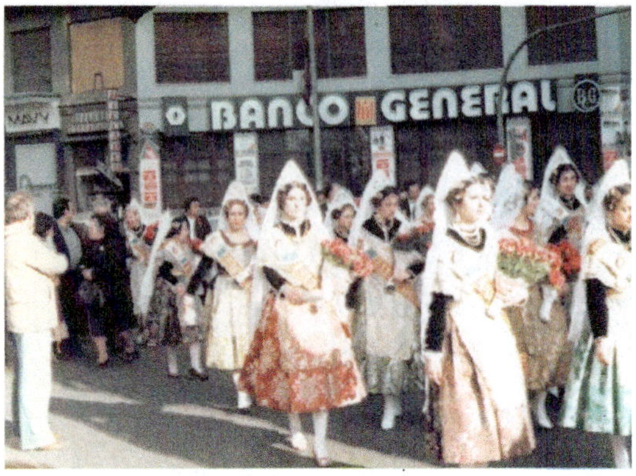
GENERAL

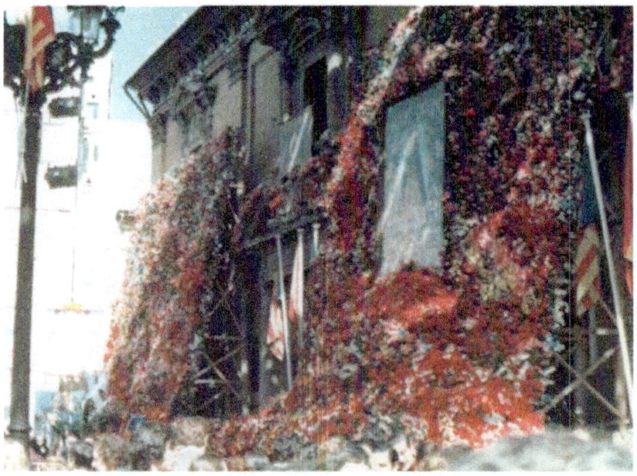

Lloret del Mar

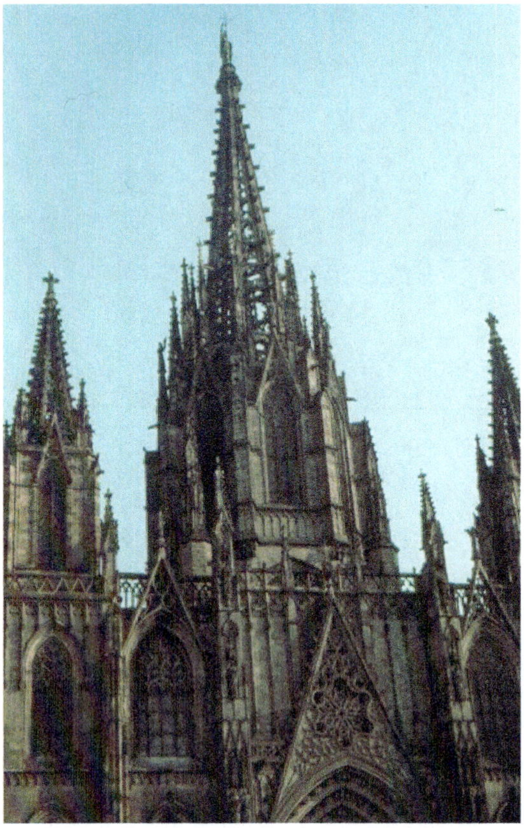

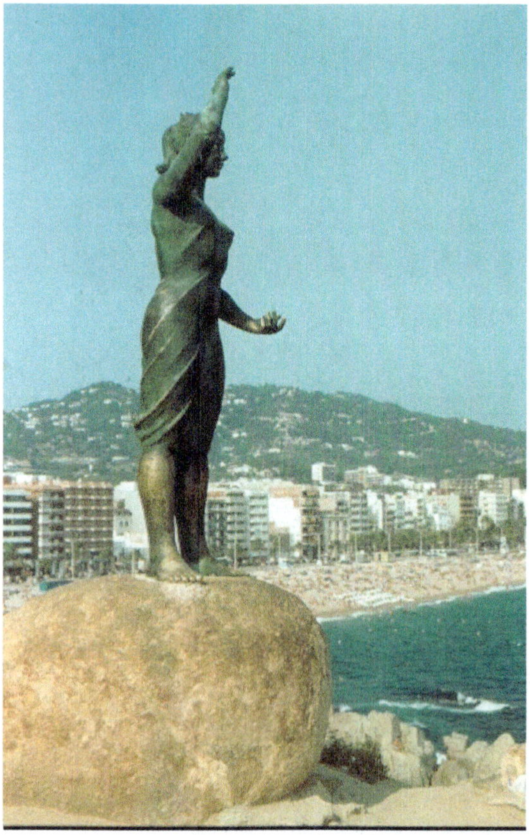

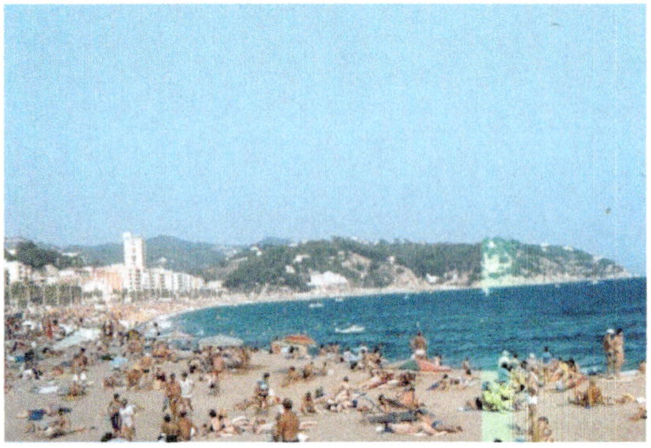

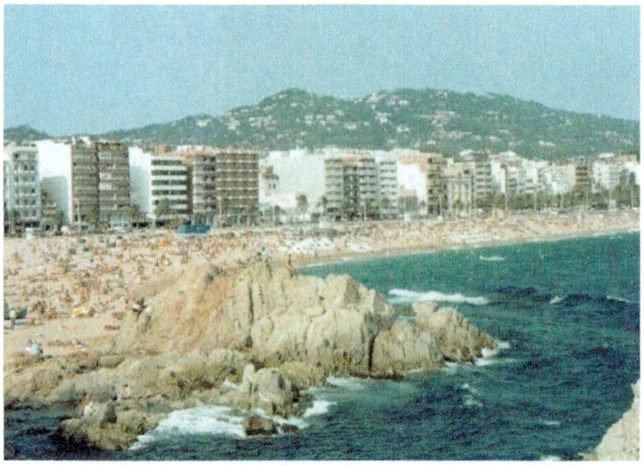

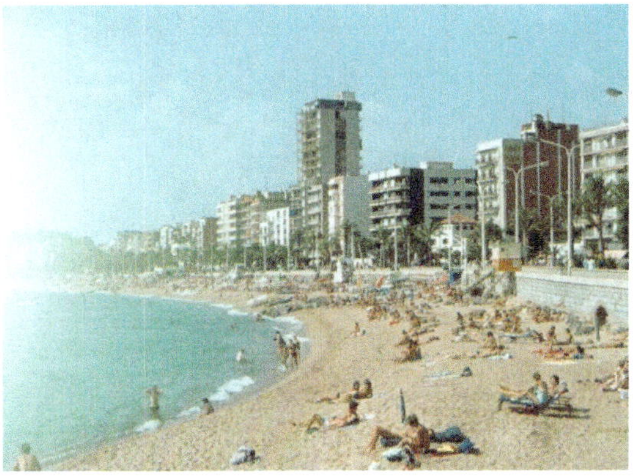

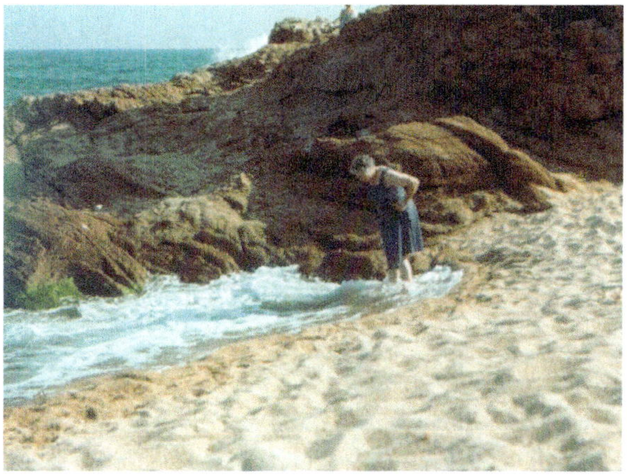

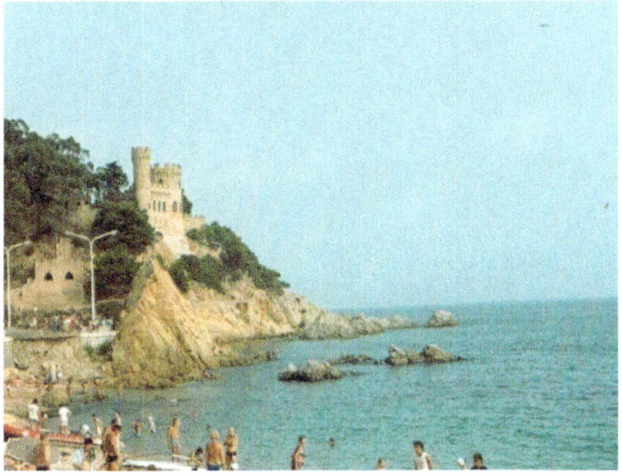

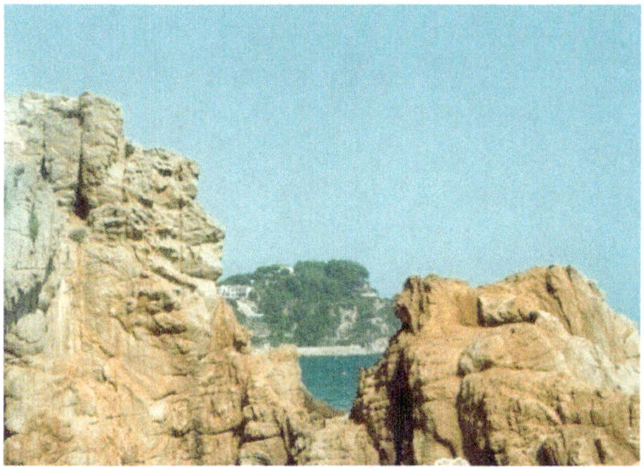

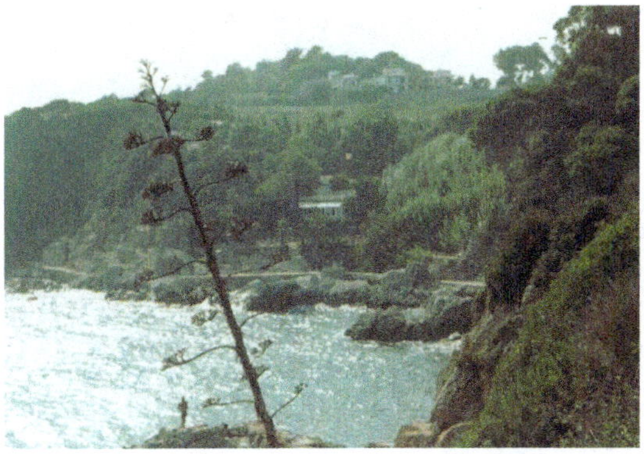

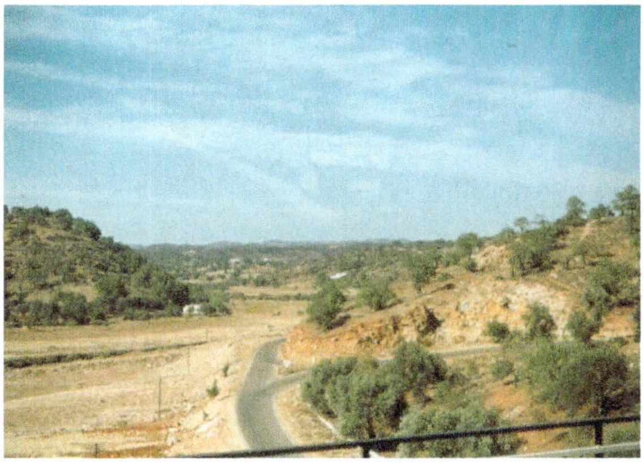

Portugal

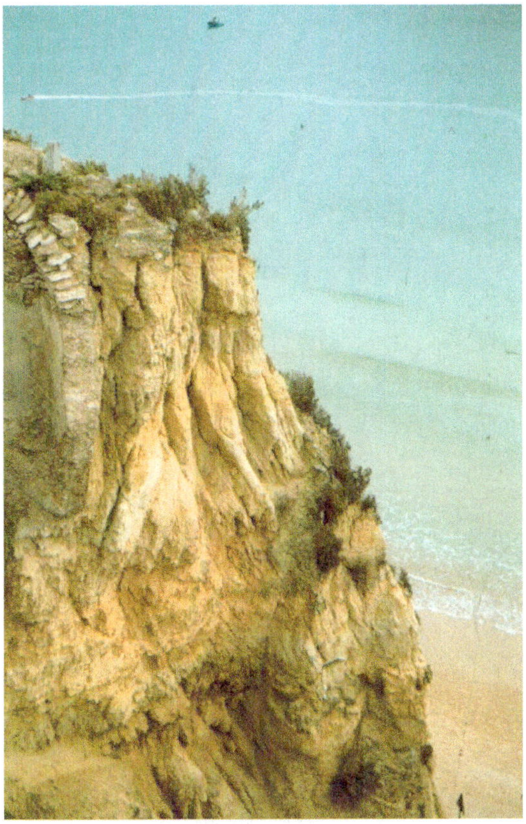

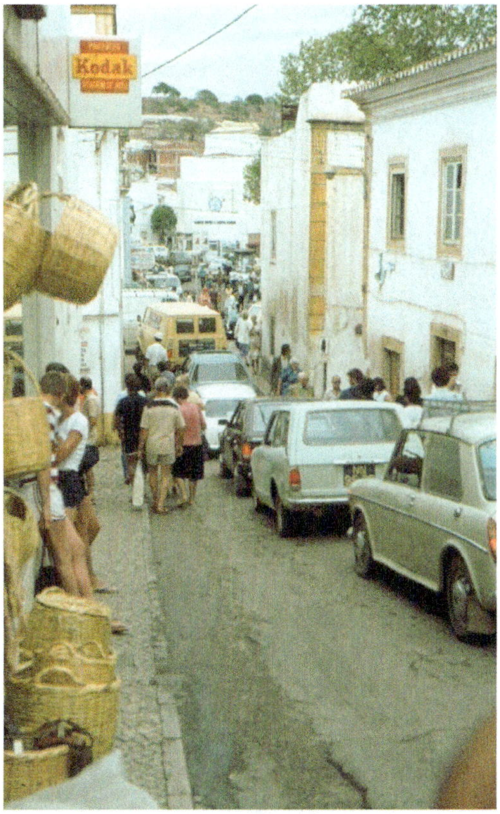
Kodak

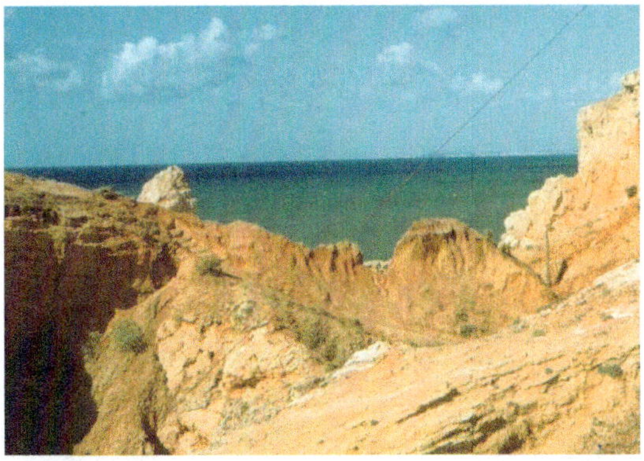

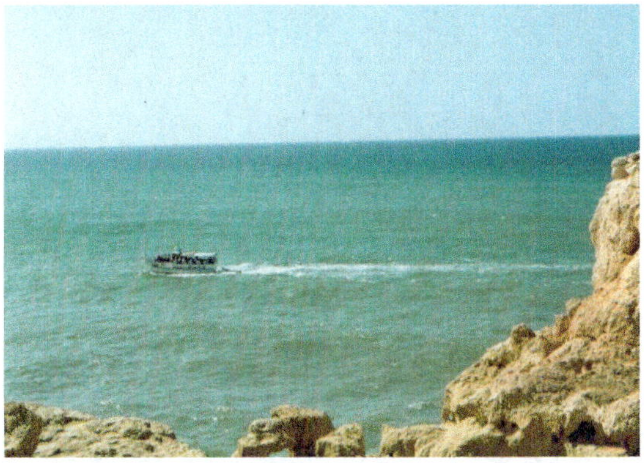

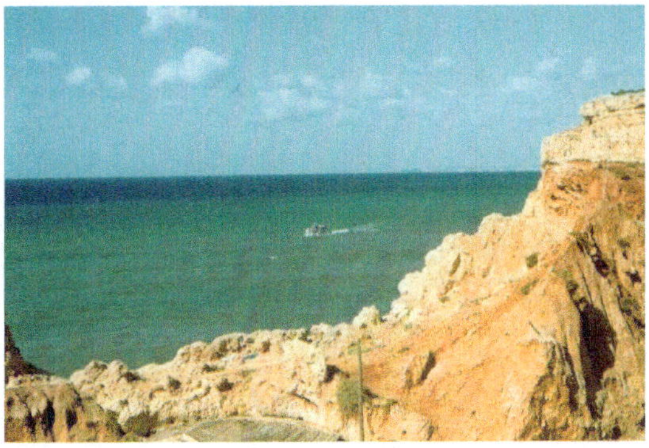

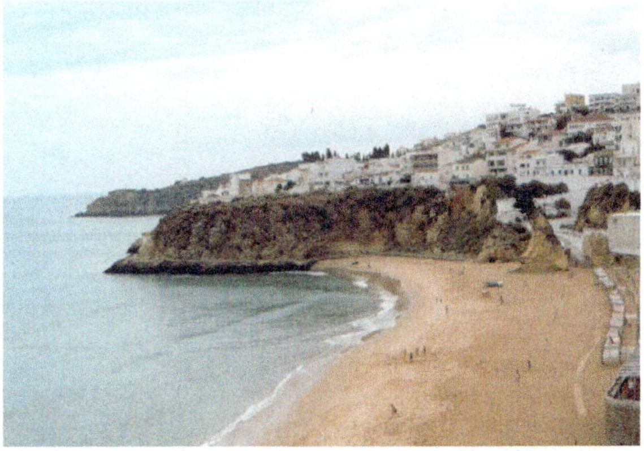

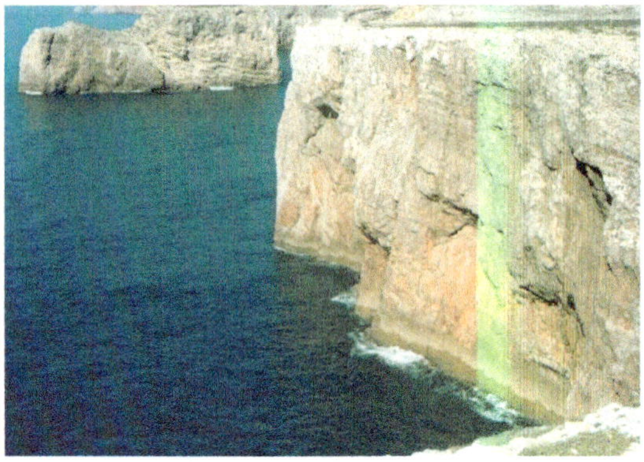

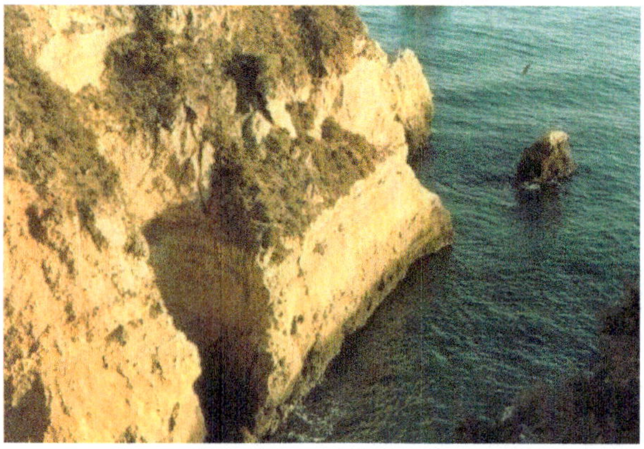

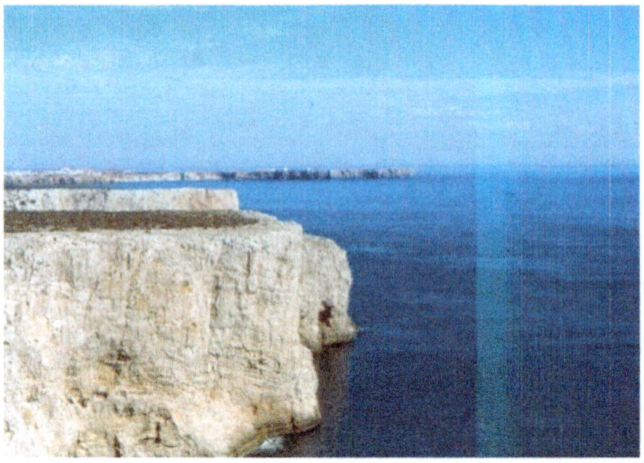

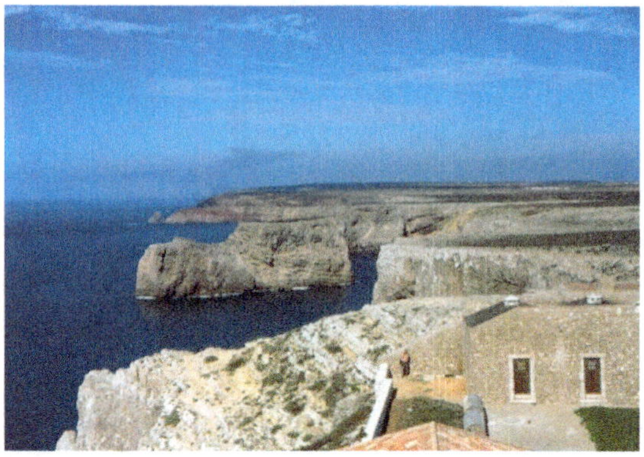

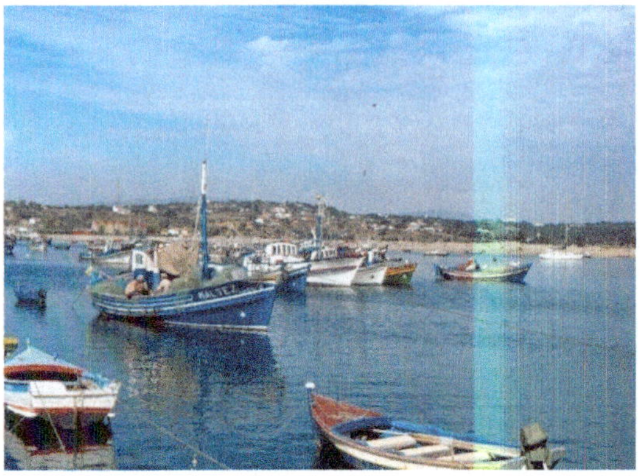

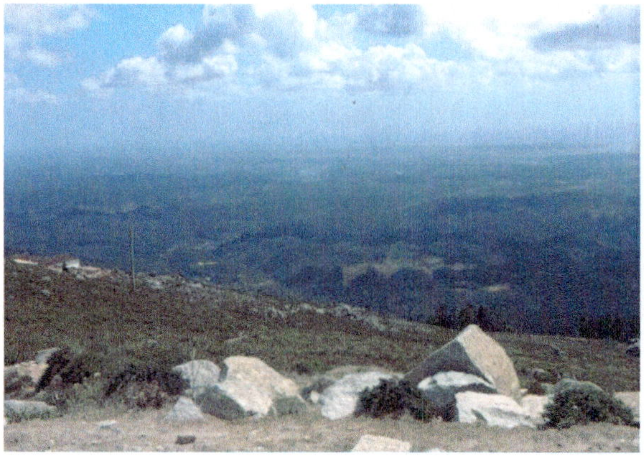

Andalucía

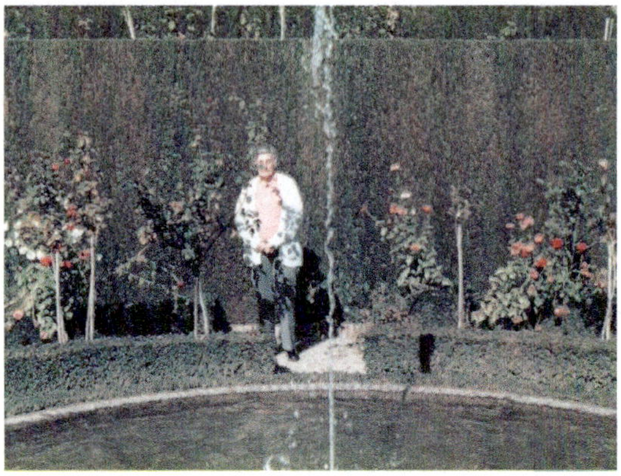

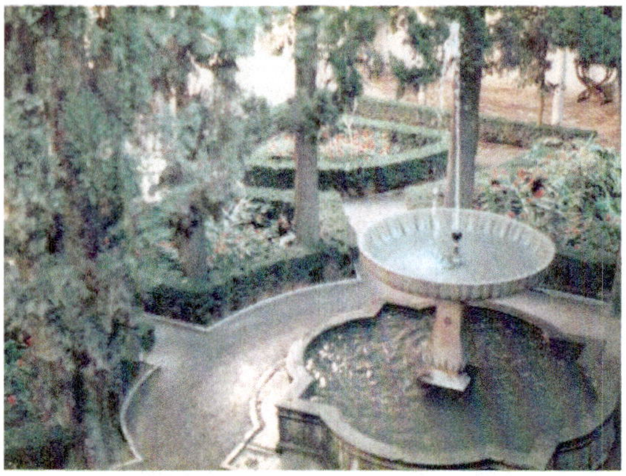

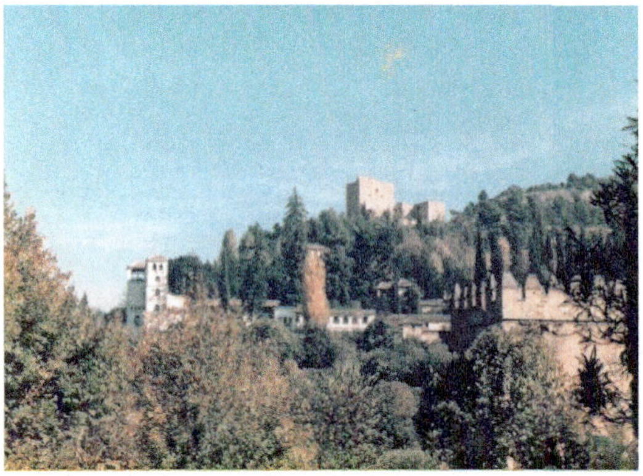

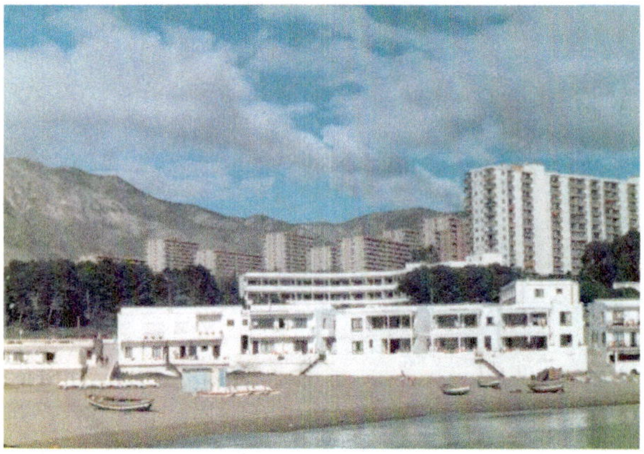

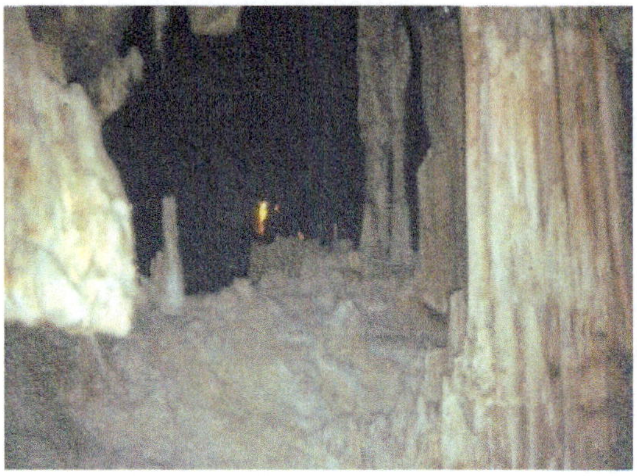

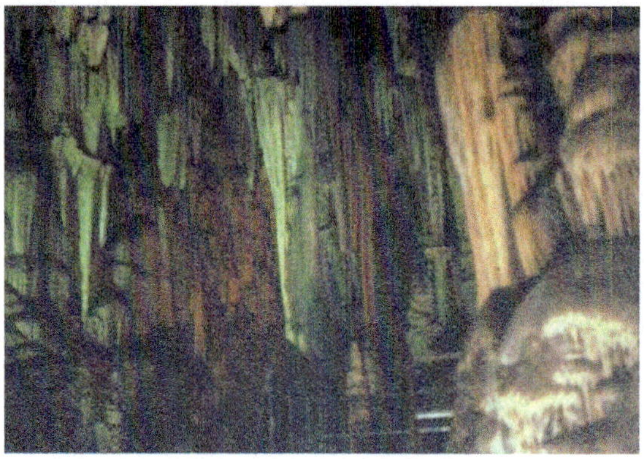

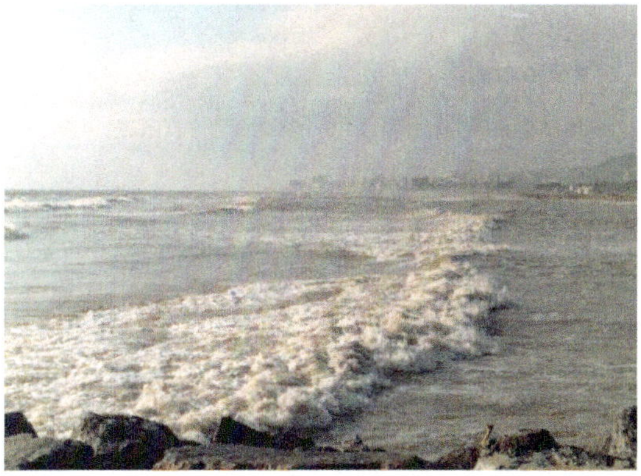

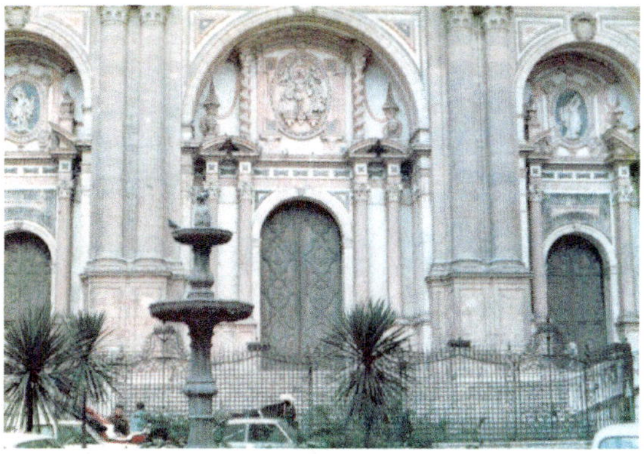

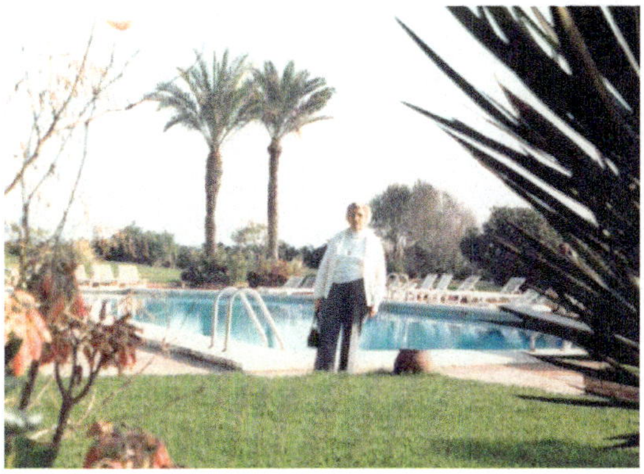

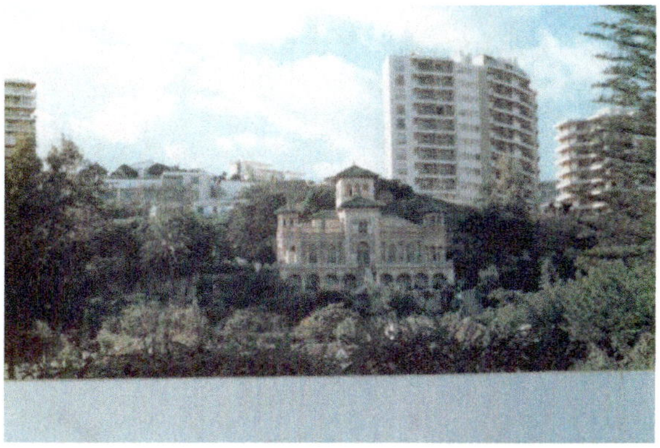

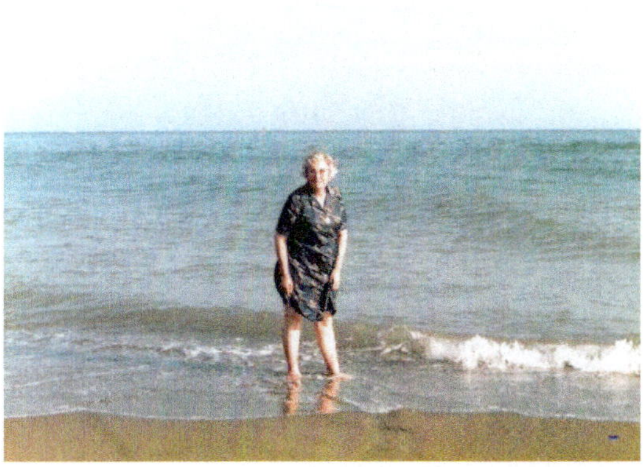

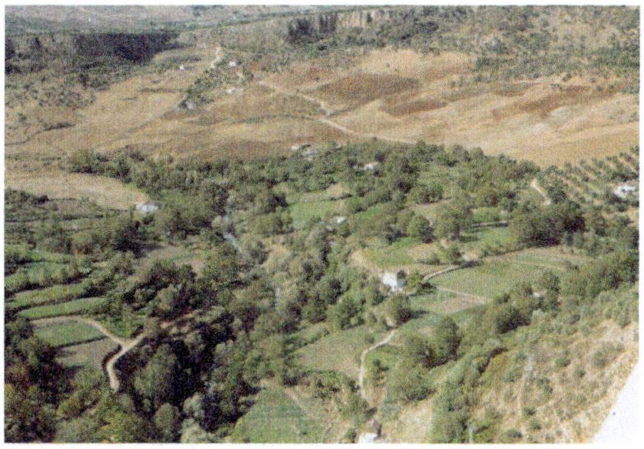

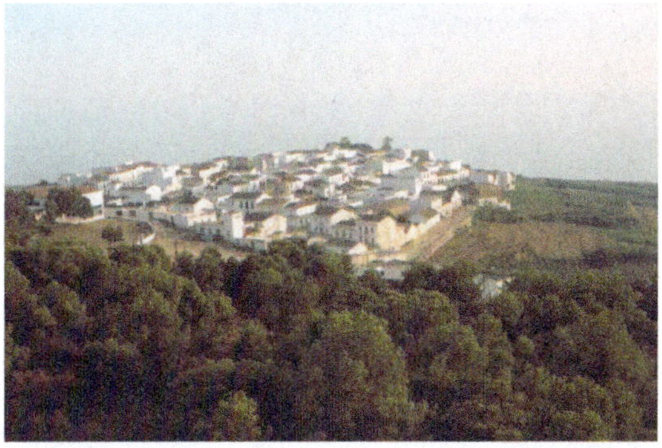

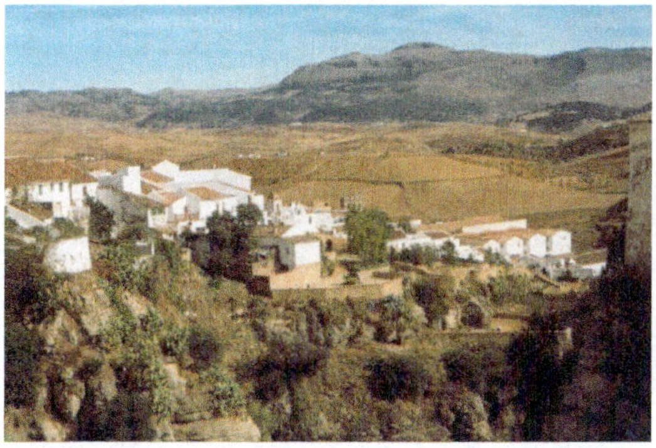

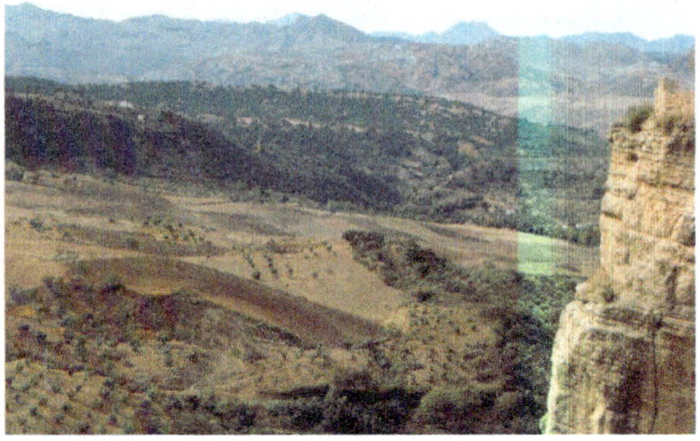

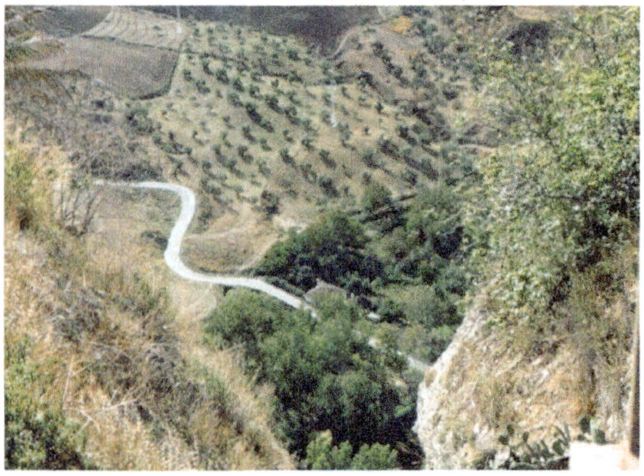

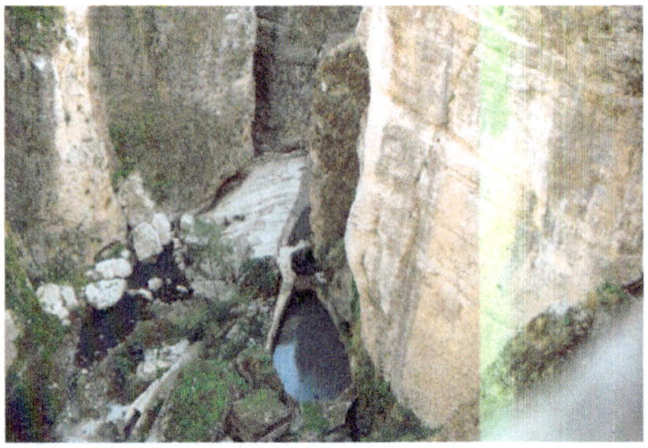

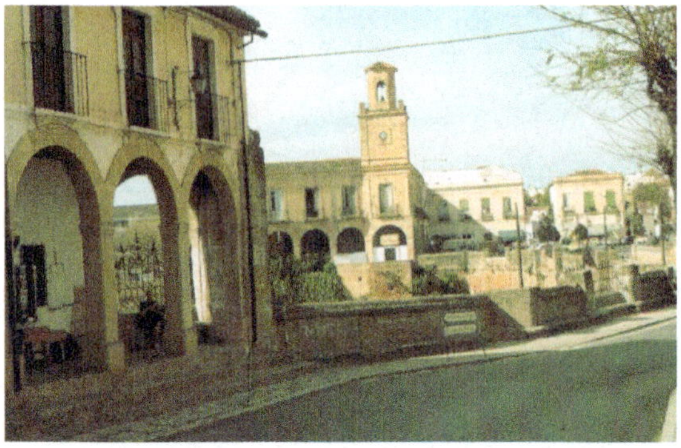

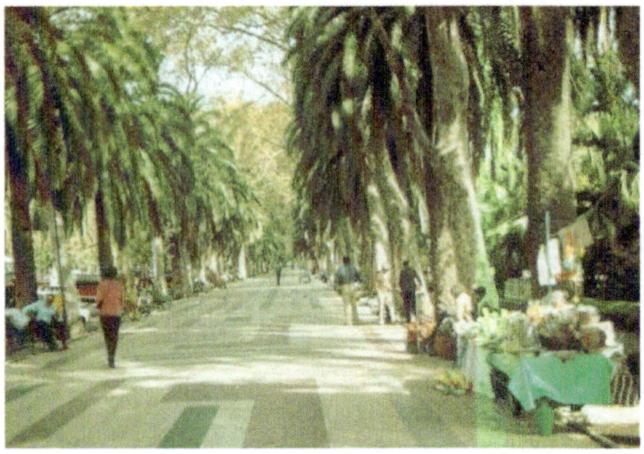

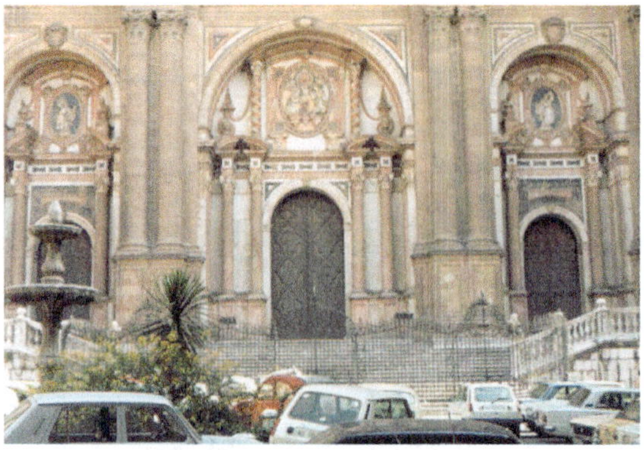

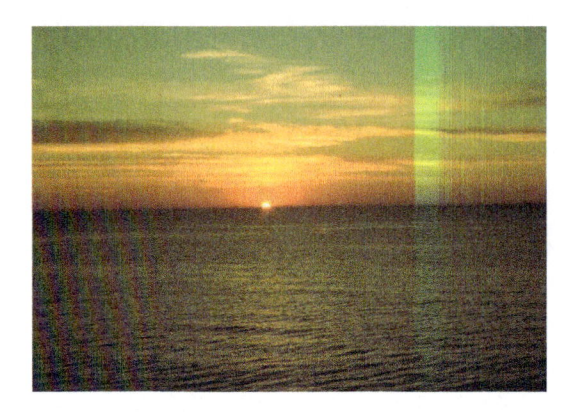

Paris

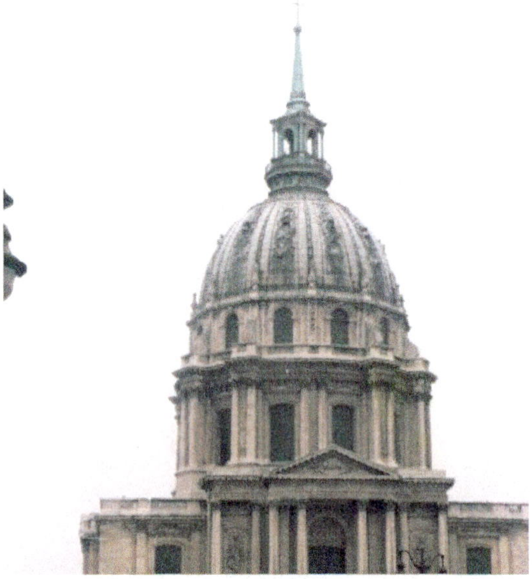

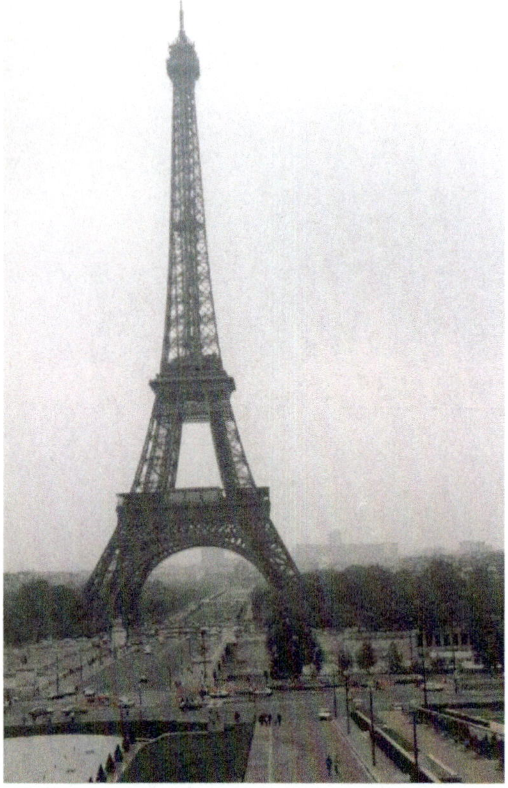

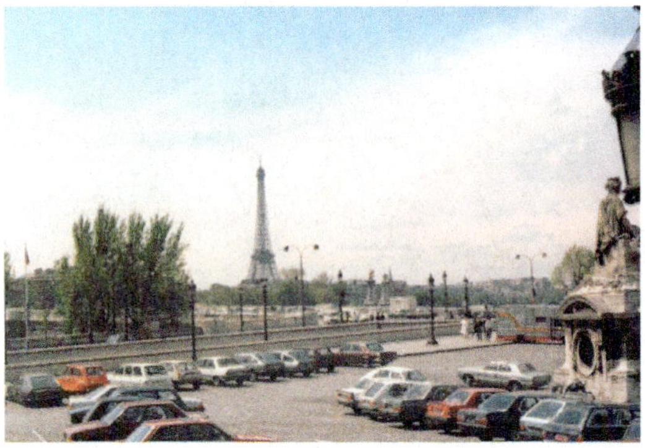

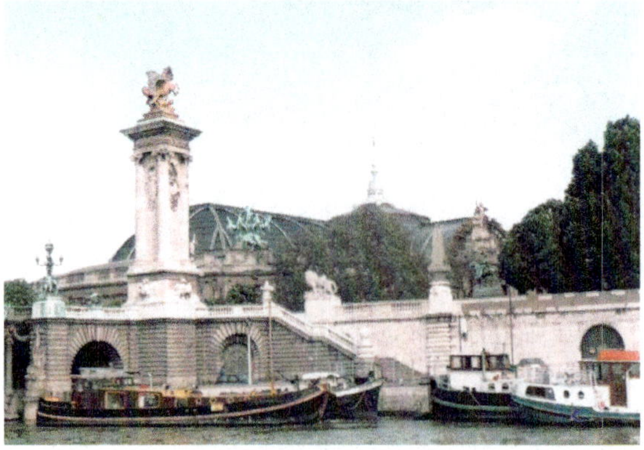

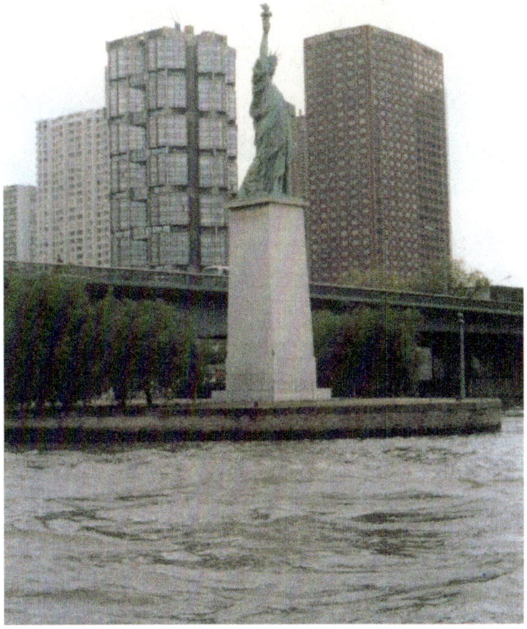

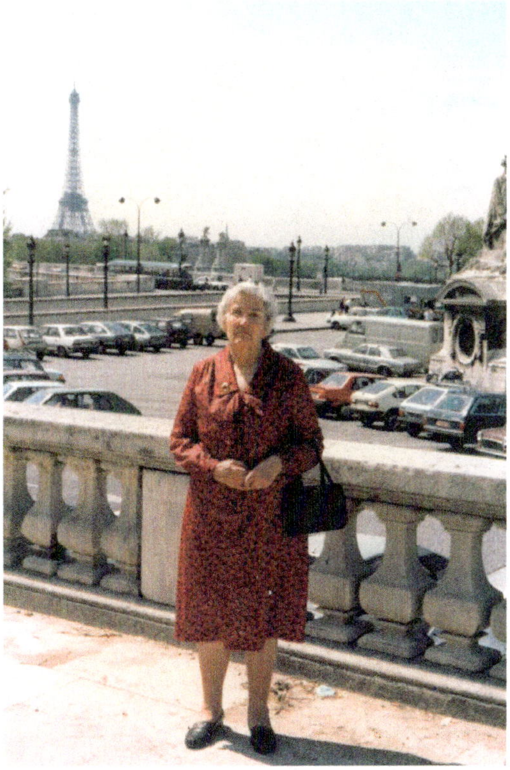

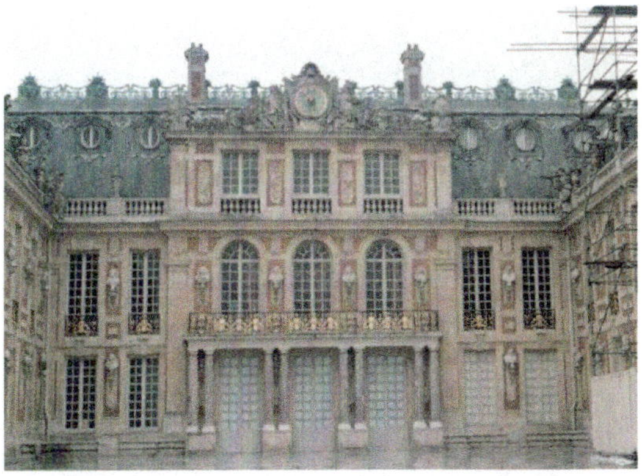

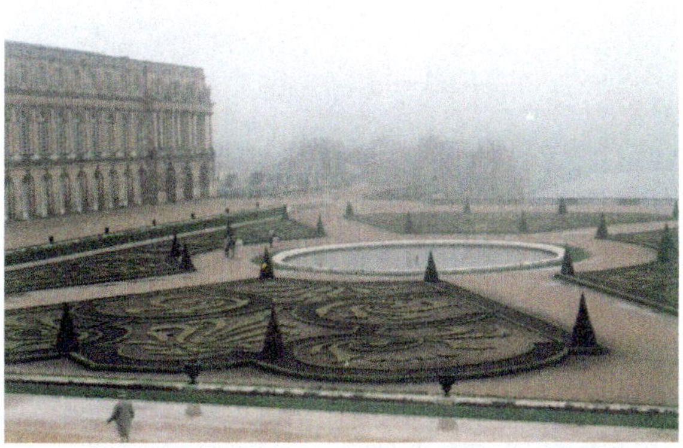

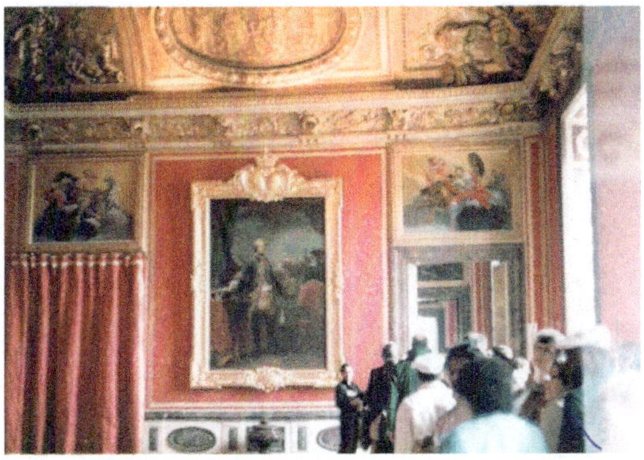

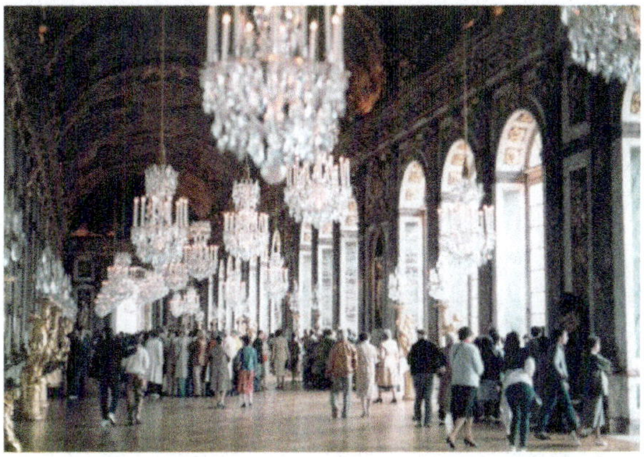

York

Lichfield

Bath

Buckingham Palace

Lincolnshire

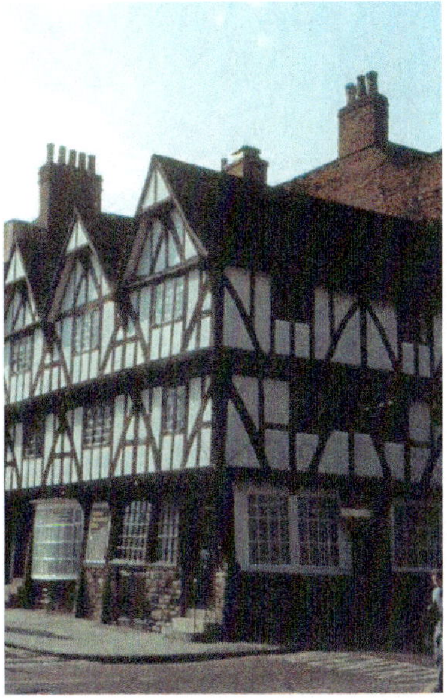

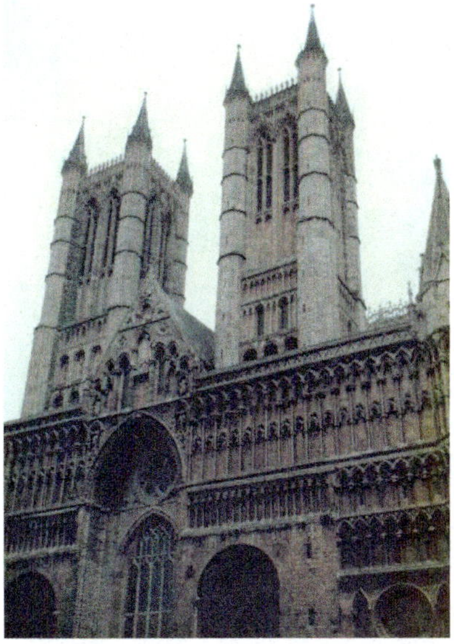

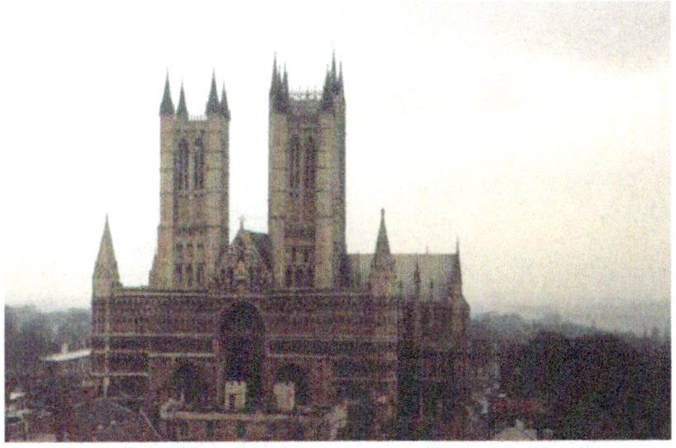

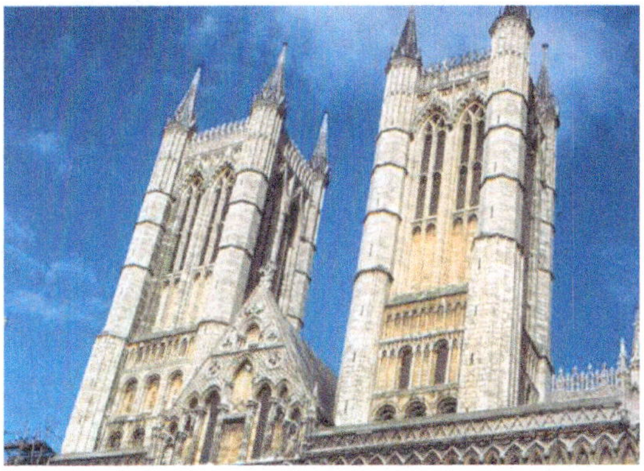

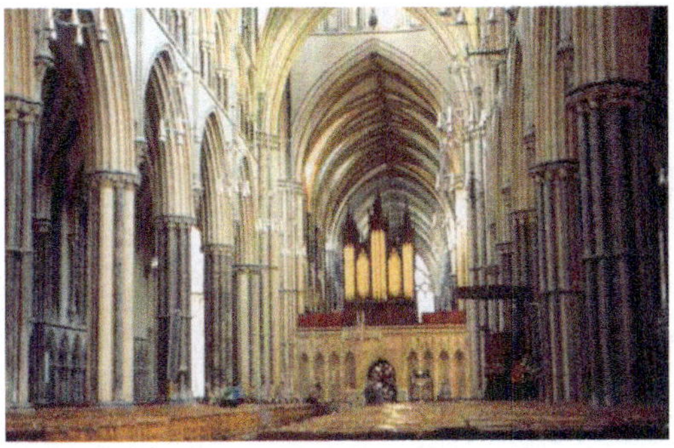

Winchester

Milton Abbas

Essex

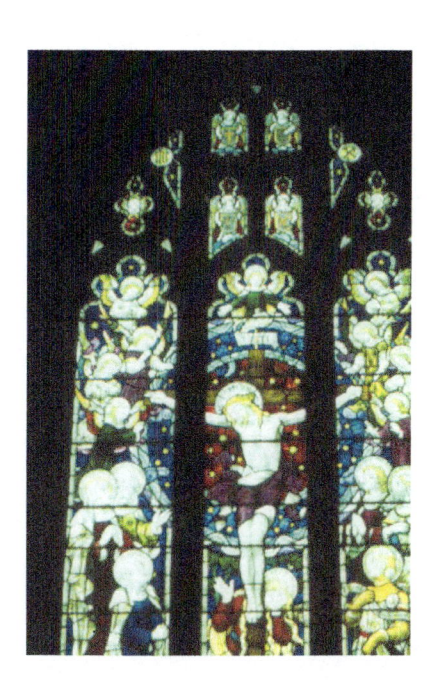

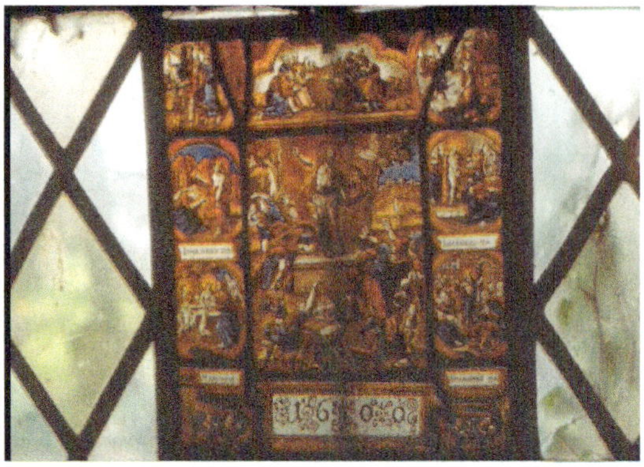

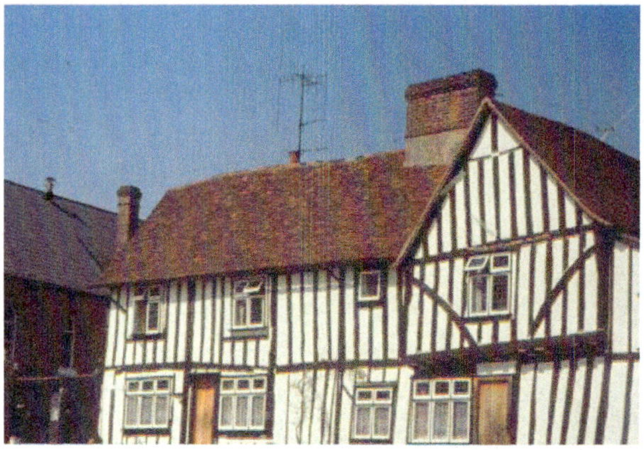

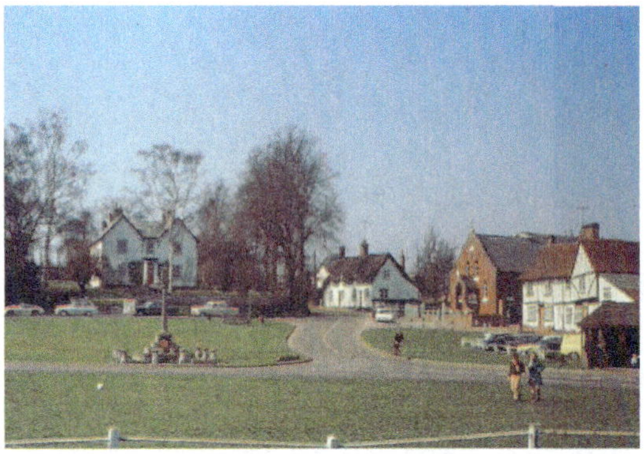

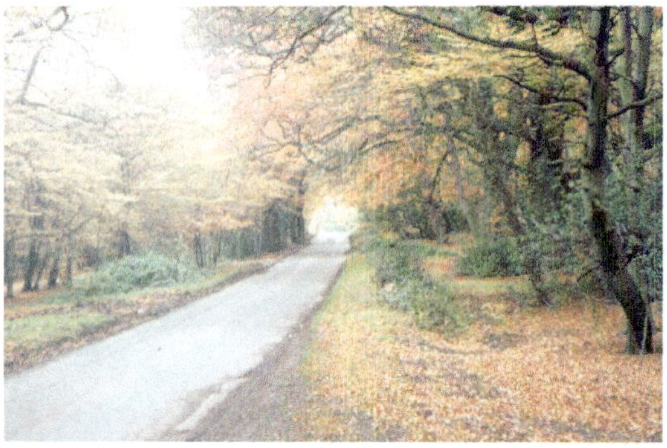

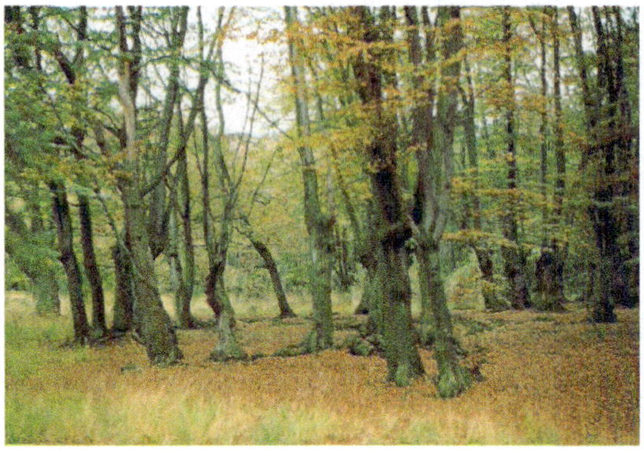

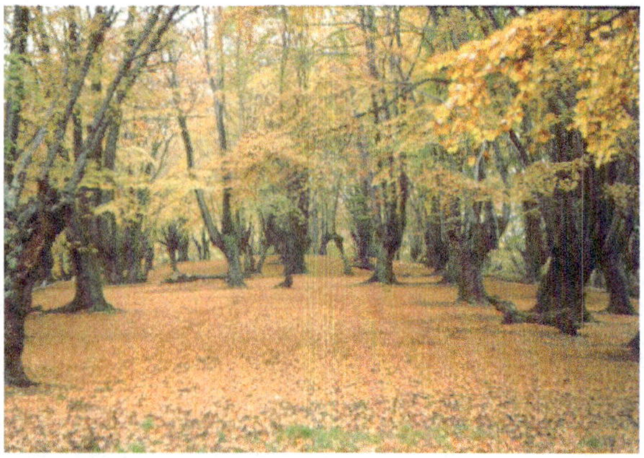

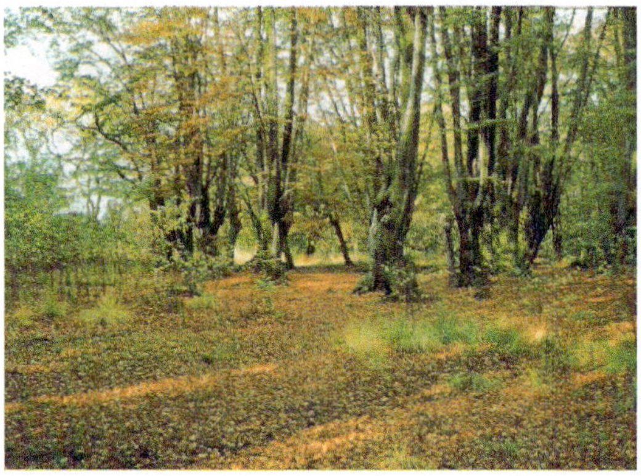

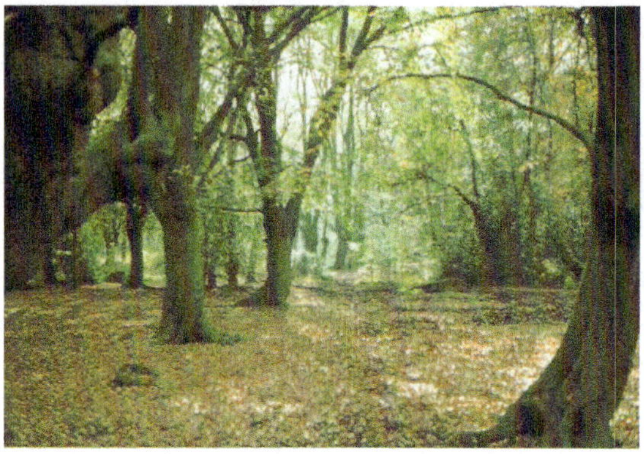

Palaces: Burleigh House, Chatsworth & Blenheim

Norfolk

Greenwich & Woolwich

Eastbourne

Southend

Derby

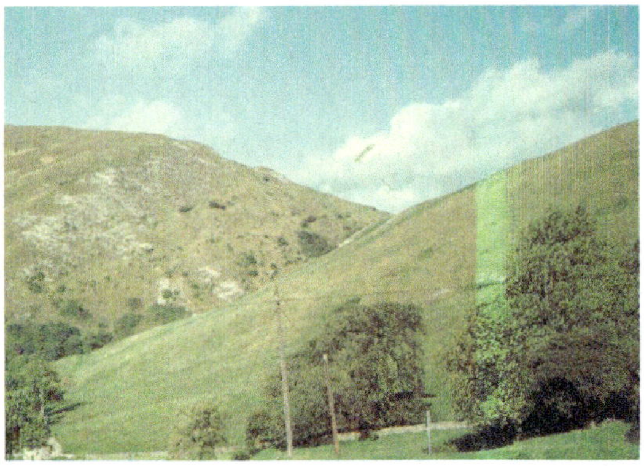

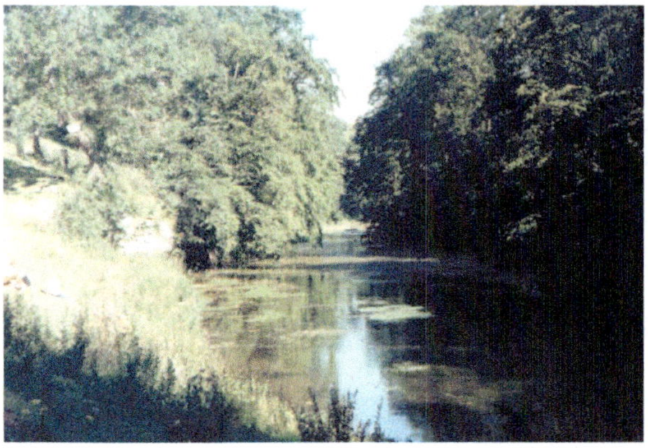

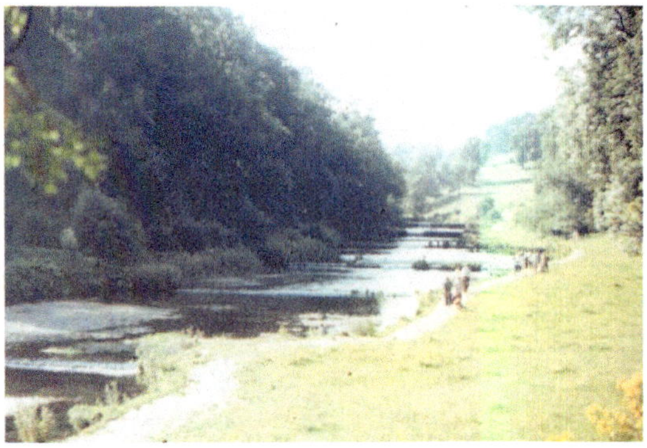

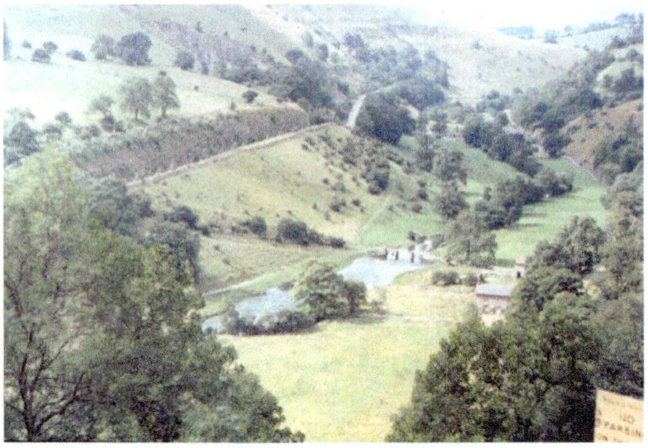

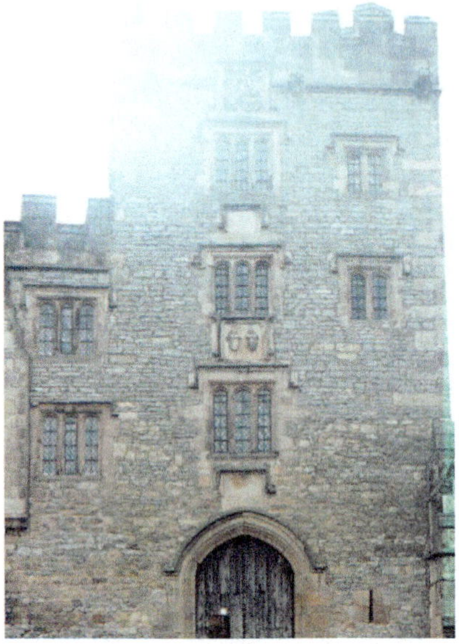

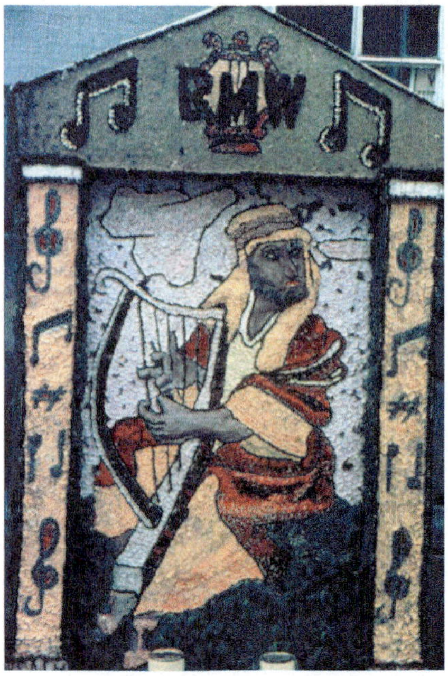

Spalding

Saville Gardens, Windsor

Kew Gardens

Chelsea Flower Show

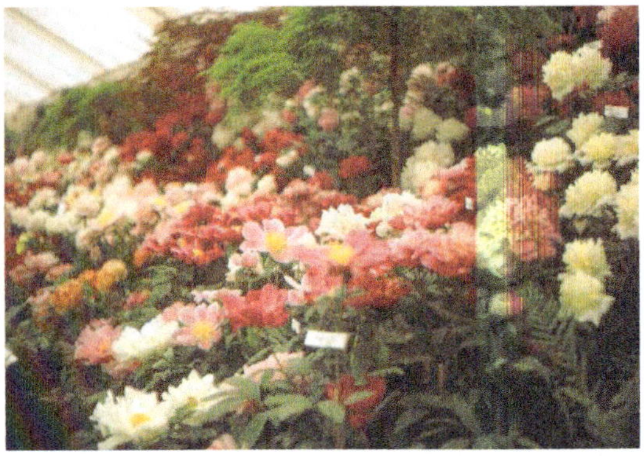

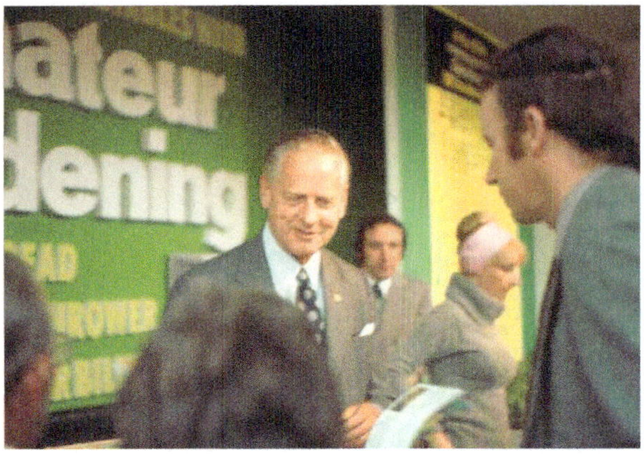
ateur
dening

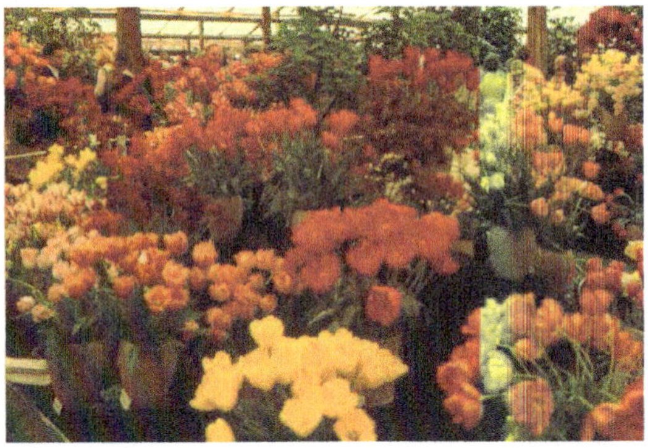

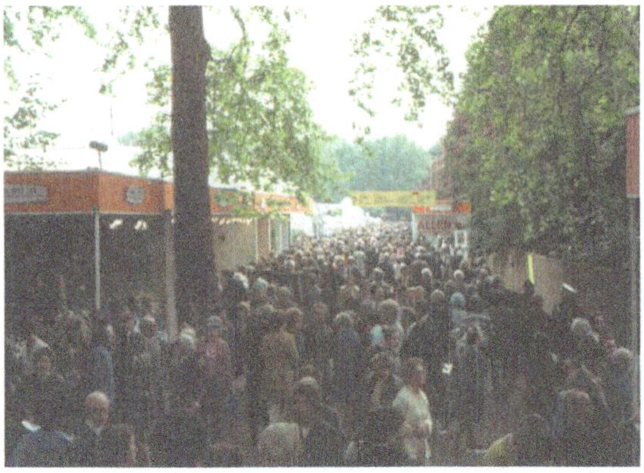

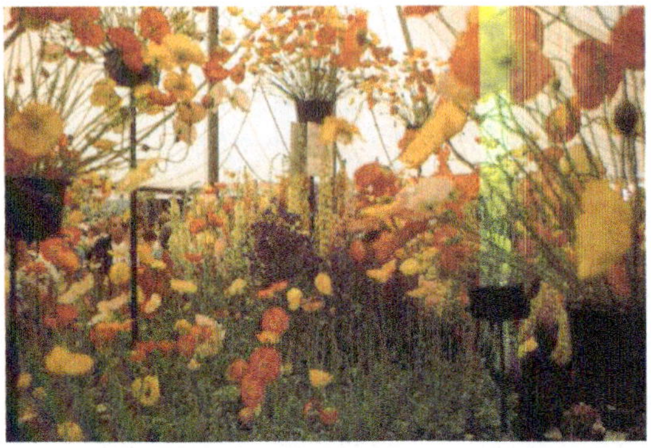

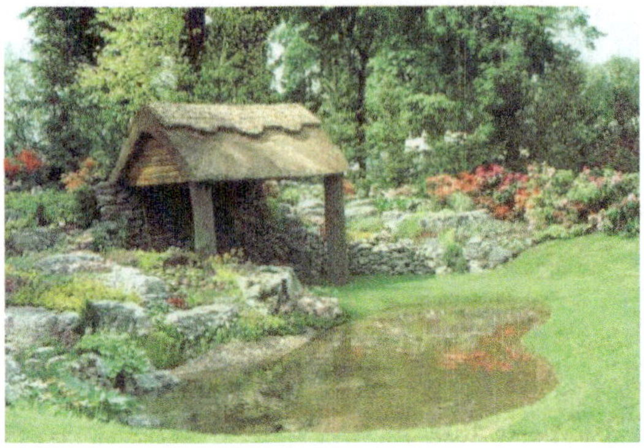

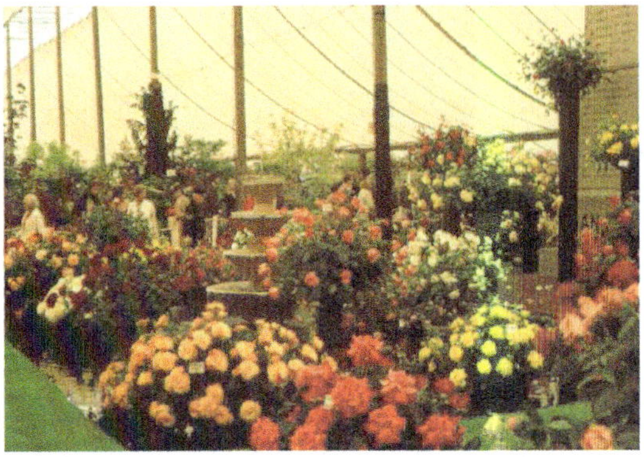

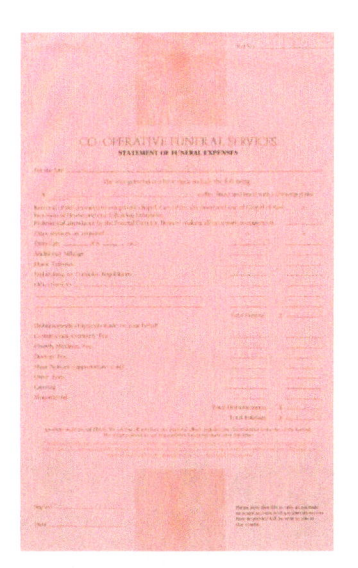

APPENDIX H

Dad's death.

APPENDIX I

Mum's cake making

Andrew's 18th birthday

Ann's confirmation

Ann & Trevor's engagement

Brian's 18th birthday

Joyce & Wally Xmas 1988

Joyce & Wally Xmas 1989

Paul Xmas 1988

Paul Xmas 1989

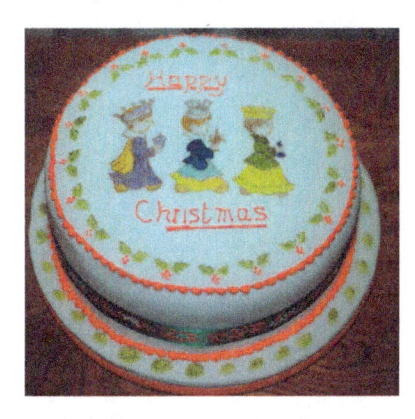

Xmas 1989

Pete Xmas 1987

Emma's Christening

Dad's 75th Birthday

Ern & Peggie's Golden Wedding

Ern & Peggie's Golden Wedding

Helen's 18th birthday

Joanna's Wedding

Joanna's Wedding

Joyce's 50th birthday

Joyce's 53rd birthday

Joyce's 60th birthday

Joyce & Wally 30th Anniversary

Joyce & Wally Retirement	Kate's 18th birthday	Kate's Confirmation
 Katharine Christening	Keith & Lynda	Laura's 18th birthday
Laura's 21st birthday	Laura's Wedding	Lynda, Ann, Keith, Trevor

Matthew Christening	 Mum & Dad Golden Wedding	 Mum's 80th Birthday
Paul's Doctorate	 Pete's 40th Birthday	 Pete's 40th Birthday
 Pete's 41st Birthday	 Pete's 50th Birthday	Pete & Jen Anniversary
 Shirley 50th Birthday	 Sue & Paul Wedding	Wally 60th Birthday

Wally's Mum's 80th Birthday

APPENDIX J

Mum's 90th Birthday Cards

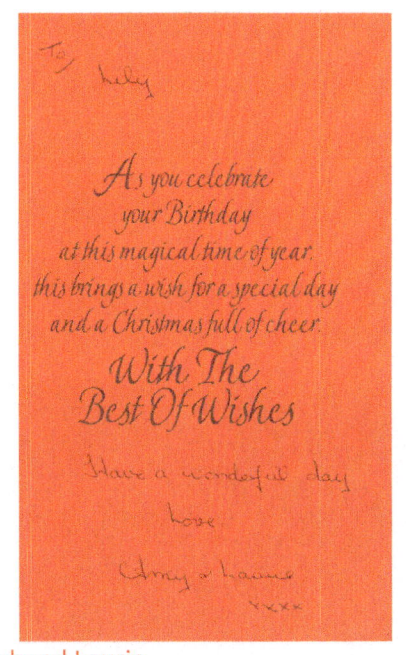

A seasonal wish from Mum's cousin Amy and husband Laurie.

From cousin Andrew Peckett.

From cousin Anne and Dennis (Arnold).

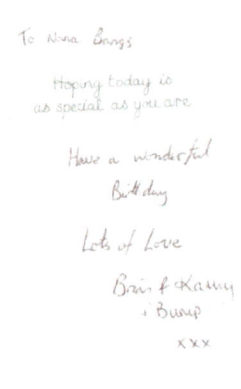

From Brian and Kathy, Anne and Dennis' son and daughter-in-law (plus "bump" meaning Kathy was pregnant at the time!).

From grandchildren Ann and Trevor, Emma and Matthew.

From family friend Dora.

90th Birthday

May your 90th birthday
be a very special day,
rich with happiness
and warm with special
moments to remember.

Wishing You
Every Happiness
Doug

From Doug, Jen's father and thus Pete's father-in-law.

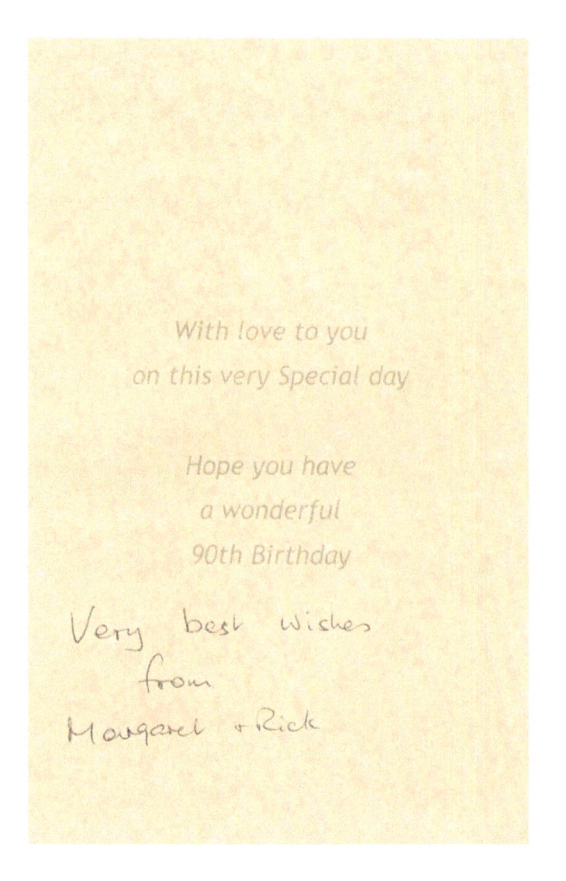

Happy 90th Birthday

San Giorgio Maggiore, Venice

With love to you
on this very Special day

Hope you have
a wonderful
90th Birthday

Very best wishes
from
Margaret + Rick

Margaret is Jen's sister, and thus Doug's daughter.

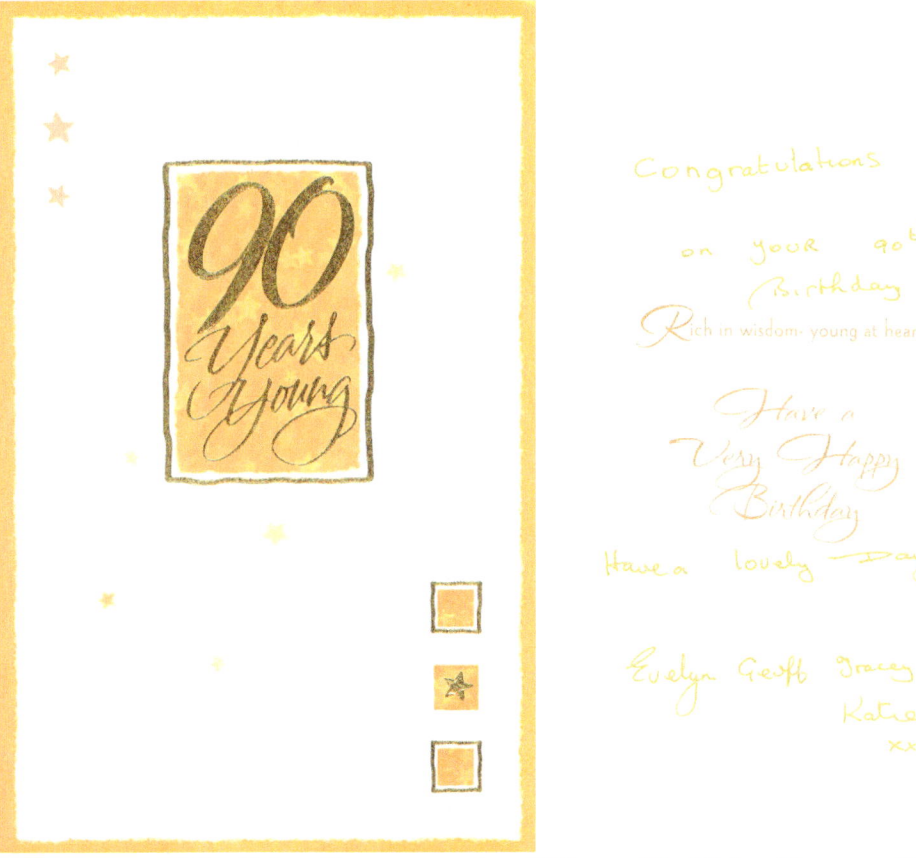

Congratulations on your 90th Birthday
Rich in wisdom, young at heart.
Have a Very Happy Birthday
Have a lovely day.

Evelyn Geoff Tracey & Katie
xxx

From Evelyn and Geoff Arnold, more cousins of Mum, with children Tracey and Katie.

Sending you warm wishes for a perfect Birthday

Happiness Always

Congratulations dear lady on celebrating your 90th Birthday. Wishing you a wonderful day.
With love from
"Topsy" (Helen)

From Helen (née) McSween, a neighbouring family and close friends for many years. Dad always called Helen "Topsy"....

... and this card is from Helen's sister Iris...

... and another McSween (as was), their sister Jean.

CONGRATULATIONS
AND
VERY BEST WISHES
FOR
A MEMORABLE BIRTHDAY.
Love
Mavis (MAC)
2004

... and yet another McSween (as was), twin sister Mavis.

To Lily

Congratulations on your
90th Birthday

With our very best wishes,

Joan and Roy

Joan and Roy are the parents of Lynda, grandson Keith's wife.

Wishing you a very happy 90th birthday

With all our love,

Keith, Lynda, Katharine & Holly
xxxxx

And here is the card from Keith and Lynda, with their daughters, Katharine and Holly.

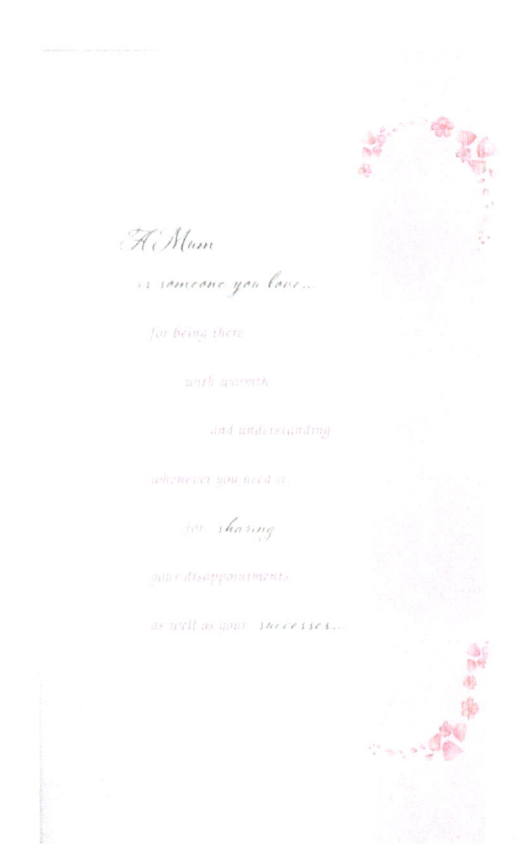

Above and following are the pages from Joyce and Wally's card.

You're such

a special person,

Mum,

and you deserve

a world

...not just

on your birthday

but all

through the year...

You are a

wonderful mum,

and you're loved

very much.

Enjoy Your
Special Day,

With all our love, Mum
Joyce + Wally
xxxxxxxxxxx

From granddaughter Kate and husband Andy, and Andy's daughter Chloe.

From granddaughter Laura, husband Jim and their three children.

Many happy returns for your 90 birthday!
Love
Małgorzata

From Paul's Polish sister-in-law, Malgosia.

To Aunt Lil

Wishing you the kind of day
that's filled with pleasant things
The kind that's long remembered
for the happiness it brings!

Happy Birthday!
Wishing you many happy returns
With all our love
Margaret + Ron
xxx

Margaret is our cousin, the daughter of Mum's only brother Albert.

ON YOUR 90TH BIRTHDAY

Dear Lillian

Moment by moment,
right from the start,
A birthday brings
memories dear to the heart.

WITH *warmest* WISHES

FOND MEMORIES OF THE TIMES GONE BY.
WISHING YOU
NEW MOMENTS TO ENJOY
IN YOUR FAVOURITE WAY.
WISHING YOU
ALL THE HAPPINESS
YOUR HEART CAN HOLD
ON YOUR BIRTHDAY
AND ALWAYS.

From
Mary and Family
(Carer)

From one of Mum's team of carers who at the time were helping her continue with her independent living in her own home.

90
Today
19th December 2004

To Mum

Wishing you a day that brings
All life's very best
A day of special happiness
That stands out from the rest

With all our love and best
wishes
on your 90th birthday.

If anyone deserves
a Happy Birthday it most
certainly is you

Many Happy Returns

from
Pete and Jen

Of course, from Pete and Jen.

On Your 90th Birthday

May all the gladness and the joy that you deserve to see Combine to make this special day as perfect as can be.

So glad it's your birthday because it's a chance to let you know how much you are thought of and what a very special person you are

Enjoy Your Day

To Auntie Lil,
Have a lovely 90th Birthday.
Lots of Love
&
Best Wishes
From
Rita, Les & Family

From Rita and Les and their family - Rita is Mum's cousin, daughter of Aunt Win, and was present at the lunch.

On your 90th Birthday

As you celebrate another Birthday milestone wishing you a day that will give you hours of happiness and many memories to treasure

Happy 90th Birthday

To Lilly Congratulations
Have a happy day
Love from Tessa.

From Tessa, mother-in-law to grand-daughter Ann.

From Wally's sister Vera and husband Roy.

APPENDIX K

Mum's Funeral remembrances

These are the cards that were sent to mark Mum's death. First, some photos of the floral tributes - there were not many flowers as most people donated, as Mum would have preferred, to the British Heart Foundation. The cards accompanying flowers are also shown below.

Dick Bangs & Lily Bourne – Their story 275

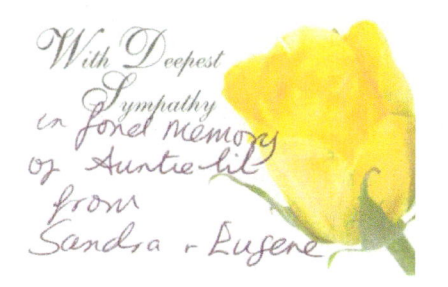

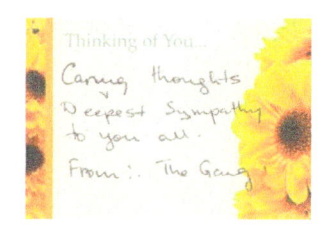

In Loving Memory

With kind thoughts of Lily from Vera + Roy

Dear Joyce and family,
 We were so sorry to hear of your sad loss. It was wonderful that she slipped away so peacefully and also that you have had so many years of happy memories to remember her by.
 Our thoughts and prayers are with you.

Thinking of you
love from
Alan + Shirley
xx

With Sympathy and Caring

Dear Joyce & Family,
 May it help
to ease your sorrow
to know that loving
 thoughts
are with you now
in sympathy and prayers.
in the loss of your
Dear Mother.
 From: Allan + Monica Florence
 & Family

Sympathy card with letter:

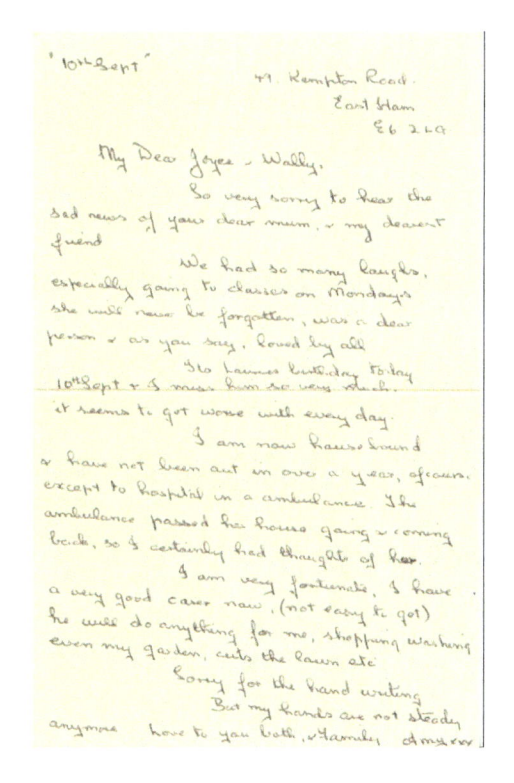

"10th Sept"
49, Kempton Road.
East Ham
E6 2LQ

My Dear Joyce & Wally,

So very sorry to hear the sad news of your dear mum, & my dearest friend.

We had so many laughs, especially going to classes on Mondays, she will never be forgotten, was a dear person & as you say, loved by all.

Its Lennies birthday today 10th Sept & I miss him so very much. it seems to get worse with every day.

I am now housebound & have not been out in over a year, ofcourse, except to hospital in a ambulance. The ambulance passed her house going & coming back, so I certainly had thoughts of her.

I am very fortunate, I have a very good carer now, (not easy to get) he will do anything for me, shopping washing even my garden, cuts the lawn etc

Sorry for the hand writing
But my hands are not steady anymore. Love to you both, & family. Amy xxx

With sympathy...
thinking of you at this sad time

Andrew Peckett

Deepest Sympathy

Treasured memories live and grow more precious with time.

To Joyce, Paul, Pete and Families

May your many cherished memories help bring you peace and comfort through all the days ahead.

We have lost a wonderful "Mum". She was always there for us and shared so many precious times with us and we will miss her. With love and our prayers to you all.

Anne & Dennis

With Deepest Sympathy

May you find comfort in the memories that are yours to cherish always...

To Joyce & family

...and may you find the courage to face tomorrow in the love that surrounds you today.

Thinking of You

We want you to know how very much we loved nana Sharing in lots of happy memories today

Love Brian, Kathy and Nathan xx

With Sympathy

"To remember is another way to love"

To Joyce & Family

When you lose someone you love
it's hard to bear the sorrow,
And it takes strength and courage
just to try to face tomorrow.
But now the words of others
and their warm concern for you
Help sustain you day by day
and be of comfort, too.

Love from
Dora, Phil & Deborah

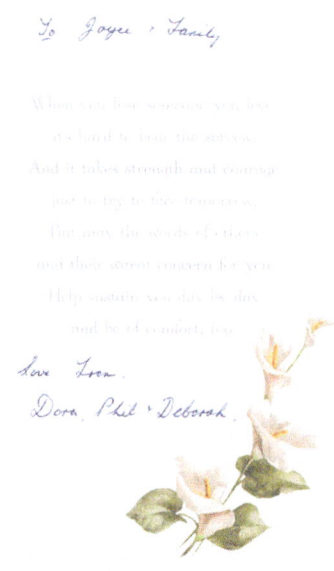

With Sympathy

From Eva and Terry

God Bless You At This Sad Time

To Joce, Wally, Paul, Ursula, Pete and Jen

May your faith bring you strength and comfort in this time of loss.

Our thoughts are with you all at this time.

Fred and Pat.

With Sympathy

Thinking of you and sending sincere sympathy at this sad time.

From Helen + Peter.

A dear lady always remembered with great affection.

With Sympathy

From Iris
to you and all the family at this
sad time when words are so
inadequate

To Joyce & Wally

Expressing *sincerest*
sympathy to you
at this *difficult time.*

So sorry to hear about
your mother. She was
a lovely lady

Ivy & Eric

Thinking of you
   with deepest sympathy
      in your time of sorrow.

With Sympathy

Many thoughts are with you at this time of sorrow.

Sending deepest sympathy to you in your sad loss.

To dear Joyce & Wally,
from, Joy & Roy

*For Your Family
In Sympathy*

To Joyce Wally Family

*In sorrow for the one who is gone.
With love for the ones who grieve.*

HOPE EVERYTHING WENT OK
SPEAK TO YOU SOON
LOVE FROM
JEAN & FAMILY
XX

In Sympathy

No matter how long
the shadows
cast by sadness,
Love and hope
can lift them.

With Deepest Sympathy
In Your Loss

Jean & Tom Scriven

With Sympathy

May such a special life
always be remembered

Dear Joyce and Wally
Our thoughts and
prayers are with
you at this time.
So glad to know
that your Mum was
happy in her last
months with such
caring friends
much love
Joan & Roy

To: Joyce, Willy & family

Thinking of you

lots of love
Lynn & Graham
— xxx —

Dear Peter,
My condolences to you and your family in your grief at the loss of your mother. My thoughts are with you now

Małgorzata

4.09.2009.

Thinking Of You

Hope it helps you to know that special thoughts are with you now.

With deepest sympathy to you and your family.

Mavis & Family

With Deepest Sympathy

"Shared times, shared memories, shared joys— these special things keep a loved one close."

Paul, Joyce & Peter

Wishing you strength for today and comfort in the days ahead, knowing how much your loved one meant to so many.

Thinking of you all at this sad time.

The McEwen family

With Sympathy

Joyce, Wally, Paul, Urszula, Pete + Jen

So sorry to hear about the death of your Mum. I have many fond memories of Tea at Hattersley Gardens. A very kind lady.

With deepest sympathy

Love from Michael + Lizzie

In Sympathy

It's very hard
to bear the pain
when loved ones pass away
but thoughts from
those who care
will bring
you strength
and peace today

And though there are no special words
to heal the pain you feel
each sympathetic word and thought
is genuine and real

Here's hoping you find comfort
in knowing others care
for in this time of sorrow
friends and loved ones will be there

One day you'll come to see
you'll never really be apart
because the ones you love
will stay forever in your heart

Thinking of you Joyce

With love
Pat + Roman

With Sympathy

Dear Joyce & Wally
So sorry to hear your loss, just to say our thoughts are with you and your family.

Special thoughts are with you

Love always
Paula, Darren,
Christopher
&
Abigail
x x
x x

May Memories Comfort You

No one who is remembered is ever truly gone.

At this sad time
with heartfelt sympathy

May you be comforted by the thoughts of those who care.

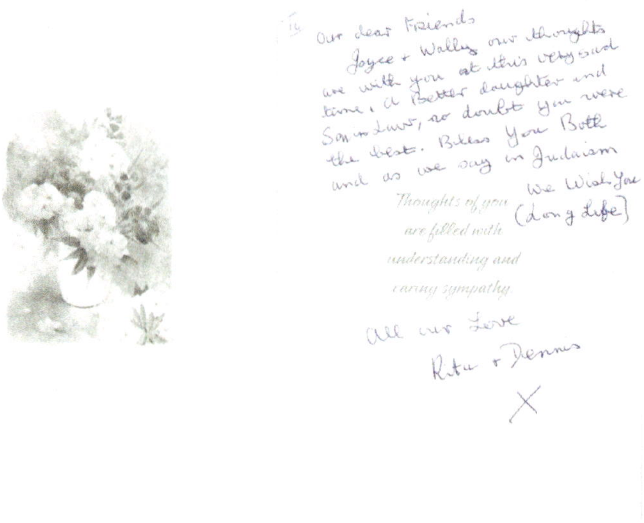

To Our dear Friends Joyce & Wally, our thoughts are with you at this very sad time. A better daughter and son-in-law, no doubt you were the best. Bless you both and as we say in Judaism (Long Life). We wish you thoughts of you are filled with understanding and caring sympathy.

All our love
Rita & Dennis
x

In Deepest Sympathy

When words may not ease the sorrow...

To Joyce & Wally
Paul & Pete

So sorry to hear the sad news, pleased that she was so comfortable the last few months. Will always have some very special happy memories of dear Mum Lil.

...remember that caring thoughts and sympathy though unspoken are always there

To
Joyce, Wally, Paul, Pete

55, Cromwell Crescent
Market Harborough
Leics LE16 9JN
12.9.09

Very many thanks for understanding. Enclosed cheque for British Heart Foundation. Will be thinking of you all on Monday.
Love
Rita & Les.

To Joyce & Wally

May your memories
give you comfort

With Deepest Sympathy

from
Ron

Card 1 (With Sympathy – flower):

To dear Joyce and Wally and family –

Please know how much you are thought of at this sad time

With our love and deep sympathy, from Laura and Eugene

Card 2 (With Sympathy – lilies and candle):

To Joyce & Wally

Thinking of You

at this difficult time.

With fond memories of Nanny and our beautiful wedding cake.

From Sue, Paul, Esther & Carmen.

Deepest Sympathy

May the memories you hold

of precious past years...

help to ease the pain

and wipe away the tears.

To
Joyce, Wally & family

*Those we love deeply
are the memories of the past
For they'll always be kept
within our hearts.*

Memories are all we can say
Thinking of You

So sorry to hear your sad news.
Best Wishes,
Richard, Tanya, Errin & Roy
x

In Sympathy

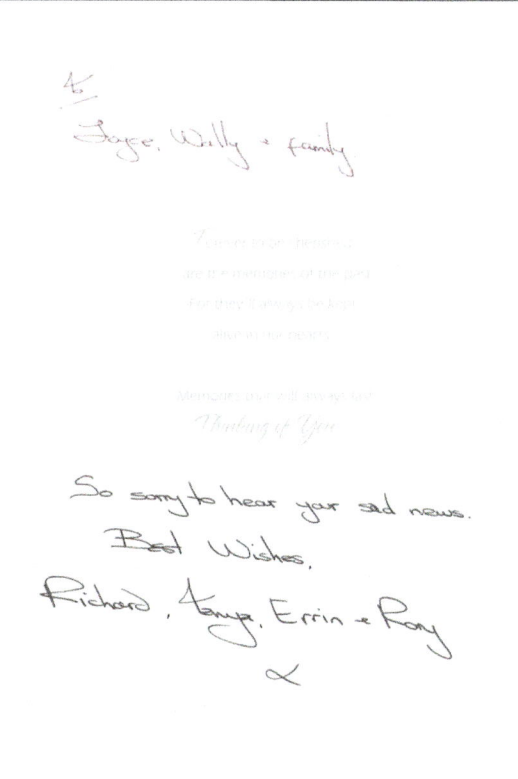

Dear Joyce and Wally,
I was sorry to hear about your Mum. At least her last few weeks were spent in a pleasant place with kind people looking after her. It must have been a comfort to you.
I will be thinking of you next Monday. Love Jessa and Julian.

*May you find some comfort
in the thought that others care*

With deepest sympathy

with sympathy
with sympathy
with sympathy

with sympathy
with sympathy
with sympathy

In Sympathy and Caring

*May your cherished memories
bring you peace and comfort
in the days ahead.*

*Please know
that many caring thoughts
are with you now.*

DEAR
Joyce, Peter, Paul.
Our Thoughts are with,
with you all at this sad.
Time. We all have Lovley.
Memories of Aunt Lil and Loved.
Her very Much.
Love. Tony, Irene, Jimmy &
Joanna. xx

TO JOYCE AND WALLY
SORRY TO HEAR THE SAD
NEWS THINKING OF YOU ALL

*Many special thoughts
go out to you today,
hoping you find comfort
in knowing that your sorrow
is deeply shared.*

Thinking Of You

LOVE
TREY

Heartfelt Sympathy

May you find comfort in knowing that others are thinking of you.

To Joyce, Wesley & family

In times of deepest sorrow
when tears may cloud our eyes,
It seems our grief is endless
but then we realise,
That sorrow is the memory
of a happy yesterday,
And memories live on and on
while sorrows fade away.

Vera & Roy
x x x x

With Sympathy

Waterlilies, Evening
Claude Monet

Dear Joyce, Paul & Peter
I was so sorry to hear the sad news of your mother's death. I have many fond memories of her. She had a long life, getting to see grandchildren + great grand children. She was very proud of all her family, and I know will be greatly missed.
Thinking of you all
With love,
Viv

In fond
remembrance
of
Lily Bangs
from
Joan & Roy
Wimbleton

On The Loss of Your Mother

At This Sad Time

To Jen & Pete

Sometimes, it helps a little
to know that friends are there,
And that's why this message
comes to let you know—
That we share in your loss
and that our friendship
is with you always.

Thinking Of You

With Love & Sympathy
Bill & Betty

Pete & Jen

Thinking of you

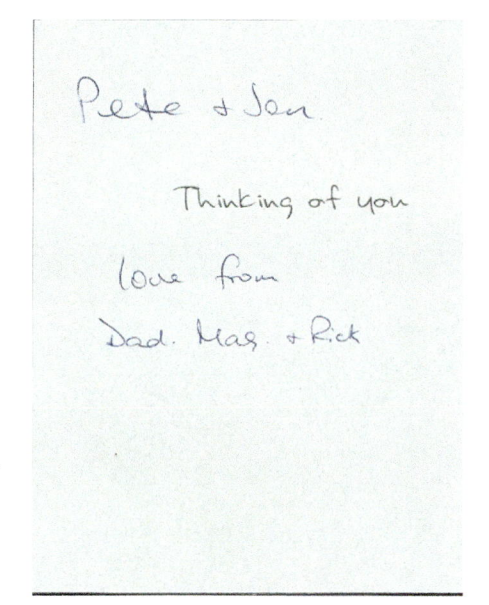

love from
Dad, Mag. + Rick

With Sympathy

Waterlilies, Evening
Claude Monet

Dear Pete,
So sorry to hear the sad news. Heartfelt condolences to you, Jenny and the family
Thinking of you
Mike & Eileen

Printed in Great Britain
by Amazon